James Fergusson is a freelance   correspondent who has written for many publications including the *Independent*, *The Times*, the *Daily Telegraph*, the *Daily Mail* and *The Economist*. He began reporting on Afghan affairs fourteen years ago. His third book, *A Million Bullets*, was the British Army's Military Book of the Year. He is married with three children and lives in Edinburgh.

Acclaim for *A Million Bullets*:

'A riveting, blistering, deeply reported narrative of the recent British military intervention in Afghanistan'
Peter Bergen, author of *Holy War, Inc.*

'The lessons drawn by Fergusson are deeply uncomfortable; but his account cannot be ignored'
Douglas Hurd, *Spectator*

'If you read anything on Afghanistan this year then read this strong, intelligent book of crafted anger and insight'
Anthony Loyd, *The Times*

'Fascinating . . . succeeds brilliantly'
Christina Lamb, *Sunday Times*

'Fergusson's book is brisk but reasoned and it feels important . . . This is not a tub-thumping polemic'
Toby Clements, *Daily Telegraph*

'A timely account . . . intelligent, balanced and a welcome addition to the growing body of literature on the current conflict'
Patrick Hennessey, *Literary Review*

Also by James Fergusson

Kandahar Cockney
The Vitamin Murders
A Million Bullets

TALIBAN

The True Story of the World's Most
Feared Guerrilla Fighters

James Fergusson

CORGI BOOKS

TRANSWORLD PUBLISHERS
61–63 Uxbridge Road, London W5 5SA
A Random House Group Company
www.rbooks.co.uk

TALIBAN
A CORGI BOOK: 9780552162838

First published in Great Britain
in 2010 by Bantam Press
an imprint of Transworld Publishers
Corgi edition published 2011

Addresses for Random House Group Ltd companies outside the UK
can be found at: www.randomhouse.co.uk
The Random House Group Ltd Reg. No. 954009

The Random House Group Limited supports The Forest Stewardship Council
(FSC), the leading international forest certification organisation. All our titles that
are printed on Greenpeace approved FSC certified paper carry the FSC logo. Our
paper procurement policy can be found at www.rbooks.co.uk/environment

Mixed Sources
Product group from well-managed
forests and other controlled sources
www.fsc.org Cert no. TT-COC-2139
© 1996 Forest Stewardship Council

Typeset in 12/15pt Granjob by Falcon Oast Graphic Art Ltd.
Printed in the UK by CPI Cox & Wyman, Reading, RG1 8EX.

2 4 6 8 10 9 7 5 3 1

For Mary

Contents

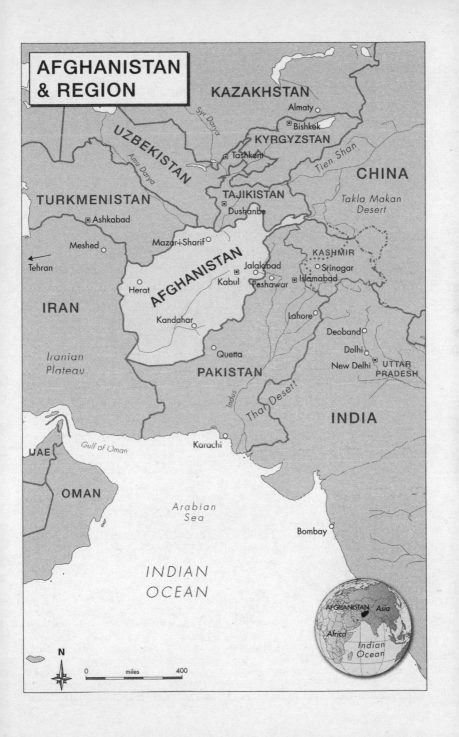

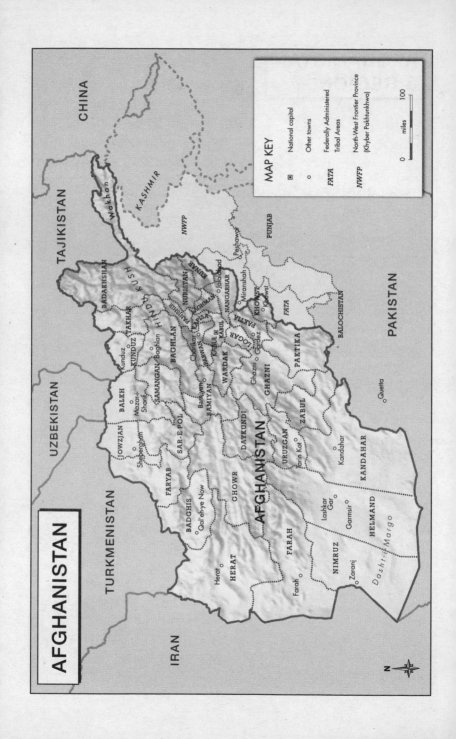

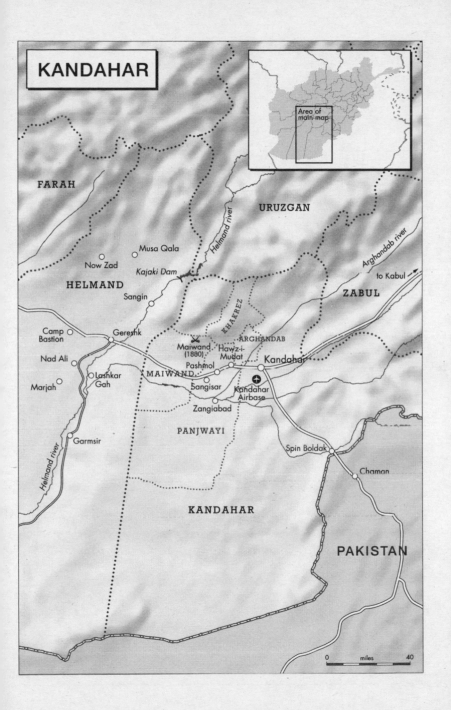

Introduction

In a previous book, *A Million Bullets*, an account of the British Army's battle with the Taliban in Helmand in 2006, I argued in its conclusion that negotiation with the enemy might be a better alternative to fighting them. Ever since – at conferences and literary festivals, in the comment pages of Sunday newspapers, on national radio and television, in private meetings with senior politicians and soldiers, even in testimony to a House of Commons Foreign Affairs Select Committee – I have repeated the axiom that no counter-insurgency in history has concluded without dialogue with the enemy. No one ever contested the assertion. And yet, nine miserable years after the campaign against the Taliban began, there has been no contact between the West or any of its allies and the insurgency's undisputed leader, Mullah Omar: not so much as a text message.

This book is written from a deep conviction that we must change tack. The insurgency is still expanding and Afghans have lost confidence in our ability to stem it, as well as in our ability to establish an alternative government in Kabul that is truly worthy of their support. A negotiated settlement with the Taliban looks increasingly like the West's only way out of the mess.

Our strategy to date has been dominated by military rather than civilian thinking, and it is failing in large part because we continue to misunderstand the nature of the opposition.

'There are those who are propagating war based on an extreme, perverted view of Islam. Those people are not reconcilable,' the former British Prime Minister Gordon Brown once remarked.[1] Yet if the problem is the 'perversion' of Islam – a characterization of their religion, incidentally, that a great many Afghans, not just the Taliban, would dispute – is reconciliation not more likely to be achieved through theological debate rather than military force? The Taliban are the representatives of an ideology as much as they are an army. It follows that we need to win arguments with them, not just battles – and we can't do that without talking to them. How much, in the end, do we really know about the Taliban and their motives? Not nearly enough, I would suggest. And yet according to Sun Tzu's *The Art of War*, the famous ancient Chinese text still taught in Nato staff colleges, 'know your enemy' is one of the first precepts of successful warfare.

In the first part of this book I have traced the origins and history of Mullah Omar's extraordinary movement from 1994 to the present day, with the aim of demonstrating that the Taliban were never quite the bearded bigots of popular Western imagination. The second part is dedicated to conversations with leading members of the so-called 'reconciled' Taliban, who are likely to emerge as key mediators in any peace deal with Omar in the future, and tackles these more immediate questions: what might such a deal look like? What would it mean for Afghanistan and the world, and how can it be achieved?

A compromise would not necessarily entail the abandonment of the West's principal goal.

'Let us not forget why we are in Afghanistan,' the US General David Petraeus said in November 2009. 'It is to ensure that this country cannot become once again a sanctuary for al-Qaida.'

Forget, for a moment, democratization, development, reform. They are all optional extras: desirable in themselves, perhaps, but nevertheless means to a greater end. Omar wants the withdrawal of foreign troops and the establishment of Sharia law in his country. In return for a guarantee to keep al-Qaida out of Afghanistan, is it unthinkable now to grant him this wish? Our policymakers assume that Omar could never be trusted to keep al-Qaida out, but how can they be sure when they have never asked him?

Western troop withdrawal, phased and carefully

timetabled, would not mean the abandonment of Afghanistan. On the contrary, the departure of our soldiers should be coordinated with a massive uplift in aid, paid for by savings from the military effort: the civilian-led development programme that we should perhaps have concentrated on in the first place. In February 2010, for the first time, the Pentagon spent more in a month on Afghanistan than it did on Iraq: $6.7 billion compared to $5.5 billion, or $233 million a day.[2] This is about three times what the Taliban government, before it was ousted, could afford to spend on civil development in an entire year. How many roads or schools or hospitals could be built with a budget as big as that? Such reconstruction could only happen with the consent of the Taliban, of course; but there is every reason to think that they would give their consent. They did in the past. The Taliban are not against Western aid and development in principle. It is the presence of infidel troops they primarily object to, and when they destroy a newly built school or well or road, it is often because they see these projects – perhaps with some reason – as weapons in a Western counter-insurgency campaign.

As an organization they have been relentlessly demonized: a byword for extremism, the most infamous religious movement of our times. They were doubtless guilty of many excesses when they were in power. Crucial questions remain about how they would treat the non-Pashtun minority should they return to the political mainstream – particularly the Hazara Shi'ites, the victims of serious persecution in the late 1990s. The footage of public executions carried out in a Kabul football stadium remains hard to comprehend in the West. We are rightly outraged by those insurgents who apparently see nothing wrong in using women and children as human shields on the southern battlefields of today.

Yet the truth is that the Taliban were never as uniformly wicked as they were routinely made out to be – and nor are they now. The original idea behind their movement was not evil, but noble. Perhaps like all popular revolutions, theirs took off in directions unanticipated by its founders, and much of the idealism that underpinned it became lost. But not, they insist, irrevocably so; and if they are convinced they could do better next time, who are we to say that they are wrong?

More to the point, the Afghans themselves now seem ready to offer the Taliban a second chance: even some Afghan women.

'I changed my view three years ago when I realized Afghanistan is on its own,' said Shukria Barakzai, an MP and one of the country's leading women's rights campaigners. 'It's not that the international community doesn't support us. They just don't understand us. The Taliban are part of our population. They have different ideas, but as democrats we have to accept that.'[3]

In 1999, Barakzai was beaten by the Taliban's religious police in Kabul when she went to the doctor's unaccompanied by her husband. If even she is prepared to consider a compromise with her former tormentors, should not the West be listening?

The Taliban made some terrible mistakes, and I do not condone them. But I am also certain that we need a better understanding of how and why they made those mistakes before we condemn them. Many worse things have happened to Afghans than the Taliban government of 1996–2001. In the context of Afghanistan's history of violence and poverty, they may well represent the least of evils. It is not as if the West's track record in Afghanistan over the last nine years is anything to boast about. Lawlessness, corruption, poppies: the Taliban arguably dealt with all these better than we have since 2001. For all their good intentions and sacrifices, our armed forces have won precious few hearts and minds in Afghanistan, while inadvertently visiting death and destruction on thousands of rural civilians and their communities.

In the end the Taliban are only people, and surely deserve to be treated as such. I know they are capable of learning from their mistakes and of changing their minds. In private arguments I have heard them do so many times. Besides: if we find their worldview abhorrent, is it not more practical to try to change it through patient argument rather than at the point of a gun? Jaw-jaw is better than war-war, as Churchill once said. Dialogue is more effective as well as more humane than bullets.

There was a time in the 1990s, often forgotten now, when even America did not consider the Taliban so bad.

A Texan oil firm once discussed building a trans-Afghan pipeline with them, openly and with Washington's blessing. We can and should learn to live with them again; and political reconciliation, currently a kind of adjunct to Western military strategy, must be placed centre stage if there is ever to be peace in the country.

Finally, a caveat: I have been writing about or reporting from Afghanistan for fourteen years now, but I do not claim to be an expert. In fact, the more I visit this bewildering, intoxicating country, the less I feel I truly understand it. There are certainly many people with a better grasp of its complexities than me. I therefore make no apologies for borrowing from the work of other writers in some sections of this book, while affirming that any mistakes are entirely my own.

Part I

1

The Tank of Islam: Kandahar, 1994

It seems improbable, given the daily drip of news of British soldiers' deaths in Afghanistan, but in 1994, the year the Taliban movement was born, that country was a far more dangerous and chaotic place than it is now. The Soviets, who ended their ten-year occupation in 1989, were long gone – and the disparate ethnic and religious leaders who once united to eject the invaders, the famous mujahideen, were now at each other's throats. In the first six months of 1994, 25,000 civilians were killed in the vicious squabble for control of the capital, Kabul: death and destruction on a scale worse than anything the Afghans had suffered under the Soviets.

The world's attention had wandered since 1989, and the renewed carnage was barely noticed abroad. The Cold War was yesterday's story, and the hottest proxy battlefield of the 1980s seemed an irrelevant backwater. There was in any case much else to preoccupy the West in 1994. Even as President Bill Clinton pulled US troops out of Somalia, he found himself drawn into an intensifying civil war in Bosnia. Boris Yeltsin invaded Chechnya, while Saddam Hussein refused to cooperate with UN weapons inspectors and sent troops to the Kuwaiti border once again. In Rwanda, 800,000 Tutsis were hacked to death by rival Hutus, a massacre that the international community seemed powerless to prevent. The suffering in Kabul was small fry compared to that. For whatever reason, between 1990 and 1996 the UN Security Council did not hold a single debate on Afghanistan.[1]

With the collapse of central government, much of the countryside had fallen under the control of rapacious bandits. Life had become particularly difficult for the rural poor – and nowhere more so than in the Pashtun heartlands of southern Afghanistan. Rival gangs of armed men had slung chains across every road around Kandahar city, stopping the traffic to demand a 'toll' before it could proceed. It was becoming uneconomical as well as dangerous for farmers even to try to take their crops to market.

Many of these bandits were minor ex-mujahideen commanders whose salaries had dried up with the ending of the war and who were unwilling, or unable, to disband their hungry followers. Others were merely criminals with an eye to the main chance. By the spring of 1994 it wasn't just farmers but the international trucking business that was suffering. The bandits laid siege with their chains to the A1 national ring road that intersected the southern provinces, a road that connected Afghanistan's main trading partners, Iran to the west and Pakistan to the east. There were fifty chains just on the 65-mile drive between Kandahar and the Pakistani border.[2] Truckers were paying more in bribes than the value of the goods they were trying to transport. The A1 was a vital artery in the national economy, and now it was all but choked off.

Some highwaymen, such as Shah Baran, a former officer in the Soviet-backed National Army, were often so stoned on *chars*, the powerful local cannabis, that they were barely able to function. One traveller recalled his dread as his car approached the chain that designated a Shah Baran checkpoint. The gang of grubby armed men huddled in blankets at the kerbside didn't move, however. They were too busy puffing from a large *chilam*. The traveller was too scared to attract their attention. More than fifteen minutes passed before Shah Baran looked up and even noticed the car.[3]

Men like these soon graduated from demanding tolls to random acts of murder, or worse. A notorious villain called Saleh, who at times commanded hundreds of men, had taken to stopping inter-city bus traffic and abducting any woman he fancied. Two young girls travelling from Herat to Kandahar were later found to have been gang-raped and beaten to death, their naked bodies thrown in a pit behind Saleh's checkpoint.

Things were no better in Kandahar city. A bloody turf war had erupted between the main local commanders,

Ustad Abdul Haleem, Hajji Ahmad and Mullah Naqib. One battle lasted for six days, turning buildings into rubble and streets into impassable mazes of trenches. Bodies lay scattered everywhere. The air was filled with thick smoke from houses burning out of control, and hundreds of shops were looted. On the sixth day, a Friday, thousands of townspeople gathered after prayers to demonstrate against the violence, but at Kabul Darwaza Square their march through the city came to an abrupt halt when they were confronted by Baru, a former mujahideen commander who had taken up position with a tank.

Baru was an odious man, corrupt and without conscience. He was notorious for marrying some girl, demanding a large dowry, then divorcing her a month later without returning the family's money. Nor was his sexual appetite confined to women. Like many mujahideen commanders, Baru kept a teenage catamite, a practice unequivocally forbidden in Islam but which is nevertheless widespread among Afghanistan's huge fighting community: a status symbol as well as a source of sexual release. The difference in Baru's case was that the catamite himself was a bandit, effetely waving a Makarov pistol at passing travellers and able to get away with anything, including murder, thanks to his feared patron. A man such as Baru thrived in Kandahar's present climate. Now, without warning, he fired a shell into the demonstrators, massacring dozens. The Kandaharis had suffered greatly during the Soviet occupation, but this was worse. The period is still remembered as *topakiyaan*: the time of the men with guns.

Not all former mujahideen had gone to the bad. Among them was the veteran fighter Mullah Abdul Salam Zaeef, who took up arms against the Russians in 1983 at the age of fifteen. He was ambushed nine times and injured twice in that war; in an attack on Kandahar airport in 1988, he lost fifty of the fifty-eight men under his command. Zaeef was no war-monger by nature but a religious scholar who greatly preferred the Koran to the Kalashnikov. But because a *jihad* had been formally declared against the Russians in 1979, it became his duty as a Muslim to take up arms against them. He was grateful, indeed overjoyed, to hang up his guns when the invaders were finally ejected.

The war had slowed rather than interrupted his studies. Now, back at home, he was able to concentrate on them properly again. In 1990 he became a father for the first time. He was forced to take a job digging roads when money became tight, but by 1993 he had found a position as the imam of a tiny village mosque. This quiet life was not to last. The rumble of artillery could often be heard from Kandahar city, thirty miles to the east. Passing travellers or visiting friends brought news of fresh chaos and atrocities there almost every day. A moment came when one of his parishioners, a young man called Abdul Mohammad who was just back from a trip to the city, told him how he had almost been killed by two armed muggers on a motorbike, one of whom he had managed to wrestle to the ground. The attack, shockingly, had happened not in Kandahar but in broad daylight on the road right next to Zaeef's mosque. Abdul Mohammad was still white and shaking from the experience.

Zaeef was a peace-loving man whose patience had been tried too much. This was the land of his childhood: he had been born in the village of Zangiabad, barely 20 miles away, and had spent most of his adult life in desperate combat with foreigners bent on subjugating his country and suppressing his religion. A million of his countrymen had died in the national cause, and for what? The Islamic society he had fought so long and hard for was disintegrating before his eyes. Some ex-mujahideen friends of his, Abdul Qudus and Neda Mohammad, were in favour of ambushing and killing the villainous Saleh, but Zaeef advised caution. He knew there were other retired mujahideen commanders who thought and felt as he did: local men alongside whom he had fought for years. Saleh and his kind were powerful; banding together again seemed the best means of standing up to them.

The networks from the war were still strong among the ex-mujahideen. The anti-Soviet resistance had coalesced around a number of politico-military organizations, or *tanzeems*, which represented every possible shade of political opinion in Afghanistan's fragmented society, from the deep religious conservatism of Gulbuddin Hekmatyar's Hizb-i-Islami to the federalism espoused by Abdul Ali Mazari's Hazara Shi'ite organization, Hizb-i-Wahdat.

Like many Pashtuns from the conservative south,

Zaeef initially fought for a unit loyal to Hizb-i-Islami. But as a man with a religious calling, he also belonged to a separate but overlapping network that, although drawn from a far wider area than the typical tanzeem, was no less tightly knit. Their bond was their faith and, very often, a childhood upbringing in a *madrasah*: an Islamic seminary, a training school for mullahs. Such men formed the grass roots of the movement that became known as the Taliban.

Contrary to common perception in the West, the movement did not emerge out of nowhere in the 1990s. 'Taliban' was no more than the plural, in Pashto, of *talib*, the Arabic word for an Islamic student: literally, 'one who seeks knowledge'. They had been a presence in Afghan village society for as long as there had been madrasahs – which is to say, since the earliest days of Islam. There had once been so many Islamic students at large, indeed, that they had created something of a social problem. A British intelligence report written in 1901 described the 'talib-ul-ilm' as 'men, chiefly young men, who contemplate following the religious profession. They flock to the shrines of the country and attach themselves to some religious leader, ostensibly for religious education. Their number far exceeds those required to fill up vacancies in village mullahships and other ecclesiastic appointments, and they are reduced to seek other means of livelihood. They are at the bottom of all the mischief in the country, the instigators and often the perpetrators of the bulk of the crime. They use their religious status to live free on the people, who are too superstitious to turn them out, even when they destroy the peace of the family circle.'[4]

In the 1980s, most madrasah students who fought against the Soviets were assimilated into units controlled by the established tanzeems, although some banded together to form their own platoon-sized fighting groups who were described, by both themselves and others, as 'taliban' even then. They were easily distinguished by their turbans that were either jet black or snow white, in emulation of the headgear worn by descending angels who, according to the Koran, came to the Prophet's rescue during one of his battles with the infidel hordes between Mecca and Medina in the founding days of Islam. They were Muslim brothers-in-arms, and their faith made them tough guerrillas who were highly valued by their regular mujahideen colleagues, both for their fighting prowess and for the galvanizing effect that their religious conviction could have on their troops' morale. At their best, taliban fighters embodied the mujahideen ideal. One mullah specialized in ambushing armoured vehicles by hiding under water in a ditch by the road, breathing from the inner tube of a bicycle tyre. They could and frequently did survive on a handful of dates when supplies ran low, and they faced Afghanistan's extremes of heat and cold in the same old sandals and *shalwar qamiz* each day.

Among the people Zaeef went to consult in 1994 about standing up to Saleh and his like was one Mullah Mohammad Omar, a former fighter born in the neighbouring province of Uruzgan to the north, but who was now living at Sangisar, a village community 25 miles west of Kandahar. In the 1980s Sangisar was home to an important mujahideen base, and both Omar and Zaeef had taken part in a desperate battle with the Soviets in the district in 1988, the type of close combat where they had picked up live grenades and tossed them back at their assailants. Zaeef was 20 metres from Omar when their position was attacked by MiG fighter jets. Omar, looking around the corner of a wall, was struck by shrapnel from a bomb – a wound that would later prove terminal to his sight in one eye.

That same night, even as Omar was bandaging himself up, Zaeef recalled how the defenders celebrated the success of their resistance with an *attan*, a physically intense Pashtun war-dance performed to the beat of a double-headed drum called a *dhol*. The men gathered in a large circle, leaping and spinning faster and faster and firing their guns in the air. It was, according to Zaeef, 'a marvellous party . . . May God be praised! What a brotherhood we had among the mujahideen! We weren't concerned with the world or with our lives; our intentions were pure and every one of us was ready to die as a martyr. When I look back on the love and respect that we had for each other, it sometimes seems like a dream.'

Omar had returned to the Sangisar base after the war, and converted it into a madrasah where he now preached and taught. He was a pious, conservative man with a reputation as a courageous but taciturn military commander. He was something of a southern Pashtun archetype in this respect. He kept himself to himself and avoided the petty politics and self-advancing turf wars that preoccupied some of his peers. As a consequence he had never been a very prominent figure in the Jihad, but he was also a clean slate, a man who had no enemies because he had crossed no one in the past, and no scores to settle on his own behalf. In the view of Zaeef and others, this was precisely the kind of man that the reconstituted band of veterans now needed as a leader. Memories are long everywhere in Afghanistan, but nowhere more so than among the Pashtuns, who traditionally put great emphasis on *badal*, the obligation to seek revenge.[*]

Omar's wife had just given birth to a son when Zaeef went to see his old comrade. His friends and the local imams had all gathered there for the traditional celebration ceremony – lengthy recitations from the Koran – and Zaeef and two other mullahs who had accompanied him joined in. After supper, they took Omar to a separate room to talk business. The plan they proposed to him was beguilingly simple: the disarmament of the people in two provincial districts west of Kandahar – Maiwand and Panjwayi – and the establishment there of Sharia

---

[*] The English proverb, 'Revenge is a dish best served cold', is a direct translation of a Pashto one that was imported into British phraseology in the nineteenth century.

law, as articulated by the Prophet Mohammed in the early seventh century.

'We told him that he had been proposed as a leader who could implement our plan,' Zaeef recalled in his autobiography. 'He took a few moments to think after we had spoken, and then said nothing for some time. This was one of Mullah Omar's common habits, and he never changed this . . . Finally he said that he agreed with our plan and that something needed to be done. "But, I cannot accept the leadership position," he said . . . "Why did you not accept it yourself?"'

Zaeef understood Omar's misgivings, for the job would certainly be a dangerous one.

'He asked us what guarantees he could have that everyone wouldn't just abandon him if things became tough. We assured him that all those involved were true taliban and mujahideen.'

He was persuaded eventually. Others had come to see him, asking for the same thing.

'In the end everything that happens depends on God,' he said.

Within six weeks of the first discussion about killing Saleh, some forty or fifty people gathered in Sangisar at a small, crumbling mud-brick building known as the White Mosque to discuss the foundation of what became known as 'the Taliban'. Omar agreed to be their commander and took a solemn oath of allegiance, a *beyat*, from all those present. No mission statement was drawn up, no articles of association written down. There didn't seem any need. No name for the movement was ever discussed, either: *taliban* was simply what Omar and his followers were. The term in its present sense, with a definite article and a capital T, was probably coined by the BBC Pashto service, which aired a report about the Sangisar meeting twenty-four hours after it happened. It was never clear how the BBC learned about the meeting, since no press release was ever issued, nor any interview given. No one, least of all Omar, ever suspected that 'the Taliban' would one day become a kind of global brand name.

Very soon afterwards the Taliban set up their own checkpoint near the village of Hawz-i-Mudat on the main road west of Kandahar. They had a few weapons but almost no money. Zaeef donated 10,000 Afghanis, which was all he had: enough, as he said, 'to buy lunch for ten people in a good restaurant in Kabul'. The group's sole means of transport was an old Russian motorbike with no exhaust pipe, a machine that could be heard coming from miles away, and which they nicknamed 'the Tank of Islam'. The movement would have folded almost before it had begun were it not for the extraordinary support of the locals. Scores of villagers came out to see the new checkpoint for themselves. They provided bread and milk and, crucially, volunteers. Within a few days the movement had over 400 new members. Money was soon no longer a problem either, thanks to donations from businessmen, particularly truck-company operators whose livelihoods depended on being able to use the road without hindrance. One man appeared at the checkpoint dragging a sack that contained 90 million Afghanis. Zaeef did not ask where such an enormous sum had come from.

The Talibs began by moving against the nearest check points up and down the road. The first was operated by an ex-mujahideen commander called Daru Khan, who fled after a short firefight. The next three bandits, Yaqut, Bismillah and Pir Mohammed, fled without any resistance at all. The fifth, Saleh, fought back at first but then also ran away, and was caught in a secondary ambush. So it went on – and with every victory, the Taliban's ranks swelled with fresh volunteers. The justice they meted out was as harsh as it was swift. Some bandits were lynched, their bodies left dangling from gibbets at the side of the road with money stuffed into their mouths to serve both as a symbol of their crime and a warning to others.

To begin with, the Taliban's ambitions stretched no further than the two districts nearest their original checkpoint, Maiwand and Panjwayi. But on 12 October, some 200 of them hid themselves in trucks and drove into the centre of Spin Boldak on the border of Pakistan, 60 miles east of Kandahar. Jumping out in front of the police station, they took control of the town in fifteen minutes. This takeover was significant. Spin Boldak was a customs post in the lucrative international trucking trade. It had been garrisoned by Mullah Akhtar Jan, a Hizb-i-Islami militiaman loyal to Gulbuddin Hekmatyar, one of the top three mujahideen leaders and, until four months previously, the Prime Minister. Akhtar Jan escaped but, in a development that boded ill for the power-brokers in Kabul, many of his men now switched sides and joined the Taliban.

The local strongmen around Kandahar could see which way the wind was blowing. Switching allegiance to the stronger side was common practice in Afghanistan, a survival tactic learned over centuries in a region where war and internecine violence are the norm. When Mullah Naqib came over to their side, unexpectedly handing over his base at Hindu Kotai on the outskirts of Kandahar city, there no longer seemed any limit to what the Taliban might achieve. Naqib was the leader of the influential Alikozai tribe and perhaps the most respected warlord in the region with an impressive reputation from Soviet times. More to the point, the warehouses at Hindu Kotai were full of heavy weaponry, including tanks. Kandahar city fell on 5 November after four days of fighting that cost fifty lives.

By now the entire country was talking about the Taliban phenomenon. News of them had spread to Pakistan, too: on 1 January 1995, 3,000 volunteers for the cause arrived from Peshawar. Ordinary Afghans tended to speak in a whisper about these turbanned avengers. Some felt repulsion at their methods, but most felt relief that here, at last, was a group who looked like they might restore some semblance of social order. The proof of the public's hunger for this was in the speed of the Taliban's success. By February 1995, just four months after setting up a single rural checkpoint, this mullahs' revolt had become a national movement that controlled nine of the country's thirty provinces.

2

The Army of Orphans: Peshawar, 1996

My first encounter with the Taliban was not in Afghanistan but in Peshawar in Pakistan, in August 1996. They were big news by then, for Omar's troops had captured half the country and were poised to take Kabul – although my original reason for being in the region was more prosaic. I was a 29-year-old freelancer, broke and scrabbling for work as usual. So when the *Sunday Express* showed an interest in a piece about Jemima Goldsmith, the English It-girl who had just married the cricketing star Imran Khan – and offered to pay for a trip to Lahore if I could secure an interview with her – I grabbed the opportunity.

This part of the trip didn't go well. I had no introduction to either of the Khans, who turned out to be in no mood to talk to the press after a honeymoon embarrassingly spoiled by a paparazzo with a telephoto lens. Their home in Lahore was a virtual fortress. I spent two tedious days loitering outside, trying to persuade a gang of *chowkidar*, or watchmen, to pass a message to their employers – and then admitted defeat.

Fortunately there was another story to pursue, although it was nothing the *Sunday Express* would be very interested in: a general election had just been called in Pakistan. Imran Khan, indeed, was contesting it with his own newly founded political party, the Tehrik-i-Insaf, or Movement for Justice, although he never got very far with it. The front-runners were Benazir Bhutto, leader of the left-of-centre Pakistan People's Party (PPP), who had unexpectedly been sacked from the prime ministership following allegations of corruption; and her main challenger, the Pakistan Muslim League's Nawaz Sharif.

I spent an extraordinary fortnight following these two around on the campaign trail. Bhutto was an electrifying orator. She was indignant at the accusations of corruption and outraged at her removal by the President, Farooq Leghari. At one point I found myself standing behind her on an open-air platform in Lahore as she whipped up a crowd of a couple of thousand, imperious and magnetically beautiful, her trademark silk headscarf billowing, somehow glacially cool in the sweltering summer sun. I assumed her self-confidence was dynastic. The Bhuttos were Pakistan's version of the Kennedys, a political family blessed with talent, tainted by scandal, cursed by assassination. Both her brothers were killed in suspicious circumstances; her father Zulfikar Ali Bhutto, who served as both President and Prime Minister, was hanged by a political rival in 1979.

It was Nawaz Sharif, though, who won the 1996 election. With his curly hair poking from beneath a Western-style pale flat cap, he looked disconcertingly like the singer Paul Simon. One day I secured a place on his helicopter for a campaign tour of the Punjab. It was a lordly way to see the country. We clattered low over vast dusty plains that shimmered in the heat. A sparsely inhabited land, I thought at first: not many votes to be had among the goatherds here. But the villages out here were all towns; by European standards, large towns. We visited four or five of them and they all seemed to pop up out of nowhere.

Some were clearly expecting the visit: we would land and be led to a stage in some makeshift football stadium that was already packed with thousands of people, all roaring their approval. The Punjab had long been the Pakistan Muslim League's heartland. Elsewhere the pilot would circle the town two or three times before landing, a technique that drew the inhabitants to their doorways and windows, pointing and clapping in anticipation of a big event. These were not places where helicopters appeared every day. In one town a crowd of several hundred suddenly swarmed on to our intended landing zone, a cricket pitch. We hovered over a sea of upturned faces, and watched their expressions turning from excitement to doubt and then horror as the machine dropped relentlessly lower. I glanced across at Nawaz Sharif, but his face was a mask of indifference. Only at the last possible moment did the crowd part and scatter, abandoning bits of shopping, a sandal or two, a bicycle with a wheel still spinning.

The day as a whole was a strange experience, thrilling and dispiriting at the same time. From the porthole of the helicopter it was hard not to view the people of Pakistan as a seething, barely controlled mass, permanently teetering on the edge of a Malthusian catastrophe. The population was in fact growing exponentially – and it still is. Since 1996 their numbers have risen by 50 million, to 176 million. By 2020 the figure is predicted to be 220 million, or about six times the number who lived here in 1950. It seemed improbable that any political system could bring order to such a society, let alone democracy. It wasn't just that the swelling population meant the voice of the people was forever being diluted. In 1996 about two-thirds of Pakistanis were illiterate, obliging politicians to campaign with pictures rather than slogans. Sharif's symbol was a lion, Bhutto's an arrow. It seemed to me that the raw enthusiasm that greeted Sharif in Punjab had less to do with his policies than with tribalism. It was politics in its crudest form.

Beyond the campaign hoopla, Pakistanis had reason to feel deeply disillusioned with their government in Islamabad. The politicians who claimed to represent them were serial abusers of the power entrusted to them. Nawaz Sharif was no better than Benazir Bhutto, for he too had been sacked from the prime ministership for corruption, three years earlier in 1993. When polling day finally came in February 1997, voter turn-out was around 30 per cent: close to a record low for Pakistan and a statistic that told its own story.

After all this my trip to Peshawar was almost an afterthought. I had British friends who lived and worked there for the aid agency Oxfam, and I was looking forward to staying with them. Peshawar today is a dangerous place, plagued by suicide bombers and officially off-limits to foreign journalists, but it was different then. It was still possible to wander the maze of bazaars for hours, shopping for carpets and jewellery and trinkets like any tourist. After the Soviet invasion of Afghanistan the city, close to the border at the eastern end of the famous Khyber Pass, became what the author Peter Bergen called 'an Asian Casablanca, awash in spies, journalists, aid workers and refugees', and it still had that edge to it. It remained the principal gateway to Afghanistan for Westerners, since there were no direct international flights to Kabul in those days. The foreign aid community was consequently huge. Some of the wide, leafy streets of University Town, the district they favoured just west of the city centre, seemed to contain nothing but NGO offices. After work the foreigners descended on the American Club, where they swapped special coupons for beers and hamburgers and, in the summer months, partied late into the night beside the club's most popular asset: a swimming pool, well shielded from the prying eyes of an easily offended public.

Peshawar was a Pashto-speaking city, and quite unlike any other in Pakistan. It had been a commercial and cultural hub for the Pashtuns since ancient times, a major crossroads on the Silk Road between China and Rome, and they still regard it as 'theirs'. The fact that it lies within modern Pakistan is considered by many as an accident of recent history, a blip in the natural order of things. The 1,600-mile Durand Line, as the Afghan–Pakistan border is known, is named after Sir Mortimer Durand, the Foreign Secretary of British India who delineated it only in 1893. The border is not just 'porous', as Nato's hard-pressed commanders still describe it. In the Pashtun mind, it is non-existent: a line drawn on a map long ago by foreigners who did not consult them on the splitting in half of their ancestral homeland.

There was little discussion of the Pakistani elections at the American Club in Peshawar that August. Instead the bar was buzzing with talk about events over the border. In Kandahar that spring, the Taliban leadership had met with a thousand religious leaders and elders to discuss policy. It ended on 4 April with a call for a new jihad against President Burhanuddin Rabbani's government in Kabul.

To cement his position as leader, Mullah Omar had a brilliant idea. In a green-marbled shrine near the centre of Kandahar lies one of Islam's most sacred relics: a plain brown cloak said to have belonged to the Prophet Mohammed himself. This ancient garment is stored in the centre of a series of locked boxes, like the tiniest in a set of Babushka dolls, and is traditionally taken out only in times of crisis; the last time had been in 1935 when a special religious service was held to counter an epidemic of cholera. At the head of a crowd of some 1,200 followers, Omar now went to the shrine, ordered the cloak to be taken out again, and climbed to the building's roof where he held it up for all to see. The crowd below was duly transfixed. They began to chant deliriously, declaring Omar 'Amir ul-Mu'mineen' – the Commander of the Faithful. Then they snatched off their turbans and hurled them at the cloak in the hope that their headgear might come into contact with it. There were so many turbans in the air that for a moment Omar almost disappeared beneath them.

It was an inspired piece of political and religious drama. The title of Amir ul-Mu'mineen had not been adopted by anyone in Afghanistan since 1834, when the ruler Dost Mohammed declared jihad against the Sikhs. By associating himself so directly with the Prophet, Omar was asking to be called the commander not just of Afghanistan's faithful, but of Muslims everywhere. For Pashtuns, there was additional meaning in the gesture. Omar was also associating himself with Ahmad Shah Durrani, whose mausoleum the shrine abuts and who acquired the cloak from the Amir of Buhkara in 1768. Durrani, still popularly known as 'Baba', the Father of Afghanistan, once ruled from Kandahar a Pashtun empire that stretched as far as Delhi.

'In his time,' according to the ornate lapis lazuli

inscription that runs around the roof of his mausoleum, 'from the awe of his glory and greatness, the lioness nourished the stag with her milk. From all sides in the ear of his enemies there arrived a thousand reproofs from the tongue of his dagger.'[1]

The whole fantastic episode was filmed by the veteran cameraman Peter Jouvenal, who happened to be in Kandahar that day looking for footage to use in a BBC *Newsnight* programme. It remains one of the very few pieces of footage of Omar in existence, and the programme that resulted was an award-winning one. Jouvenal was 150 yards away in the back of a Toyota van that had been brought to an unscripted halt by the dense crowd around the shrine. The driver, his fixer and his Taliban minder were sitting in the front. Photographing Omar was strictly forbidden, even then, but with all eyes fixed ahead Jouvenal was able to shoot the scene through the van window, peering surreptitiously through the viewfinder set at a right-angle to the camera on his lap. Omar did not put the cloak on but held it up gingerly, and for no more than a minute or so – which was only sensible considering the garment's great antiquity. It was quite a windy day, according to Jouvenal, who couldn't help wondering how different history might have been if the cloak had disintegrated in Omar's hands. He had one other wicked thought: the chanting and the turban-throwing seemed to him to amount to idolatry, a sin in Islam that the Taliban were later notoriously keen to eradicate from Afghan society.

Omar's rooftop theatrics achieved their goal. Nine months earlier, in November 1995, the Taliban's first assault on Kabul had been repulsed despite the supporting fire of some 400 tanks. This was the first significant setback Omar's troops had suffered on the battlefield, and the Kandahar gathering provided just the morale boost his troops now needed. The spring and summer of 1996 saw some dazzling military successes in eastern and western Afghanistan. The keys to the Taliban's early success in Kandahar had been surprise and speed: old guerrilla skills learned in mujahideen times but abandoned by many commanders as the country sank into civil war, and static trench warfare around the urban strongholds became the norm. Replicating their tactics in the south, the Taliban now developed a version of Blitzkrieg, with lightly armed fighters travelling in fast fleets of Toyota Hi-Lux trucks. And when this didn't work they used bribery, usually to equally good effect.

The Taliban soon renewed their attack on the capital, this time with barrages of rockets. In June, President Rabbani formed a hasty alliance with his main political rival, Gulbuddin Hekmatyar, who was appointed Prime Minister for a second time. In return, thousands of Hekmatyar's Hizb-i-Islami troops were brought in to stiffen the defence. They were experienced and well-equipped fighters who, it was assumed, were itching to avenge previous humiliations at the hands of the Taliban back in Spin Boldak and elsewhere. In the American Club, therefore, there were some who predicted that

Hizb-i-Islami would prove too great an obstacle for the zealots from the south, and that the assault on the capital would fail once again.

Pakistan's role in the war to their west was obscure. It certainly wasn't a public election issue on the campaign trail in Islamabad and Lahore, where the talk had all been about the economy and political corruption. On the other hand, it was widely suspected that the Taliban were being supported in their revolution by the ISI, Pakistan's mighty Inter Service Intelligence wing and, it was inferred, by the government too. Two years previously, after all, Benazir's Pashtun Interior Minister, General Nasirullah Babar, had publicly referred to the Taliban as 'our boys'.[2] Nevertheless, Benazir evaded the question when I asked her about Pakistan's relationship with the Taliban, saying only that she was 'monitoring events in Afghanistan closely' and that we 'would all have to wait to see what happened'. I took this to mean that support for the Taliban was, at most, a small and possibly experimental covert operation orchestrated by the ISI. It was also clear that she considered it no business of foreign journalists to pry into sensitive matters of national security. So I was surprised to discover that the Taliban were not just lurking in the refugee camps outside Peshawar, as I expected, but were operating quite openly in the city centre. They had even opened an office recently on the Old Bara Road in University Town.

Their appearance in Peshawar had sent a frisson through the foreign aid community, particularly its female members. An Australian aid worker I met described how a black-turbanned young man had squared up to her the previous week as she came out of a bakery opposite their new office. He hadn't said anything, but stared and deliberately blocked her way when she tried to step around him on the pavement. His meaning was clear: there were to be no unveiled women in *their* street. Many similar stories were doing the rounds in University Town that summer, when Western outrage at the Taliban's misogyny in general would reach new peaks. It was widely suspected that their office's location, highly visible and in the heart of the NGO district, had been chosen for its symbolic value as much as for any practical reason. Western NGOs were in practice responsible for all social welfare in Afghanistan in those chaotic days, so this was taken by some as a direct challenge to that status quo, as if to say: 'We'll be running Afghanistan *our* way now.'

Were they serious? One morning I borrowed an interpreter from the Oxfam office and went to the Old Bara Road to find out. The Taliban office was small and dilapidated: a hastily converted shop, I guessed. Three or four men with beards and black turbans squatted by the entrance watching the passers-by in the street, like so many perching crows. They rose and followed me inside, where another half-dozen men loitered. It was hard to make out what their purpose here was, for there appeared to be no work going on. There was one desk with a telephone on it but no other obvious office equipment, no paperwork, computers or even type-writers. I glimpsed a rack of Kalashnikovs locked behind a grille in a cupboard in a corner, but otherwise the atmosphere was strangely like that of an underworked East London minicab office.

My interpreter and I were shown to some grubby floor cushions. Tea was brought and eventually their leader appeared. His name, he said, was Amruddin; like nearly all the men here, he was from Kandahar. He was a young man with a straggly beard, clad head to toe in black and outwardly indistinguishable from the others – until you looked at his eyes. These shone with the light of religious conviction so intense that you sensed at once that he needed no other badge of authority. Their clarity was startlingly emphasized – *italicized*, perhaps – by dashes of thick black kohl painted on the lids beneath. He sat down cross-legged on the carpet, and the others all copied him until they had formed a semi-circle around us, silent and expectant, like schoolboys waiting for a story from their teacher. I supposed that as former madrasah students, they gathered this way almost by default.

Despite his transcendent piety, Amruddin was evidently not a senior figure. He took a long time to answer my questions, and when he did it tended to be with the shortest of platitudes. I came away with the impression that he understood almost as little as I did about what they were really doing in Peshawar. The ostensible reason was to 'help our Afghan brothers' still living in the refugee camps that surrounded the city: 'The religious duty of every Muslim,' he said.

I asked if their mission was supported by the Pakistan government.

'The Pakistanis are our brothers – they are Muslims like us.'

'And the ISI – are they also your brothers? Are they giving you money and weapons for your fight against Kabul?'

'The ISI are Muslims too.'

'But you are trying to impose Sharia law in Afghanistan. Not everyone wants that in your country. Is it what the ISI wants?'

'We have imposed nothing but peace on the people of Afghanistan,' he replied. 'Our success is due only to the fact that the people want us to succeed.'

Amruddin's words were polite, yet the crowd round about him were increasingly unnerving. Their initial curiosity about who I was and what I might want had given way to barely suppressed impatience. Our encounter was not going to be a long one. They were young men, all of them, and there was an almost bovine quality to their stares, a passive-aggressive *hauteur* that I could not quite fathom. I wondered if I was being subtly mocked. I had no beard then, which must have seemed freakish to them. They were foot soldiers in their move-ment, simple people who I was sure had seen few if any Westerners before coming to Peshawar. For my part it was the first time I had seen men wearing eye-liner –

actors and drag queens excepted. It was only much later that I realized how common the practice was among Pashtuns, and that wearing it was not necessarily an exercise in male vanity.* Only one thing was clear to me: they believed with total certainty that they were the coming power in the region – and that the West had better watch out. But what were they really doing here in Peshawar?

Pakistan's corrupt political climate had more to do with their presence than the foreign aid community imagined. In times of political weakness it was the leaders of the enormous armed forces – the seventh largest in the world – who had always stepped up to fill the void of leadership. The generals saw themselves as the guardians of the nation: its soul, its backbone, its only real source of moral fibre – and their country's body politic was undoubtedly lacking that in the mid-1990s. In 1999, Pakistan was to experience its third military coup in half a century when General Pervez Musharraf seized power from Nawaz Sharif. The Taliban could only have opened an office in Peshawar with the permission and collusion of the ISI.

---

* Kohl, the Arabic word for stibnite, a naturally occurring sulphide of antimony, has been used throughout the Middle East since ancient Egyptian times at least in order to improve the vision of the wearer. The custom is mentioned by Pliny the Elder as well as in the Old Testament. The Prophet himself advocated smearing each eye with it three times before going to bed every night, according to the *hadith*.

The department had grown powerful during the 1980s, when they functioned as the CIA's main conduit for dollars destined for the mujahideen. Peshawar was the nerve centre of an enormous support operation. The ISI did not just provide arms to the insurgents over the border, they also trained them how to use them: perhaps as many as 95,000 fighters over the decade. Out of the seven main mujahideen groups, Gulbuddin Hekmatyar's Hizb-i-Islami was the one they most favoured, though all of them benefited from ISI largesse at one time or another, including many future Taliban – even Mullah Omar. The ISI had carried on supporting Hekmatyar after the Soviet retreat, hoping that he would establish a friendly and stable regime to their west, but by 1994 it was becoming all too obvious that their protégé had failed. As a consequence, the ISI had switched horses to an organization that appeared to have a much better chance of restoring stability: the Taliban.

Quite when the ISI switched horses is still hotly debated. Some Afghans believe the revolt was an ISI-sponsored project from the very start. Others say that it was as spontaneous and home-grown as Mullah Zaeef claimed, and that the ISI did not become involved until later when the odds on the Taliban succeeding had short-ened to a near certainty. Either way, their approval of the movement was implicit in the mere existence of the Taliban's Old Bara Road office in August 1996.

ISI sympathy for the Taliban cause was not in itself surprising. The relationships forged on the training grounds in the heat of the Soviet war were not easily dismantled. Indeed, the former ISI chief Lieutenant-General Hamid Gul, who headed the department from 1987 to 1989, is known in Pakistan as 'the father of the Taliban' and remains openly supportive of their cause to this day. He heads a generation of ISI officers who continue to make a distinction between Omar's organization and the so-called 'Pakistani Taliban', who are bent on the overthrow of the Islamabad government: a goal never shared by Mullah Omar, whose ambitions have always been confined to his own country. Omar was among those trained by 'Colonel Imam', the nom-de-guerre of Brigadier Amir Sultan Tarar, who had in turn been taught his guerrilla skills by US Special Forces on a course at Fort Bragg, North Carolina. He still remembers his former protégé with fondness. Now sixty-five and living in retirement in Rawalpindi, the garrison town that abuts Islamabad, Tarar told a British reporter in January 2010 that Omar was 'a good man. He is for his country, not for any mischief.'[3]

If certain military hearts were with the Taliban in 1996, so were many minds, for there were some sound strategic reasons for backing them. The first of these was that Pakistan was still hosting at least 1.4 million refugees from the Soviet war.[4] A source of growing social tension in the border areas, these Afghans were understandably reluctant to return to a country of lawless violence. With their promise of restoring stability, the Taliban appeared to offer the best chance of luring them home again.

The second reason was to do with India. Since 1947 Pakistan has fought no fewer than four wars with its vastly stronger southern neighbour, most of them centred on the disputed territory of Kashmir. India was a Pakistani obsession, the prism through which all military strategy was and is still seen. The ISI was convinced that India sought to encircle them by seeking power and influence in Afghanistan. This fear was not wholly without foundation. India does take a close interest in Afghanistan, spending $1 billion in direct aid there in 2009 alone. Helping an overtly Sunni Muslim – and Pashtun – regime into power in Kabul promised to eliminate the encirclement threat once and for all. The policy was part of what Pakistan's generals call 'strategic depth' which, at its most literal, offers somewhere for their forces to fall back upon in the event of an Indian invasion, a mountainous hinterland ideal for conducting a prolonged guerrilla resistance campaign.

This was always a high-risk strategy. It was popularly said that the ISI had given birth to a tiger when they created the Taliban; the question was, did they have that tiger by the head or by the tail? The Islamic revolution the ISI sponsored was supposed to be confined to Afghanistan, but it ended up spreading to the Pakistani side of the porous Durand Line. The ISI could not have anticipated al-Qaida's attack on New York, or the subsequent US invasion of Afghanistan, or the resulting displacement of al-Qaida into Pakistani territory. Forced to deal with this domestic terrorist threat, from 2004 the

Pakistani Army found itself drawn into a vicious counter-insurgency of its own.* If anyone today enjoys 'strategic depth' in the region it is the Afghan Taliban in north-west Pakistan, not the other way round: a classic case of the biter, bit. In April 2010, as if to underline that point, Omar's former trainer Colonel Imam was briefly kidnapped while travelling in the border areas by members of a formerly unheard-of militant organiz-ation, the Asian Tigers, who were reportedly hoping for a high-level prisoner exchange; one of his travelling com-panions, the ex-ISI agent Khalid Khawaja, was murdered before Colonel Imam was released.

But all this was unimaginable in the summer of 1996. Few in Peshawar had even heard of al-Qaida then, let alone the Pakistani Taliban – a phrase unknown before 2002 when the Tehrik-i-Taliban Pakistan, the umbrella movement of the Pakistani Taliban, was founded. Instead, naturally, the bar-chatter was all about Mullah Omar. His movement was on the cusp of taking over the whole of Afghanistan. How would the international community deal with his strange new regime – and vice versa?

The mainstream development community's politically correct, gender-aligned culture couldn't have been more starkly opposed to the Taliban worldview. The West's

* To date, more than 3,000 Pakistani soldiers and policemen and some 12,000 militants have been killed, while an estimated 7,000 civilians have died and a further 3.4 million of them have been dis-placed. (Source: South Asia Intelligence Review.)

initial response to the Taliban was shaped – hijacked, almost – by outrage over their treatment of girls and women. Unicef, the United Nations Children's Fund, led the charge in November 1995 when it cancelled all its education programmes in areas under Taliban control, arguing that the Taliban's insistence on segregated class-rooms was a violation of schoolchildren's human rights. The *burqa* was becoming a potent new international symbol of female oppression, and a string of powerful American women began to speak out against it: Barbara Bush, Madeleine Albright, Hillary Clinton. Mavis Leno, wife of NBC's top-rated nightly news-show anchor Jay Leno, donated $100,000 to an anti-Taliban lobbying campaign.

But among some aid workers there was a whispered, alternative view that intrigued me. Stuart Worsley, for instance, a programme director with Care International who had begun working in Afghanistan in early 1991, thought the Taliban represented an opportunity for greater cooperation with the West.

'There is a big difference between what the Taliban say and what they actually do,' he told me. 'Some of the edicts that come out of the madrasahs are pure Monty Python, and very often the guys on the ground choose not to enforce them.'

He had been all over Taliban-held Afghanistan, and observed that women were not always automatically beaten for showing their faces. Nor, he said, was the education of girls over the age of eight universally banned, as had almost constantly been reported. In their rush to demonize the Mullahs, in other words, it seemed the West was guilty of greatly oversimplifying what was going on.

The key to the Taliban's astonishing recent success, Worsley thought, was that they generally sought to govern by consensus – imposition being a tactic that seldom worked in Afghanistan, as the Russians found to their cost. He recalled that in the eastern town of Ghazni recently, the populace had complained about a Taliban proposal to convert a local school into a madrasah. The Talibs had immediately backed down.

'The enforcement of rules usually depends on local tradition,' he said.

For the NGOs, developments over the border were far from negative in practice. It was true that the rights of girls and women were being trampled on, which was unacceptable to anyone who believed those rights to be universal and absolute. Yet at the same time, even female aid workers admitted that the Taliban had dramatically improved security in many rural districts. The mullahs were not against foreign development projects per se. In many areas, indeed, they actively encouraged the foreigners and their work. It was therefore possible now for aid workers to travel to the remotest villages, in some cases for the first time in years, without fear of rape, murder, or having their expensive 4x4 vehicles stolen at gunpoint.

Worsley was effectively agreeing with Amruddin's

claim that the Taliban had 'imposed nothing but peace'. The Afghans were exhausted by war; he confirmed that their enthusiasm for the order and security brought by the Taliban was largely genuine. Talking to Afghan shopkeepers and others in the markets of downtown Peshawar over the previous days, I had come to much the same conclusion. Most striking was an encounter with a taxi-driver called Mahmud Amin, a former Hizb-i-Islami supporter who said he had once worked as a driver for the party leader, Gulbuddin Hekmatyar himself. These days, however, Amin was defiantly pro-Taliban.

'All Afghans are – except for some educated Kabulis who still think like the communists.'

Amin lived in Nasir Bagh, an Afghan refugee camp of 100,000 on the edge of Peshawar. He said he intended to return to Afghanistan as soon as the Taliban had unequivocally conquered the country, an outcome of which he and apparently everyone else in Nasir Bagh had little doubt. The harshness of the edicts streaming from Kandahar was a small price to pay for the improvements in security the Taliban had brought about.

'They were quite right to ban music,' he said. 'People had learned some very bad habits.'

He went on to define two kinds of music: the kind where men play instruments and women dance, which was 'disgraceful', and the kind where men play and young boys dance: 'That's perfectly OK.'

This was a weird inversion of Western norms, but I

was beginning to grasp that it wasn't the Taliban who had invented it. Their strange attitude towards boys, towards sex, towards cosmetics, even, was part of a tradition far older than what the West had labelled 'Islamic extremism'. It was in fact as much to do with the ancient culture of the Pashtuns as with Islam; and the Taliban creed was a grass-roots marriage of both. An enlightened handful of aid workers in Peshawar, Stuart Worsley among them, understood almost instinctively that in the long run it would be more productive – at least in terms of furthering the work of the development agencies – to work with the Taliban rather than against them, because they were part of the grain of society.

The racial origin of the Pashtuns is still hotly debated by genealogists. They have almost certainly occupied Afghanistan for longer than any other of the country's peoples; the Greek historian Herodotus referred in the fifth century BC to a race of 'Pactyans' who had lived in the Kandahar area for five hundred years even then. Some scholars believe Pashtuns have ancient Greek ancestry. Another popular and persistent theory is that they are descended from one of the lost tribes of Israel who were scattered by the Assyrians in the eighth century BC. With their large and frequently hooked noses, many Pashtuns certainly resemble the Jewish archetype. The idea is taken seriously enough that, in early 2010, a team of geneticists from the Institute of Technology in Haifa began studying blood samples taken from members of the Pashtun Afridi tribe in a bid to demonstrate a link. The effect on the Muslim world if the scientists succeed can only be guessed at.

Pashtun warriors had banded together for military purposes since at least the thirteenth century, when they conquered much of northern India, but they were not politically united until the early eighteenth century, when the Kandahar-based Hotaki dynasty rebelled against the Persian Empire. They remained in control for the following three hundred years, a period when almost every ruler of Afghanistan was a Pashtun. Other races were regarded as interlopers, and therefore as intrinsically inferior. The Dari-speaking Tajiks – Dari is a dialect of Farsi – remain forever associated with the Persians whose rule the Pashtuns had rejected. The Turkic-speaking Uzbeks were merely settled nomads from the Asian plains to the north. The Hazaras, who today account for perhaps 9 per cent of the population, were particularly discriminated against. With their pronounced Asiatic features they were said to be descended from the Mongol army of Genghis Khan who invaded in the thirteenth century. In the nineteenth century, a camel's life was set at six times that of a Hazara, while a Pashtun's life was worth 1,000 camels.[5]

The Pashtuns were the undisputed overlords, and their legendary past continues to play to their strong sense that Afghanistan is their land by right. Between the seventh and nineteenth centuries, after all, the term 'Afghan' – a Persian corruption of the Sanskritic 'Ashvaka', the name of a tribe who lived in the Hindu

Kush during the Iron Age – was used interchangeably with the word 'Pashtun'. 'Afghanistan' in its modern sense only came into use in 1919; before then, the country was known by the British as the specifically Pashtun 'Kingdom of Kabul'.

Today there are some 42 million Pashtuns, 25 million of whom live in north-west Pakistan, making up around 15 per cent of that country's population. The remaining 17 million live mainly in the south and east of Afghanistan, accounting for perhaps 42 per cent of the total there[6] – the largest single ethnic group, and well ahead of the next most numerous people, the Tajiks, who account for 27 per cent.

Unlike the country's other inhabitants the Pashtuns remain a defiantly tribal society, divided into about sixty major tribes incorporating more than 400 sub-clans. They are proud of their status as the largest tribal society in the world, and this is key to understanding both them and the Taliban movement they spawned. The Pashtuns principally define themselves by the unique Indo-Iranian language they speak – Pashto – and by a strict adherence to their ancient tribal customs, which are collectively known as the *Pashtunwali*, the famous 'way of the Pashtuns', an honour-based behavioural code that still regulates all social intercourse. It is by keeping to this code that the Pashtuns have ensured the homogeneity of their society for so long.

'Customs are subtle chains with which the primitive man tries to keep intact the pattern of his society,' observed the poet Ghani Khan, one of the twentieth century's most famous Pashtun poets, in 1947. 'They are his school and radio, prime minister and preacher . . . [A Pashtun] knows his customs before he knows how to eat. It is bred in him. It is mixed in his bones and works in his liver. He does not have to go to a learned man in a wig to know the law against which he sinned. He knows it as soon as he does it. He is his own judge and jailer. His ancestors have seen to it that it is so.'

Ghani Khan noted that Pashtuns have thousands of customs – for death, birth, marriage, love, hate and war – all of which are ultimately geared to a common purpose: the protection of the integrity of the tribe. It is every Pashtun's duty to defend his tribe's *Zan*, *Zar*, *Zameen*: women, gold and land. Many Taliban beliefs are rooted in this tribal imperative. For example, the strict sexual propriety of women that they insist upon is a modern interpretation of the ancient custom that prescribed death for elopement or adultery – part of what Ghani Khan called 'a subtle system of selective breeding'.

'[The Pashtun] must breed well if he is to breed fighters,' he wrote. 'The potential mother of the man of tomorrow is the greatest treasure of the tribe and is guarded jealously. He does his duty by his people. He will play true to his blood even if he breaks his heart and his neck in the bargain. He will walk to the gallows with proud steps with his hands covered with the blood of his wife or sister. And the admiring eyes of his people will follow him, as they always do those who pay with their life for a principle.'

Treating extramarital relations with such extreme intolerance not only kept the tribal gene pool pure but also preserved sexual health: an important consideration in an era when there was no cure for syphilis. The system, Ghani Khan acknowledged, was 'hard and brutal, but it works . . . Death to him who dares to risk the health of his tribe. It is treachery and sabotage which you also punish with death.'

The teachings of Islam often overlapped with such traditional Pashtun thinking, and the Taliban had clearly assimilated elements of both in the formulation of their ideology. Working out which was which was evidently going to be of critical importance to those foreign aid workers who hoped to go on working in Afghanistan; for on 11 September 1996, the Taliban captured the eastern stronghold city of Jalalabad – the gateway to Kabul.

Reinforcements for the defence of the city had been promised by the Tajik leader Ahmed Shah Massoud, but he arrived too late. The opium-dealing governor of Jalalabad, Hajji Abdul Qadir, fled to Pakistan, and the remaining garrison surrendered without a fight just two days later. Massoud hurried to block the pass leading to Kabul, taking up position 30 miles east of the capital in the small market town of Sarobi, whose approaches he heavily mined. The Taliban, led by Mullah Bor Jan, simply drove one vehicle after another at a fixed point in the eastern defences until a path through the minefield had been cleared. And each vehicle, according to the rumours in Peshawar, was manned not just by a single brave driver but by a crowd of up to thirty men, all waving flags and singing to Allah – such was their fervour for martyrdom and a passage to Paradise.

This was something new, even in a country as devoutly Muslim as Afghanistan. The mujahideen had often given their lives for the jihadist cause in the 1980s, but never so wantonly. There was no tradition of martyrdom for its own sake in Afghanistan; when self-destruction was called for in the campaign against the Soviets, it generally had a point. In pure military terms, moreover, the Sarobi assault seemed the craziest waste of manpower.

Two weeks later, on the night of 26 September, Kabul finally fell. The American Bar pundits were wrong: the seasoned fighters of Hizb-i-Islami could not match or cope with this level of religious zeal, and nor could any other mujahideen militia. With the exception of the north, the country now belonged to the Taliban. A new era had begun. But any quiet optimism that a Taliban government would bring a better Afghan future was quickly qualified, if not quashed. On the 27th, the Taliban breached every diplomatic protocol when they entered the United Nations compound in Kabul, where Mohammed Najibullah, the Soviet-era President, had been sheltering since 1992. In a grisly echo of their earlier tactics in the south, and to widespread international condemnation, Najibullah was tortured, castrated, and hanged from a lamp-post outside with his genitals stuffed in his mouth.

It was a terrible moment of truth for the world. The Taliban, a movement founded on a noble pledge to establish peace and justice for Afghanistan, had just demonstrated that it was also capable of the worst kind of savagery.

'It had to happen,' said Mullah Mohammad Rabbani, appointed the same day by Omar as the head of a six-man council charged with running the capital. 'He killed so many Islamic people and was against Islam and his crimes were so obvious. He was a communist.'

The world sucked through its teeth at this paradox. How could anyone behave with such callous disregard for the conventions of the civilized world, for other cultures, for human life itself?

In later years, apologists for the Taliban would argue that Najibullah's murder had never been a part of their plans for the takeover, and that it was Pakistan who had insisted on his elimination. This was because Najibullah was a close ally of India, where his wife and children had taken up sanctuary in 1992. It is sometimes alleged that Abdul Razaq, the Taliban mullah who led the five-man hit squad into the UN compound, was acting on the direct orders of the ISI. But this still did not explain the Taliban's extraordinary blindness to the value of human life which, as their battles for Sarobi and else-where showed, included their own.

Their particular interpretation of Islam provided only part of the answer. The Taliban were also the product of their country's experience of modern industrial warfare, which was surely unique. The human cost of the decade-long Soviet occupation alone was staggering. Out of a population of perhaps 15 million in 1989, over a million were killed, over four million were wounded, and five million were turned into refugees. Because there had been no real peace in Afghanistan since the 1970s, no Afghan under the age of twenty-one in 1996 had any memory of peacetime at all. For this brutalized generation, displacement, poverty and violent, premature death had all become the perverted norm.

Just as significantly, a large number of the Taliban's foot soldiers were orphans: a class of people with special resonance in Islam, since the Prophet himself had lost both his parents and grandparents by the age of eight; he was raised by an uncle named, appropriately enough, Abu Talib. Millions of Afghan children lost their parents as well as their homes in the 1980s. The ancient ties of family, village and tribe that might have swept these orphans up in the past were in many cases permanently fractured. There are few actual orphanages in this part of the world, either in Afghanistan or in the frontier regions of Pakistan where most refugees ended up. Something had to be done with these children, and a common solution – at least for the boys, since girls were generally excluded from the possibility – was to send them as wards into an Islamic madrasah, which was often the only institution beyond the extended family prepared to take them in.

The madrasah system was the incubator of the Taliban movement. In the majority of the big madrasahs in Pakistan, the curriculum follows the Deobandi school of thought, which takes its name from a still-flourishing religious college established in the town of Deoband in Uttar Pradesh, northern India, in 1866. The Deobandis are dedicated to the propagation of Sunni Islam, an expansionist programme founded without apology on the learning of the Koran by rote. At 80,000 words the Koran is about a tenth of the length of the Bible, although memorizing even this much takes years of dedicated work – particularly since the text must be studied in its original language, a poetic and elliptical seventh-century Arabic. (Although the Koran has been translated into almost every language on the planet, convenient local versions are rejected by most Islamic scholars, and certainly by the Deobandis. Muslims believe that the text of the Koran was handed down to Mohammed directly from Allah. It follows that translations must be inferior – perhaps dangerously so – because no human scholar can match the perfection of holy writ.)

The key to memorizing anything substantial is mental discipline, which the Deobandis foster through the iron regulation of all personal behaviour. Some madrasah children are brought up with a strictness that makes the London workhouses described by Dickens look like luxury hotels. Children as young as four are made to study in exchange for their daily bread, and they do not eat if they fail in their task. In some cases they are chained to their lecterns. These Asian Oliver Twists are taught almost no other subject, and they are kept at it for as long as there is daylight to study by, chanting and rocking back and forth on their crossed legs in long serried ranks on the floor. There is no privacy and precious little free time. Every activity is prescribed. Since 1900 the Deobandis have issued nearly a quarter of a million *fatwa*, or edicts, governing the minutiae of daily life: more than any other Islamic school of thought in the world. Drawn either directly from the Koran or from the *hadith*, the body of interpreted 'sayings' of the Prophet, these regulations are themselves considered the will of Allah. Any child breaking the rules can expect to be beaten or, possibly worse, thrown on to the streets to fend for himself.

By the mid-1990s the orphan boys of the decade before had grown into joyless young men of fighting age. They were tough and disciplined and there were many, many of them.* Despite the decades of war, Afghanistan's population is growing just as fast as Pakistan's: 8 million in 1950, 20 million in 2000, close to 30 million today.[7] The Koranic knowledge of this lost generation may have been unparalleled, but they were also ignorant and deeply

---

* Afghanistan is an extraordinarily young nation anyway: in 2000 the average age was just sixteen, compared to thirty-eight in Europe. (Source: *The Times*, 3 July 2009, Richard Ehrman, 'The Forces of Democracy Can't Beat the Power of Demography'.)

suspicious of everything that lay beyond the madrasah walls – including, and perhaps particularly, women. How could it be otherwise, when they had been segregated according to gender all their lives and taught nothing but Scripture? Raised without the love of parents or family, and cut loose from the traditional tempering influence of their tribal communities, there was nothing and no one to counterbalance the inevitably skewed view of the world engendered by such an education. No wonder they sometimes fought like religious automatons. The Taliban were the world's first Army of Orphans.

Madrasahs have gained an evil reputation in the West, where they are often derided as insidious 'mullah factories' that do nothing but propagate terrorism. Their image was certainly not helped by an incident in 2007, when the pro-Taliban imam of Islamabad's Red Mosque called for a suicide-bombing jihad against the government. A lengthy siege of the mosque-and-madrasah complex by the Pakistani Army ended with the deaths of hundreds of students. The link between some religious schools and the Taliban is not contested. The immense Dar-u-Uloom Haqqania madrasah near Peshawar, for instance, is sometimes called 'the Harvard of the Taliban movement'. In 1998, notoriously, its headmaster Sami ul-Haq shut the college down and sent the entire student body – as many as eight thousand young men – over the border as troop reinforcements for the Taliban.

The size of colleges like Haqqania is not typical. A

madrasah is traditionally a small annex to a mosque, a place for the discussion of the Koran's finer points outside the hours of formal worship. Most madrasahs, and almost all of those in Afghanistan, remain small. But in Pakistan in the last twenty-five years, many madrasahs have become much larger than the mosques they used to service. Religious education, often generously subsidized by Arabian petro-dollars, has become a very big business. The number of madrasahs in Pakistan has outpaced even that country's exploding population, and continues to soar. In 1947 there were just 137 of them. These days they number in the thousands, a development that the West perhaps understandably views with suspicion and alarm. In 2006 Islamabad alone had 127 madrasahs, with a new one opening every week.[8]

And yet to criticize the madrasah system as a whole is to strike at one of the foundations of Islam, a faith to which religious education has been crucial for almost 1,200 years. Western policy-makers have sometimes struggled to understand that the vast majority of madrasahs are not sinister breeding grounds for terrorists. The oldest madrasah in the world, the Jami'at al-Qarawiyyin in Fez, Morocco, has been operating benignly – and continuously – since it was established in 859; and even the students at Haqqania are encouraged to play cricket.

In 2002, soon after the Taliban were defeated, the then US Defense Secretary Donald Rumsfeld embarked on a victory tour of his newly conquered territory. He arrived at the northern town of Mazar-i-Sharif in a giant C-17 transport aircraft with an entourage of Secret Service men and, according to a British SAS officer stationed in the city and who witnessed it, 'a brilliant double dressed in a conspicuous Macintosh', who emerged and waited at the top of the aircraft steps while the real Rumsfeld was hustled off the aircraft by another exit.

The SAS officer was then detailed to escort the American around the city.

'He had these dead, cold doll's eyes, and he kept asking questions about madrasahs,' he recalled. 'He wanted to know where the nearest one to our base was. I had to tell him that we didn't know of a single madrasah in Mazar, which is a liberal, multi-ethnic city, not a Pashtun one . . . I doubt there's a madrasah within 150 miles of the place.'

Rumsfeld's armoured motorcade passed the famous Blue Mosque in the city centre: the shrine of the Prophet's son-in-law Hazrat Ali from which Mazar-i-Sharif, the 'Tomb of the Exalted', takes its name. Rumsfeld jabbed a thumb at it and turned to the SAS officer once again.

'Is *that* a madrasah?' he wanted to know.

This was not quite the silly question it appeared. The shrine does have a small 'house of learning' attached to it. But it is also an integral part of the whole blue-tiled complex, a national monument that appears on the backs of banknotes. To call it a 'madrasah' in the sense that Rumsfeld meant it was a bit like describing the Chapter House at Westminster Abbey as a bomb factory.

'No, sir,' replied the exasperated SAS officer drily – perhaps a little too drily. 'That is the fourth holiest shrine in the whole of Islam.'

'Young man,' Rumsfeld snapped, 'may I remind you that you are a junior officer in the British Army – while I am the United States Secretary of Defense?'

3

'Try Not to Hurt the People!': Kabul, 1996–1998

In April 1997 I boarded a small Red Cross cargo plane that flew once a week from Peshawar to Mazar, where it delivered supplies to the handful of aid agency missions based there. It seemed a likely place to find a good news story. With the fall of Kabul, Mazar was now the only town of any size not under Taliban control, and the de facto headquarters of the new Northern Alliance – a shaky coalition of Uzbek, Tajik and Hazara Shi'ite militias who had failed individually to resist the southerners' advance.

I made my way by bus to the local headquarters of Oxfam, a small compound just west of the city centre that rented a few rooms to itinerant journalists like me. The previous year I had written a commentary piece for the London *Independent* entitled 'The Peace Brought by the Taliban'. This was largely an exercise in devil's advocacy, although it had a serious point: it seemed to me that the West's righteous fist-shaking at the Taliban's treatment of women was in danger of obscuring the positive side of the new regime, particularly the benefits of improved security. The article quoted Care International's Stuart Worsley at some length. Arriving at the Oxfam compound at last, I was amazed to see this very article, pinned up in pride of place next to the reception desk. Worsley was evidently not alone in seeing the Taliban's plus-side. I was just silently congratulating myself when I heard a man harrumph loudly over my shoulder.

'I'd like to meet the idiot who wrote that damn piece of crap,' he boomed, in a heavy Australian accent.

'Well, um, I think it might have been me, actually.'

We made friends in the end. He was a photographer, recently arrived from Kabul: the gruff epitome of a seasoned war correspondent and, as I later learned, a legend on the Afghan circuit. Two years previously he had been out on the front line near the capital, filming a mortar crew in action against the Taliban forces besieging them. The crew were amateurs who kept thrusting their shells into the launch tube instead of gingerly dropping them in.

'I knew it was wrong at the time,' he said. 'It was an accident waiting to happen.'

He had backed away fast, but too late. One of the shells exploded in the launch tube, obliterating the crew and badly wounding him too. He was evacuated from the country and spent months in rehabilitation: a career-ending moment, his family thought. Yet here he was, back in Afghanistan again, a self-confessed addict to a country famous for its ability to get beneath a Westerner's skin.

He made me glad I had chosen to try my journalistic luck in Mazar rather than Kabul. The Taliban, he said, had made it so difficult for foreign media to operate there that he had decided to flee for the relative freedom of the north. Every journalist arriving in the capital these days was assigned a local fixer-translator by the newly established Interior Ministry. These fixers, he explained, were in reality spies for the new regime, who kept a tight grip on where their foreign charges went and whom they spoke to, and even decided what they could and couldn't film or photograph. This 'service' was not optional, and an exorbitant (and non-negotiable) daily fee was being charged for it. It sounded no place for an impoverished freelancer like me.

The clumsiness with which the Taliban handled the press in the early days was an important factor in the hardening of the West's attitudes towards them. Restrictions on foreign journalists' freedom to operate encouraged neither objectivity nor much analysis of what made the Taliban tick. Instead, the Taliban unwittingly handed the foreign media a telegenic scare story about 'Islamic fundamentalism' that most journalists found impossible to resist: a public relations own-goal that the leadership would later come to regret.

When, for example, an edict was issued banning the

watching of television, the Taliban authorities in Kabul decided to reinforce the point by impaling stacks of television sets on poles at the entrances to the city. For good measure these carcasses were sometimes draped with audio and video tape that had been ripped from their housings. The tape was like metal seaweed: long, shiny brown strands that fluttered beautifully when it was windy, their surfaces winking in the sunlight and visible for miles across the moonscape of the capital's hinterland. The Afghans have always liked a good flagpole. Foreign correspondents such as the BBC's John Simpson could hardly be blamed for filming them – discreetly, of course, from the back of a car. 'Welcome to Kabul,' Simpson gravely intoned, 'capital of the most fundamentalist government in the world.' It was great television, a news shot that played directly to the West's growing sense that the Taliban really were from another planet.

Yet this kind of reporting does not satisfactorily explain the complex socio-political reasons behind such a Draconian edict. Islamic 'fundamentalism' was only a part of it. The Taliban were also driven by a straightforward fear of television and the corrosive effect it could have on society: exactly the same fear that the West experienced throughout the 1960s and '70s. In Britain this was most famously expressed by the anti-television campaigner Mary Whitehouse, who blamed programmes like *The Benny Hill Show*, *Doctor Who* and even the children's story-reading slot *Jackanory* for a collapse in the nation's morals. There was more than a hint of

Mary Whitehouse about Omar, an austere mullah from the most conservative part of the country.

It was hardly surprising if he was behind the times. Like everything technological, basic television came very late to Afghanistan, in the 1980s. Afghan society was still coming to grips with the new medium when satellite television arrived in 1991. The civil war that raged in Kabul from 1992 destroyed its electricity supply, but with the arrival of the Taliban in 1996, power was miraculously restored. The capital's bazaars were suddenly flooded with electronic goods imported from China, cheap and shamelessly cloned. The return of television threw open a window on to an outside world that astounded Afghans, and millions of them were now badly hooked. They watched anything, without discrimination: cheap Italian game shows, soap operas from Brazil, twenty-year-old American crime series like *Kojak*. In the Taliban's view, the citizens' time would be much better spent praying in the mosque. The stricter sort of mullah naturally thought the television habit was a direct enticement to apostasy.

Kojak was one thing, however. The Taliban were far more troubled by another kind of imported show which was easily the most popular in Afghanistan: the steamy, Hindi-language romances of Bollywood, the Mumbai-based film-making centre that outstrips the world in productivity. Afghans, the inhabitants of a dun-coloured land, were drawn to Bollywood like magpies to tinsel. I saw the power these movies held over the people for myself, once, in a Mazari *chaikana* – a teahouse – where a hundred or so men had crowded around a set suspended from the ceiling, gazing in open-jawed silence as a scantily clad starlet sashayed around a Mumbai car park filled with expensive sports cars.

Bollywood threatened society's morals far more seriously than comparable material from Europe or America. It made a big difference to the Taliban that this licentiousness was going on not in the other-worldly white West but right here in south Asia, a few hundred miles to the south-east, among men and women of a skin colour worryingly like their own. In Pashtun society, women do not dance semi-naked in car parks, or even go out in public much unless veiled and accompanied by a husband or relative. This challenge to the Pashtun sense of female decorum, furthermore, came not from some random regional neighbour but from Hindu India, the mortal enemy of the Taliban's brother Muslims in Pakistan. According to *namus*, one of the tenets of Pashtunwali, the honour of women must be defended at all costs: another means, perhaps, of controlling men's desire for them. The poet Ghani Khan observed that a Pashtun 'cannot think of love without marriage. If he does, he pays for it with his life – and therefore all his love poetry is about those who dared it. The Pashtun may shoot the lover of his daughter but sing to the glory of love.' Bollywood's invasion was cultural rather than military, though not necessarily less dangerous for that in the Taliban's eyes. It played to the old Pakistani fear of encirclement by India – as well as to the old Pashtun suspicion of any foreign interference in their country.

In times of external pressure the Pashtuns have historically survived by turning inwards, falling back upon and rigorously upholding the ancient cultural values that had served them so well in the past. Loyalty to the Pashtun nation, or *hewad*, is another important tenet of Pashtunwali, as is the obligation to defend it against any type of foreign incursion. Protecting Pashtun culture, the *dod-pasbani*, from disintegration or dilution by outside influence is also important. For this reason, an ability to speak Pashto is considered not just important but essential. Not speaking it is often taken, quite unfairly, as an inability to comprehend anything to do with Pashtun culture. International television, with its assumption of global values and its tendency to linguistic homogeneity, endangered both the hewad and the dod-pasbani.

The demands of Pashtunwali alone were probably motivation enough for Omar to approve the banning of television, although there was also no shortage of justification to be found in the Koran – at least in the way the Taliban interpreted it. Early Islam forbade the portraiture of all living things on the grounds that it encouraged idolatry, and both Hollywood and Bollywood, with their attendant and highly developed celebrity cultures, undoubtedly smelled of that. The

Taliban's ambition to turn the clock back to the time of the Prophet was often problematic, though. As Mary Whitehouse discovered, controlling television in the modern world is like trying to turn back waves on a beach.

In time, the Taliban learned that it was more useful to exploit the power of Western information technology rather than to try to destroy it. By 2001 even Omar was developing his own website in Kandahar. The Taliban made propaganda films, appointed clever press spokesmen, courted television channels such as al-Jazeera, and learned to manipulate public opinion in myriad ways that continue to bamboozle the Nato Coalition today. They were capable of adaptation when necessary, in other words. However literally some among them were inclined to interpret the Koran, the rules could still be relaxed. The emotive tag of fundamentalism, with all the crazed inflexibility implied by that word, and which the Western media bandied about so often and easily in the early days, was never quite accurate or fair.

This is not to say that they weren't sometimes guilty of terrible intolerance. In 1997 the leadership was still at the bottom of a steep learning curve, and by their own later admission they made many mistakes. The sum total of their ambition when they started out in 1994 had been to save two small provincial districts from bandits. Now they found themselves in charge of an entire country, almost, and they were frankly struggling to cope. Like the Americans in Iraq in 2003, the Taliban sought regime change. Also like the Americans, their preparations for running the country once they had taken the capital were almost non-existent. In fact, forming a government themselves had never been a part of their agenda. The idea rather was to install one that would govern according to Sharia law, and then to go home. But 'mission creep' within the movement, combined with the pressures of civil war and the influence of their Pakistani and Saudi sponsors, drove them much further than they first intended. In that sense, the Taliban were the victims of their own success.

Before 1997, most of the leadership had never even been to Kabul, a city whose customs and mores were very different from those of conservative Kandahar. It was the most outward-looking city in the country, a seething, multi-ethnic conurbation of perhaps a million and a half people in 1997, about half of whom were ethnic Tajiks and only a quarter were Pashtun. It wasn't just television that kept its citizens entertained. Kabul in the past had been a city of music and flowers, of cinemas and night-clubs. The children flew kites, the men gambled on partridge fights. In the 1960s, female students at the university had worn trousers, even mini-skirts. In the 1970s, the city had been a popular staging post on the hippy trail from Europe to India.

Kabulis had also flirted with Western modernity earlier, in the 1920s, under the modernizing Shah Amanullah, who had been the city's Governor before he ascended the throne. He kept a fleet of Rolls-Royces,

introduced co-education in schools, and promoted a constitution based on equal rights for women. He
campaigned against the burqa and even decreed that
Afghan men in the capital had to wear Western clothes,
complete with a European hat. For all these reasons,
Omar both distrusted and disliked Kabul. He might
have been expected to take up residence in the Arg,
Kabul's presidential palace, but instead he appointed his
close colleague Mullah Mohammad Rabbani to head the
six-man 'advisory council' while he remained in splendid
isolation in Kandahar. In the seven years he controlled
the country, he visited the capital just twice.

This aloof style created a problem for the administration in Kabul before it had even begun to govern. No
country is easily ruled from two capitals at once. As the
Amir ul-Mu'mineen, Omar considered it his primary
role to set the spiritual tone of his revolution; the business
of actual government was generally left to others.
'Everything that happens depends on God,' he said when
he had accepted the leadership in 1994 – and it turned out
that he really meant it. Mullah Rabbani was the de facto
Prime Minister responsible for the day-to-day running of
the government. Since Omar chose not to show himself,
Rabbani also became the domestic and international
public face of the Taliban. At the same time, Omar had
no intention of loosening his grip on the revolution he
had created. All key government officials had either to be
nominated or approved by him. Rabbani's job ultimately
was to interpret and implement the orders that now

began to stream northwards from Kandahar, where all the important decisions were taken. It was a highly inefficient command and control system that caused tension from the start.

Schooled at a madrasah in the Kandahari village of Pashmol, Rabbani was a former mujahid who had fought the Soviets alongside Omar. He had taken part in the destiny-laden attack on Spin Boldak, and was reputedly an excellent tactician and field officer who still commanded the loyalty of thousands of fighters. Even so, he was no firebrand but a 'soft, gentle, humble man – the kind who always makes himself "small" in a meeting,' a contact who knew him told me. He was naturally revered by his mullah peers.

When the Taliban first took Kabul, Rabbani had favoured negotiating a peace with the Northern Alliance government under the auspices of the United Nations. He agreed to a ceasefire, and proposed calling a *jirga* of *ulema* – an assembly of religious scholars – who would thrash out a constitution agreeable to both sides and that would incorporate the Sharia law the Taliban craved. As a sign of good faith he even withdrew the heavy weaponry surrounding Kabul, and might have seen a peace deal through were it not for Omar, who flatly rejected any such proposal. It was almost certainly a Taliban rocket that broke the ceasefire: 'The moment they turned from liberators into a warring faction just like any of the others that preceded them,' according to Peter Jouvenal. Whether the rocket was fired on orders from Kandahar is still disputed. Many Afghans insist the ISI had a hand in it, for by this stage of the campaign there were many reports – never verified – of Pakistani military 'advisers' among the Taliban ranks. Nevertheless, it was clear enough that the Amir ul-Mu'mineen had no interest in compromising with the warlords of the north.

For Mullah Rabbani, loyalty to the Amir had to come first. He was forced to go back on his word to the United Nations and to the ulema, and to declare that the Taliban would be taking power alone and without consultation. With this move, a rare chance to put an early end to years of internecine strife was lost – or at least that chance was never put to the test. Rabbani died of liver cancer in April 2001.

Mullah Rabbani's greatest fear was that he might lose control of Kabul, a development that would spell disaster for the Taliban project. Showing any weakness could encourage fresh insurrection from the non-Pashtun community, who were still far from defeated in the north and east of the country. The strength of the Taliban at its inception was that everyone knew each other – a small band of brothers held together by mutual trust and a common goal. Yet by the end of 1996, so many people had joined the cause that its leaders were no longer sure who was actually in their ranks.[1] The certainties of the early days were gone. Factions had grown up, even within Omar's inner circle. Mutual trust was replaced by a climate of suspicion.

Some Taliban officials – though not all – reacted by clamping down on Kabulis and their immoral, big-city ways with unprecedented harshness. One of the worst was Rafiullah Muazzin, the head of the Amr Bil Marof Wa Nai An Munkir, the infamous Office for the Propagation of Virtue and the Prevention of Vice. Some of the edicts he issued in Omar's name were so bizarre that they have passed into international folklore. As well as television, Rafiullah outlawed 'the British and American hairstyle', music and dancing at wedding parties, and the playing of the drum. Chess, cards and partridge-fighting, a national pastime, were early casualties because they encouraged gambling and distracted people from the mosque. Not content with banning women from the workplace and hiding them under burqas in public, the windows of private homes were now ordered to be white-washed to prevent anyone from accidentally peeking in. Tailors were forbidden from taking female body measurements. Women were also stopped from playing sports, from washing clothes in the streams that run through the city, from wearing nail varnish, even from wearing 'squeaky shoes'. This insistence on sexual propriety seemed deranged to most Kabulis. In Britain, we joke that Victorians covered the legs of pianos to prevent inappropriate stirrings. In Afghanistan, there were reports from the countryside that stallions had been forced into trousers.

Rafiullah's edicts were publicized on Radio Sharia, the Taliban's new music-free radio station. They were then enforced by his deputy, the terrifying Maulawi Inayatullah Baligh, whose 100-strong squad of religious inspectors carried out their duties with the zealousness and, apparently, the impunity of Hitler's Brown Shirts in the 1930s. Despite his title – a *maulawi* is a kind of senior mullah – Baligh was really a career bureaucrat who had served in the deposed previous government: a little man with an unhealthy liking for the big stick. 'Whenever we catch them doing immoral things, we can do anything we want,' he told one foreign journalist. 'We can execute them, we can kill them.'[2] His squads would set up spot-checks in the city centre to measure the length of beards. Beard hair, they decided, had to be long enough to poke through the gaps of a clenched fist. They also inspected the more private parts of the human body, for cleanliness is next to godliness in Islam, and the Prophet advised that all pubic hair should be shaved. The damage done to the Taliban's image by all this was incalculable. Internationally, the floodgates of opprobrium were now opened.

One of the most celebrated confrontations on the issue of women's rights came when Emma Bonino, the Italian European Commissioner for Humanitarian Affairs, visited the Indira Gandhi mother and child clinic in Kabul. When some journalists accompanying her began filming the proceedings, the Taliban ordered the whole party arrested.

'It is the policy of the Taliban that no unrelated man may take pictures of women,' said Hajji Habibullah, a security official.

Bonino was incandescent, even after the Taliban's Deputy Foreign Minister, Sher Abbas Stanakzai, had apologized.

'He said that these questions [of women's rights] would be decided when they had brought peace and security to the country,' she said. 'I said that if they did not take care of women's health now, what are you going to provide peace and security for – dead bodies?'[3]

The Taliban's testy relationship with the international aid agencies reached a new low in July 1997 when these were ordered to close their offices, which were scattered around the capital, and relocate en masse to a complex of abandoned student dormitories on the bombed-out university campus. The move was ordered 'for the foreigners' own protection', although it looked like blatant provocation to the aid agencies. Some feared that, far from improving their security, a concentration of foreigners in one place would actually make them more vulnerable to attacks and kidnappings. They also complained that they could not afford to renovate the dormitories, which had been uninhabited since 1992.

Many aid organizations were already struggling to staff their operations thanks to the Taliban's ban on local women working, which had itself caused much heart-searching in Western capitals. To go on operating under such a ban was to collude with a grave affront to civil rights, but if they quit the capital and its 750,000 inhabitants out of principle, what would become of the estimated 200,000 of them who were dependent on subsidized food, medicine and clothes? The foreigners bore the main responsibility for much other essential work besides. But the relocation order proved the final straw. When the EU Commission in Brussels urged the many aid organizations associated with it to leave Kabul, a mass exodus got under way.

Human rights organizations, meanwhile, were in full cry over the judicial killings taking place at the Ghazi football stadium – a venue that particularly outraged the West because it had been paid for with aid money from the European Union. Smuggled video footage of these executions found its way into the mainstream Western media, confirming the Taliban's new status as international pariahs. The stadium was always packed with spectators at these grisly events, which made it look as though the authorities were using executions as a form of public entertainment. The battle-lines were drawn. From 1997 on, the Taliban were almost universally portrayed in the West as a regime beyond comprehension or redemption.

'We are dealing here with a failed state which looks like an infected wound,' the UN envoy Lakhdar Brahimi remarked in 1998. 'You don't even know where to start cleaning it.'[4]

But there was another view of the Taliban regime, which was that it was not, actually, failing in 1998. Nor, necessarily, was it in need of the cleaning services of the UN. The Taliban used the same metaphor when they described their mission to 'cleanse' the country of evil and corruption, and in some respects they were doing a pretty good job.

'No one really *liked* the Taliban,' said one Western correspondent who reported from Kabul for much of the 1990s. 'They were never the answer to Afghan government. But they were very clever at carrying out Omar's promises – unlike, these days, us Westerners, who make lots of promises we don't or can't keep. The Taliban did and still do carry out their promises. They very nearly *did* get rid of the warlords and the corruption they brought. They even got rid of the poppies in the areas they controlled. And Kabul and other areas were disarmed. A lot of Westerners got very cross about women's rights in the 1990s, but the Taliban's strictures were nothing compared to the rape and slaughter that were going on before. I think it is important to see the Taliban at that time in this context. That is how almost all ordinary Afghans remember them.'

He knew more than he perhaps cared to about life in pre-Taliban Kabul.

'January 1994 was the worst, when Dostum [the Uzbek leader] changed sides ... the slaughter of innocents caught up in the fighting was appalling, ghastly. Hundreds upon hundreds were killed and badly injured, week by week. A million people fled Kabul, mostly on foot, carrying what they could. The city's hospitals were full to bursting. I didn't see a single Afghan smiling for months.'

One of the West's central misunderstandings about the

Taliban was a failure to see that their conservatism differed from the rest of the country not in kind, but in degree. Women had always been abused by Afghan men – and not just by Pashtun men, either, but in the villages of Tajiks, Uzbeks and Hazaras too. The main difference was that the Taliban were more systematic than the mujahideen ever were in the way they exerted their power; and when their religious police beat a woman with their switches for showing her ankles, they did so openly, in public. It certainly didn't look good. But the maltreatment of the capital's long-suffering women came as less of a shock to most of them than the horrified West ever properly grasped. Beatings, however cruel and outrageous, were also infinitely preferable to murder and rape: common crimes in the years preceding the Taliban, but which virtually disappeared once they were in charge.

Even the apparently barbaric judicial killings at the football stadium were not quite as they appeared. The Taliban were anxious that Sharia justice was not just done, but seen to be done. The people who filled the stadium were not there for their entertainment, but at the insistence of the authorities. The first ever execution in Kabul, interestingly, was not of some apostate but of a young member of the Taliban who had tried to disarm a citizen and ended up shooting him. This was perhaps a deliberate show of impartiality, the Taliban's way of demonstrating that everyone was equal under Sharia law. The accused – whom neighbours from his area suggested was a teenager with learning difficulties – was despatched by a single shot to the head in accordance with *qisas*, the Sharia equivalent of the Old Testament principle of an eye for an eye. The audience – and the young Talib – were submitted to a lecture on the virtues of Sharia justice for two whole hours before the fatal shot was fired.

The executions were grisly, but there weren't actually that many of them: dozens, rather than hundreds, were carried out in the years of Taliban rule. 'The West made a great fuss about it but we don't seem to object much when the same thing happens in Saudi Arabia,' commented the Western correspondent who witnessed several of the killings. 'And it was pure hypocrisy, coming from America! There have probably been more judicial executions in the state of Texas than there ever were under the Taliban.'*

The regime was accused of brutality, but it was not they who had invented the penalties of Sharia law. In the execution cases, furthermore, it was not they but almost always a bereaved relative who carried them out. This, too, was in accordance with the retaliatory principle of qisas. In fact, the system prefers forgiveness to retaliation; the death sentence is supposed to be applied only as a last resort. At the second public execution in Kabul, the Taliban repeatedly asked a man whose son had been

---

* The state of Texas has put 447 people to death since 1982, according to the Texas Execution Information Centre.

killed in a knife fight if he would not pardon the two accused, who had been brought on to the pitch in chains in the back of a Hi-Lux truck. The man glanced across at them and insisted that he would not, before marching over and swiftly sawing off their heads with a butcher's knife. When a convicted thief had his hand chopped off it was done surgically by a doctor in a balaclava. The thief would then be rushed off to hospital in the back of a pick-up truck to have the stump treated and sewn up. The real point, perhaps, was that these punishments were effective. The dismembered hands were sometimes hung up in the town as a warning to others. Crime very soon tailed off. It wasn't long before you really could leave your keys in the ignition of your car and know that no one was going to steal it.

Most Westerners only saw what they wanted to see, and read the Taliban wrong from the start. An edict preventing kite-fighting, for example, seemed typical of the Taliban's joylessness, and became famous in the West following the publication in 2003 of *The Kite Runner*, the best-selling novel by Khaled Hosseini that was later turned into a film. But the Taliban had no interest in persecuting children. The reason was that kite-flyers tended to stand on the roofs of buildings, which often afforded a view into the enclosed compound home of the next-door neighbour – and potentially therefore of unveiled women. Children flying kites at street level were rarely molested by the religious police.

The Taliban did not wish to antagonize the West. On

the contrary, the regime always craved international recognition from the United Nations, and was often sensitive enough to respond to legitimate criticism. In October 1998, for instance, it banned the use of land-mines. The move was partly self-serving. As a movement that had always been on the offensive they naturally had a healthy fear of anti-personnel mines, vast numbers of which continued to be sown by the Northern Alliance. But genuine humanitarianism played its part in the decision too, according to Guy Willoughby, the Director of the Halo Trust demining agency.

'We had a perfectly sensible working relationship with them. We liaised over which village areas they wanted us to work in and they were always pretty straight to deal with.'

The mullahs had not intended to provoke an exodus of foreign aid agencies when they ordered the relocation of their Kabul offices, and certainly never ordered them to leave the country. The United Nations agencies themselves, together with the International Committee for the Red Cross, were in any case exempt from the relocation order, while the Halo Trust simply weathered the storm, judging its mission to be too important to abandon over a point of principle. Between 1996 and 2001, Willoughby's 1,400 staff were able to remove over 40,000 mines in areas away from the front lines in a demining programme that actually accelerated slightly over the Taliban period.

'They were no problem to work with if you didn't wind them up. We didn't put in female managers for the hell of it ... Actually, we didn't have any female managers. Our deminers had to grow longer beards, and our programme managers had to hide their music cassettes under their car seats at checkpoints, but so what? It was no big deal.'

He was highly critical of Emma Bonino and her famous visit to the mother and child clinic in 1997, which he said had hardened European attitudes to the Taliban and led to the withdrawal of EU funding for Halo.

'She infuriated the Taliban and that was completely unnecessary. They were tough, unpleasant people, but it is a question of context. You can't compare them with what went before. Halo operated in Afghanistan between 1992 and 1996 when West Kabul was being destroyed. That was a truly dreadful period: a fact that is still being airbrushed out of history.'

There was evidence that the leadership were genuinely baffled at the West's outrage over their treatment of women. In Pashtun culture, women had never had the same rights as men. Restricting them to their homes, the Taliban argued with complete sincerity, was as ever necessary 'for their own protection' – by which of course they meant for namus, the protection of the honour of women. Kabul had been very over-filmed and the West had assumed that what was going on there was replicated across the country, although this was never the case. In safe rural areas, for instance, women were permitted and able to go out unaccompanied by a relative, just as they had always done.

The Taliban leadership did not see themselves as oppressors of women but as their defenders. Before 1996 it was not uncommon for Pashtun tribal feuds to be resolved through a trade-off of women – a tradition known as *swara*, which often ended in a forced marriage. This was only one of the instruments of badal, or obligation to seek revenge, available under Pashtunwali. In some instances, women were simply executed in settlement of the blood-price. It is often forgotten that Mullah Omar issued an edict putting an end to both practices.

At the same time, he seemed strangely reluctant to actively promote women's rights in Kabul, or even to rein in the religious police's worst excesses. The main reason for that was the war. Taliban leaders repeatedly told the writer Ahmed Rashid that 'if they gave women greater freedom or a chance to go to school, they would lose the support of their rank and file, who would be disillusioned by a leadership that had compromised principles under pressure. They also claimed their recruits would be weakened and subverted by the possibility of sexual opportunities and thus not fight with the same zeal.'[5]

And yet many girls did go to school under the Taliban. Indeed, several Western NGO workers thought it probable that more Kabuli girls were educated under the Taliban than in the preceding era, if only because school education of any kind was impossible during the violence of the early 1990s. Private tuition also carried on in people's homes. The leadership had no ideological objection to girls' education in itself; what they most minded about was the corrupting influence of co-education. Girls, and indeed female teachers, were forbidden from attending mixed schools, and the education of many undoubtedly suffered as a result. Of course this was discriminatory, for it was never the boys who were told to stay away from their formerly co-educational establishments. Yet the Taliban always said they intended to build new, single-sex schools for girls. The fact that they never did was due to the lack of money rather than ideology. The regime was always cash-strapped, and simply could not afford such projects while they were busy with the war.

Omar appreciated that at least some types of female education were essential. For instance, he was happy to sanction the setting up of a training programme in rooms at the central hospital in Kabul, where female medical students could study to become doctors; some 1,200 of them graduated. Meanwhile Qari Barakatullah Salim, a well-known public figure famed for his sung recitations of the Koran, was permitted to run a large girls-only school in the centre of the capital throughout the Taliban period. He employed twenty-six teachers who taught over seven hundred girls aged seven and above. This was no madrasah but a regular secondary school, with a curriculum that included maths, English, even biology.

'The Taliban were always suspicious of foreign influence in education, and their suspicion grew worse as the foreigners' demonization of them deepened,' Salim told me. 'But they had no problem with girls' schools so long as they had no association with foreign NGOs or access to their funding. Islam says that girls should be educated. The Prophet himself was married to an educated businesswoman, Khadijah. The Taliban leadership understands that no nation can survive without education; it is essential to humanity. We are as beasts without it.'

His main difficulty in those days, he remembered, was 'an extreme lack of money. We were privately funded with small donations from the parents. We had just enough to pay the teachers' small salaries ... There was nothing at all for books and pens and other essential teaching materials.'

However reminiscent of Nazis the roaming squads of religious police might have been – and the comparison was made, even by the United Nations, after an edict was issued ordering that Kabul's tiny Hindu community should mark themselves out by wearing a piece of yellow cloth on their shirt pockets – the repression of the people was never comparable to Germany's treatment of Jews. A Taliban spokesman, Abdul Hakeem Mujahid, retorted that the yellow markers were 'for the Hindus' own protection so that they can be recognized and not be bothered about the length of their beards, or not heeding the call to prayer'. He even claimed that the edict had not been a Taliban idea, but had been requested by the Hindus themselves.

Even at the height of their zeal, the religious police

Above: Is this Mullah Omar? The leader of the Taliban is so elusive that the authenticity of even this famous photograph is in question; it was supposedly taken soon after he lost an eye in a Soviet aerial attack in 1988. The last known television images of him were taken in secret by a British cameraman as he was declared Amir ul-Mu'mineen, the 'Commander of all the Faithful', in Kandahar in April 1996 (*right*).

Above: The Taliban's secret weapon was speed. Fleets of Toyota trucks allowed them to conquer a third of the country in just four months.

Right: Mullah Mohammed Rabbani, the Taliban 'Prime Minister' in Kabul, was the public face of the movement from 1996 until his death in 2001.

Below: Jalaluddin Haqqani (*left*), once described by US Congressman Charlie Wilson as 'Goodness Personified'. Mullah Dadullah (*centre*), 'a brave young man who never knew fear', according to Mullah Abdul Salam Zaeef (*right*), who was nicknamed 'the smiling Taliban'.

Above: Taliban troops in action north of Kabul in October 1996. It took two attempts to oust the Mujahideen government.

Below: The Taliban found much of the city they now occupied in ruins following years of vicious Mujahideen infighting; not even the Darulaman Palace was spared.

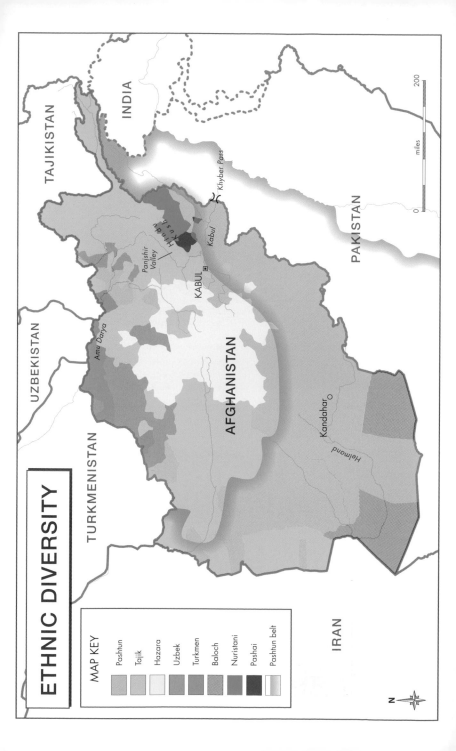

ETHNIC DIVERSITY

MAP KEY

- Pashtun
- Tajik
- Hazara
- Uzbek
- Turkmen
- Baloch
- Nuristani
- Pashai
- Pashtun belt

TURKMENISTAN

UZBEKISTAN

TAJIKISTAN

INDIA

PAKISTAN

IRAN

AFGHANISTAN

KABUL

Kabul

Khyber Pass

Hindu Kush

Panjshir Valley

Amu Darya

Kandahar

Helmand

0   200
miles

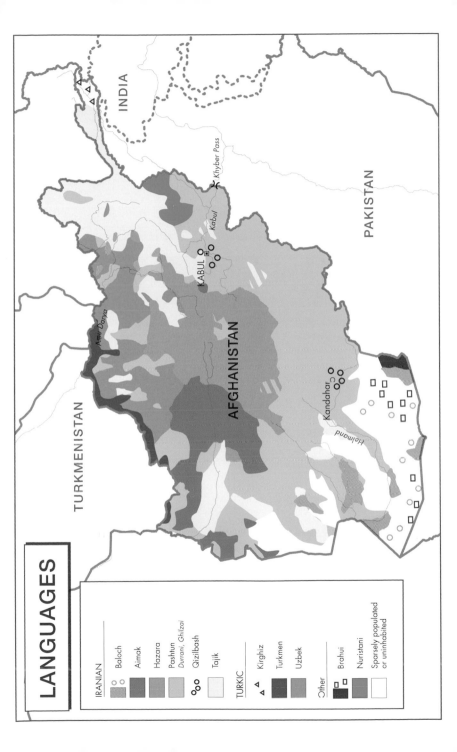

LANGUAGES

IRANIAN
- Baloch
- Aimak
- Hazara
- Pashtun
  Durrani, Ghilzai
- Qizilbash
- Tajik

TURKIC
- Kirghiz
- Turkmen
- Uzbek

Other
- Brahui
- Nuristani
- Sparsely populated or uninhabited

TURKMENISTAN

AFGHANISTAN

PAKISTAN

INDIA

Amu Darya

Helmand

Kabul

KABUL

Kandahar

Khyber Pass

Above: Women who failed to wear the burqa in public risked a beating from the religious police (*right*).

Below: Smashed sets on display in Kabul. Westerners were baffled by the new regime's attitude to television ...

... yet Kabulis did not necessarily share the West's outrage. The Taliban brought much-needed security, and girls' education was not universally banned, as was often reported (a private classroom in 2001, *below*).

Above: Only the Tajik leader Ahmed Shah Massoud continued to resist in the north of the country (*far right*, with his aide, the future presidential candidate Abdullah Abdullah, in white); he was assassinated in 2001.

Below: Hizb-i-Islami leader Gulbuddin Hekmatyar emerges from the Blue Mosque, Mazar-i-Sharif, February 1998.

Mystery still surrounds the disastrous decision to destroy the fourth-century Buddhas of Bamiyan in 2001. Mullah Omar had previously declared them a potentially important source of tourist income.

were not allowed to forget that their mission was to protect the public. On 30 July 1998, for example, an AFP reporter watched them hurl dozens of televisions and video players out on to the street as they mounted yet another raid on the city's electronics shops. As they worked their way down the street they were followed by their commander in a pick-up truck, a Maulawi Qalamuddin, who yelled at them over a loudspeaker mounted on the cab: 'Try not to hurt the people!'

Mullah Omar remained majestically indifferent to foreign criticism of his regime. Even so, in December 1996 when Radio Sharia announced that 225 Kabuli women had been beaten in a single day for violating the new dress codes, he was persuaded that things had gone too far. In some cases, people had been beaten with electric cables. A letter of 'advice' was circulated around the capital's police stations reminding the lawmen that they should not be 'cruel'. 'Such kinds of punishment and beating,' went the text of Omar's letter, 'need the permission of the Imam and Emir, otherwise the doer of such actions will be punished under qisas.' Radio Sharia promptly stopped publicizing the punishments.[6]

The following year, Omar found it necessary to reiterate an order that the Taliban were on no account to 'harm civilians' – an indication that some people were in fact being unnecessarily harmed. The leadership, it seemed, were not always in control of the foot soldiers who underpinned their movement, as the girls' school headmaster Qari Barakatullah Salim confirmed.

'The Taliban authorities were very nice but some of the lower ranks gave me problems. At one time they "requisitioned" my car – for governmental use, they said. But I got it back immediately when I complained to their superiors.'

The truth was that the rank and file often acted independently of their leaders. Some of them were little more than a revolutionary rabble, with an understanding of the new ideology that was often no more than skin-deep. Even the mullahs in charge held a variety of views. Mullah Yar Mohammed in Herat, for instance, was regarded by that city's inhabitants as a relative moderate. When he heard how the religious police had broken up a women's demonstration using hoses from the Fire Department, he was outraged and made a point of denouncing the practice at a public meeting. In Kabul, too, the repression of the people was often far more haphazard than it was usually portrayed abroad – and that cut both ways. The rules could be bent, and frequently were. It was also possible to hoodwink the authorities, for the Taliban were often unworldly people. According to Peter Jouvenal, even a Kabul brandy distillery managed to remain open by arguing that its product was essential for medicinal purposes.

The experience of a Kabuli fortune-teller, Mohammed Jakub Siddiqim, was equally suggestive. Fortune-telling is a well-established tradition in Afghanistan, where superstition and Sufi mysticism have thrived for centuries. The ancient fire-worshipping religion of Zoroastrianism was founded here in the fifth century BC; and the legacy of that and other ancient beliefs was never entirely rooted out by the arrival of Islam. This did not stop the Taliban leadership from trying again now.

Siddiqim, who came from a family of Arabs who emigrated to Afghanistan in the nineteenth century, operated from a small scruffy office lined with posters of tropical islands, one of dozens of such fortune-telling shops scattered across the city. His main skill, palm-reading, was advertised by an enormous yellow hand painted on the window. He had wisely closed up his business the moment the Taliban captured Kabul – unlike several other fortune-tellers, who paid a high price for their lack of clairvoyance.

'I know a couple of them who were beaten by the Vice and Virtue people,' Siddiqim said. 'Hoo-hoo! They were so sore, their wives had to massage them with hot bricks for a week!'

The religious police made inquiries, however, and soon tracked Siddiqim down to his home, where he was arrested and bundled into a truck.

'Those people were the worst. They were taking me to the police station to beat me. But I had prepared for this moment by memorizing some "special verses" from the Koran, which I recited to them.'

The Talibs were so impressed that they turned the truck around and took him home again, apologizing and kissing his hand; they even told Siddiqim's father to look after him because his son had a 'special gift'. Even the Vice and Virtue police, it seemed, had a respect for the old traditions.

'They told me that fortune-telling was against Islam,' said Siddiqim, 'but I told them that I wasn't fortune-telling: I was only reading what was there.'

The following morning the squad leader came back to see Siddiqim for a private consultation – and the morning after, and the morning after that.

'After two weeks I had to ask him to stop coming, because the neighbours were starting to suspect that I was working for them!'

4

The Government that Might Have Been, 1998–2000

The Taliban were often depicted as amateurs – a collection of incompetent country mullahs who were almost wholly unsuited to the task of running a country. Very few in the movement, it was true, had any previous experience of government, but the charge that they were all incompetent was inaccurate. The capital's infra-structure was in ruins when they arrived. Many government offices had been looted, departmental budgets were often non-existent, and most of the civil service had fled. From this unpromising start the Taliban were able to establish an administration that, for all its faults, functioned as an internationally recognizable government for over five years. Not even the imposition of United Nations sanctions in 1999 could destroy it.

At least some of the Taliban's ministers proved capable of learning on the job – and as they did so, the tension between Kandahar and Kabul became more acute. Mullah

Omar's decrees were fine in theory, but it wasn't him who had to put the re-creation of a seventh-century Sharia state into practice. A class of 'career Taliban' grew up in the capital that was far divorced from the lofty idealism of Kandahar. In time, Mullah Omar's edicts began to be taken as standards to aspire to rather than laws actually to be applied – in the same way, perhaps, that some southern European countries treated directives from the EU Commission in Brussels in the 1980s and '90s.

Mullah Zaeef was a competent Taliban administrator who was uncomfortably caught between the worlds of Kabul and Kandahar. The former village imam ran a banking system, three government ministries and the transport sector before becoming the ambassador to Pakistan in 2000: an entire political career shoe-horned into the space of six dizzying years. It began in the western city of Herat, which the Taliban finally conquered in September 1995 after a six-month campaign. Zaeef, still nursing a leg wound received during the fighting around the city, was put in charge of its banks by Mullah Omar. This was an important job because Herat was the gateway to Iran, and its mujahideen overlord, the so-called 'Prince of the West' Ismail Khan, had enriched the city through the taxation of cross-border trade.

Zaeef was a reluctant banking official, though, and missed the quiet life in his mosque. One day in August 1997 he simply quit, and drove home to his wife and family in Kandahar in a borrowed government car. But he was too useful to the regime simply to be allowed to retire. People of his quality were thin on the ground, and the Taliban were now in charge of Kabul. A month after his return he was again summoned to see Mullah Omar.

'Mullah Saheb Amir ul-Mu'mineen wanted me to become the administrative director of the Ministry of Defence,' Zaeef recalled in his autobiography. 'He wrote a letter of official appointment for me, and even though I no longer wanted to work for the government, I could not turn him down. I had taken an oath in Sangisar to follow and stand by him, so if he needed me in Kabul then I would go.'

Like many Taliban mullahs he had never been to the capital before, and when he got there he found his new ministry in chaos. There was no budget and most of the offices were empty. In fact there were so few staff that he was rapidly promoted to Deputy Defence Minister and put in charge of all financial and logistical affairs. Many of the new Taliban ministers were former military commanders, and thus liable to be pulled from behind their desks at short notice and sent into the front line against the Northern Alliance, for the war effort was always Kandahar's first priority. When Zaeef's boss, Mullah Obaidullah, was wounded in a battle north of Kabul, Zaeef found himself in charge of the entire ministry for a stretch of nine months. Using the banking skills learned in Herat, Zaeef designed two budgets, the second of which was used to fund the requirements of the troops on the front lines. This was submitted mostly in cash from Kandahar, and amounted to about $300,000 a week.

Compared to the billions swallowed by the American war-machine today, this was an extraordinarily small sum of money. The Taliban's greatest problem throughout their time in power was that they were broke – and it was this more than anything that prevented the Kabul government from ever becoming a truly effective civil administration. According to Zaeef, the Taliban's annual budget for the entire country never exceeded $80 million, the lion's share of which naturally went on the war. The money left over for civilian expenditure, he said, was 'like a drop of water that falls on a hot stone, evaporating without leaving any trace'.

Considering this dire lack of resources, the Kabul government's achievements were actually remarkable. The absence of official corruption meant that a little money went far. They were often ingenious in the way they spent it, and they were highly motivated. They did more than restore the electricity grid and the main roads in the capital. Zaeef progressed from the Ministry of Defence to that of Mines and Industries, where he oversaw the building of new industrial parks in five cities. The production of fertilizer, cement, coal, salt and marble all increased significantly. The natural gas and oil industries in the north of the country, where productivity in some cases was down by 80 per cent after years of neglect by the mujahideen, were overhauled and even began to attract foreign investment.

Then there was the matter of opium production. There has been much debate about the Taliban's true attitude to poppies. They have long been accused of hypocritically denouncing the trade in public while privately exploiting it to fund themselves and their war. At certain times and in certain places, it is true that poppy production went on as usual. During their years in power, gaining military control of the country was their first priority. Then as now, poppy-farming was the economic mainstay of hundreds of thousands of farmers, as well as an important source of income for many warlords and tribal leaders whom the Taliban could not afford to alienate: precisely the dilemma faced by the International Security Assistance Force (ISAF) in their counter-insurgency bid to win hearts and minds a decade later on.

The leadership always said they intended to eradicate poppy-farming when the civil war was won. They made their position on the drugs trade clear on 10 September 1997, when the Foreign Ministry issued a statement reminding 'all compatriots' that 'the use of heroin and hashish is not permitted in Islam. They are reminded once again that they should strictly refrain from growing, using and trading in hashish and heroin. Anyone who violates this order shall be meted out a punishment in line with the lofty Mohammed and Sharia law.'[1] Ten days later, a clarification was issued banning the cultivation and trafficking of opium as well.

The ban was not very effective: opium production rose

slightly over the next two years. In July 2000, however, Omar himself decreed a total ban on poppy cultivation. The following year, just 8,000 hectares of poppy were planted: the lowest on record, and less than a tenth of the area under poppy the year before. Bernard Frahi of the United Nations Office of Drug Control called it 'one of the most remarkable successes ever' in the fight against narcotics. Critics pointed out that the ban was not quite all it seemed. Gretchen Peters, the author of a study of the Afghan poppy trade, described it as 'the ultimate insider trading con'. The price of opium on Afghanistan's borders rose almost overnight from $28 to as much as $400 a kilo. And the Taliban, who continued to collect customs revenue, apparently made no attempt to destroy existing stocks.

Did Omar cynically exploit his position as Leader of All the Faithful to increase his regime's revenue from drugs? Guy Willoughby, the Director of the Halo Trust, thought that it was the West, not the Taliban, who were 'cynical and unhelpful' in their response to Omar's anti-poppy edict. Today's Taliban, meanwhile, naturally argue that they were just getting on top of the issue when their government was ousted.

'We are the only ones who managed to reduce the harvest,' the Taliban's Mullah Abdul-Basit told me in 2007. 'Mullah Omar issued a fatwa against it. We were succeeding in abolishing it. We couldn't stop it all at once – the process is slow, like weaning a child off breast-feeding – but we were getting there when the Americans came.'

Since ousting the Taliban, the West has spent billions on various schemes to control the growing of poppy, with very limited success. It is an awkward fact that production in each of the last seven years has been higher than in any of the seven years of Taliban rule. Over 90 per cent of the world's heroin continues to originate in Afghanistan, and two-thirds of that originates in Helmand, now the main focus of Nato's counter-insurgency. As Gretchen Peters observes, if Helmand were a separate country it would still be the world's leading opium producer, with the rest of Afghanistan in second place.

Perceptions matter in Afghanistan; and the Taliban at least established in the minds of the people the principle that the opium trade is morally wrong according to Islam. Drug money today corrupts the Karzai government as never before, and threatens to ruin the West's mission to stabilize the country. In the future, poppy-growing looks just as likely to be suppressed by fatwa as by Western-funded 'alternative livelihood schemes'. Afghans used to argue that heroin was exclusively a Western vice, and therefore a problem for the West to solve alone; selling heroin to infidels was sometimes seen almost as an act of war. Not any more. A 2007 survey for the UN identified nearly 50,000 heroin users in the country, and an additional 150,000 who use opium: a new and persuasive reason for the Afghans to address the poppy issue for themselves.

It is fascinating to speculate how Taliban Afghanistan

might have developed had fate and al-Qaida not intervened. Given more money, and perhaps even the support rather than the enmity of the international community, what might the regime not have achieved? However incredible it now seems, there was a time when even the United States saw the positive in the Taliban.

'They control more than two-thirds of the country, they are Afghan, they are indigenous, and they have demonstrated staying power,' the US Assistant Secretary of State Robin Raphael told a closed-door UN session in New York in November 1996. 'The real source of their success has been the willingness of many Afghans, particularly Pashtuns, to tacitly trade unending fighting and chaos for a measure of peace and security, even with several social restrictions. It is not in the interest of Afghanistan or any of us here that the Taliban be isolated.'

The US were even ready to do business with the regime – always the ultimate seal of American approval – via the giant American oil firm Unocal. Zaeef himself oversaw a contract competition between them and another oil firm, Argentina's Bridas, involving the construction of an 890-mile, $2-billion pipeline that would carry natural gas from newly discovered fields in Turkmenistan through Afghanistan to the lucrative markets of Pakistan and beyond.

Unocal's engagement with the Taliban was no secret. To this day, many Afghans believe that the CIA colluded with the ISI in the creation of the Taliban, and even that

Unocal secretly provided weapons for Mullah Omar's assault on Kabul, purely in pursuit of American energy interests – although there is no evidence for this. Washington's support for Unocal was, in fact, overt. In 1996, Unocal opened an office in central Kandahar, along with a $900,000, 56-acre training camp for the local workers who would build and operate the pipeline; similar camps were established in Herat and Mazar. They were assisted in this by the Rand Corporation's Zalmay Khalilzad, an Americanized Pashtun from Mazar who later became the most senior Muslim in George Bush's administration and, from 2003 to 2005, the US ambassador to Afghanistan. Unocal also hired Thomas Gouttiere, a former Peace Corps volunteer in Afghanistan in the 1960s who had gone on to found an influential Center for Afghan Studies at the University of Nebraska.

In December 1997, and with the full approval of Washington, a delegation of Taliban officials travelled to Unocal's headquarters at Sugar Land, Texas, where they stayed in the home of one of the company's vice-presidents, Marty Miller. This visit represented the high-water mark of US–Taliban relations. Miller treated them royally. They were taken to the zoo and the Nasa Space Center, and went on a shopping expedition to the Super Target discount store. They reportedly played with a Frisbee in Miller's garden and, because it was Christmas time, asked searching questions about the meaning of the star on the top of the Miller family tree.

The delegation was led by Mullah Mohammed Ghaus, the acting Foreign Minister. In 2010 Gouttiere, who helped arrange the visit, remembered Ghaus as a 'relatively reasonable guy' who 'felt the government under the Taliban should be like any other government, with a responsibility towards the rest of the world'. There were many Taliban who thought like Ghaus in Kabul: the acceptable, outward-looking face of the movement. The Sugar Land meetings proved that there was common ground between the Taliban and America, and that dialogue between the two sides had once been possible.

'It is always better to talk than to fight,' Gouttiere said.

The pipeline deal failed, though. Many forces were militating against its success. The first of these was that the project was dependent on the Taliban establishing peace in the north – and this they were still struggling to do. The Taliban had taken over the southern two-thirds of the country with relatively little bloodshed, but as they moved northwards into the traditionally non-Pashtun areas, resistance increased and their progress was dramatically slowed. In the spring of 1997 I hitched a ride on an army helicopter to the Northern Alliance's western front. The hold was filled with teetering crates of Iranian-made mousetrap mines, small, cheap, plastic contraptions powerful enough to take a man's leg off below the knee.

The mines were destined for Ismail Khan, a Tajik mujahideen leader and the former governor of Herat, who had taken to the hills with his followers, vowing to recapture the fief from which he had been ousted by the Taliban. I met Khan, an impressive guerrilla figure in his snowy-white shalwar qamiz and a beard to match, in his field headquarters near the Murghab river in Badghis province close to the border with Turkmenistan. If the Taliban tried to build a pipeline, he told me fiercely, he wouldn't hesitate to blow it up. Khan was later betrayed and captured by the Taliban, who transported him to Kandahar, where he was said to have been kept buried up to his neck in a pit. (He escaped in 1999, and later regained the governorship of Herat and joined the Karzai government; today he is the Minister of Energy.)

It was allegations of brutality such as this, almost all of them associated with the war against the non-Pashtun northerners, which today raise the gravest doubts about what might happen if the Taliban were allowed to return to power. The war became more vicious as it went on, and as it did so the tenor of the revolution began to change. What started out as a movement for national peace and security looked increasingly like one more militia bent on establishing ethnic hegemony. The Taliban were a Pashtun movement, and for all the overlay of Sharia idealism, killing and vindictiveness were a historical characteristic, a part of the Pashtun psyche.

'When the Pashtun is a child his mother tells him: "The coward dies but his shrieks live long after," and so he learns not to shriek,' the poet Ghani Khan wrote.[2] 'He is shown dozens of things dearer than life so that he will

111

not mind about dying or killing. He is forbidden colour-
ful clothes or exotic music, for they weaken the arm and
soften the eye. He is taught to look at the hawk and
forget the nightingale.'

A string of accusations that Taliban soldiers
committed serious human rights abuses have never been
satisfactorily answered. The worst of these concern the
Hazaras, the people with the longest history of persecution by the indigenous Pashtuns. As Shi'as rather
than Sunnis they were always marked out for discrimination, and it seems certain that some Taliban now
took their supposed apostasy as a reason for killing them.
A massacre in Yakaolang district in January 2001 went
on for four days. Witnesses told Human Rights Watch
that the Taliban had detained about three hundred
civilian men, including staff from local humanitarian
organizations, before herding them to assembly points
around the district where they were shot by firing squad
in full public view.

The most serious flashpoint was Mazar, the stronghold city of the ethnic Uzbek leader Rashid Dostum.
Being so close to the old Soviet border, Mazar had
escaped the worst of the disastrous physical and psychological effects of the Jihad. Its ethnically mixed
population – which included a large number of Hazaras
– had known little sectarian strife, and its culture and
values were wholly different from those of the south. I
spent much of April 1997 on the Northern Alliance front
lines, and it seemed inconceivable to me that the Taliban

would be able to fight or bribe their way to power here. The morale of Dostum's troops looked too strong. By day they patrolled their lines on tanks, and even on horses specially trained not to flinch when an RPG was fired at the gallop over their heads. By night they sat around their camp-fires, exchanging insults over their field radios with the Taliban sentries posted a mile or two away.

I reckoned without Dostum's ally, General Malik Pahlawan, who suspected his boss of murdering his brother, and wanted revenge. At the end of May, in a deal secretly brokered by Pakistan, Malik changed sides by betraying Ismail Khan to the Taliban. The Northern Alliance's western flank abruptly collapsed, some 2,500 Taliban fighters poured through the breach, and Dostum fled. The last city in the country to withstand the Taliban's advance was now in their hands. Various regime leaders flew in to declare victory. So did the Pakistani Foreign Minister, who on 25 May called a press conference to announce his country's first formal recognition of the Taliban government. Saudi Arabia and the UAE immediately followed suit.

The celebrations were premature. Much to the embarrassment of the Pakistanis and Arabs, the Taliban occupation of Mazar lasted just one week. The invaders apparently forgot how far they were from their southern home, and the degree to which their previous territorial gains had depended on public consent. Soon after they arrived, a Taliban mullah called a public meeting to announce the familiar terms of the new regime: women to be banished to their homes, mosques to be taken over, all schools to be shut down, along with Balkh University – the last one functioning in the country, with a student body that included 1,800 emancipated young women. There was no concession in any of this to the city's special status as the most liberal in the country. The mullahs even wanted to ban partridge-fighting, a particularly popular sport in the north. There were angry murmurs of protest as the audience dispersed. Later, when squads of Taliban spread out into the suburbs to collect weapons, the Hazaras refused to be disarmed. A firefight began that quickly spread to every neighbourhood. Some six hundred Taliban, many of them fresh recruits from the madrasahs of Pakistan and wholly untrained in urban warfare, were killed.

When Mazar fell for the second time in September 1998, it was in the Hazara neighbourhoods where the Taliban allegedly took their worst revenge. Mullah Niazi, a man implicated in the killing of President Najibullah, and who led the new attack on Mazar and subsequently became the city's governor, declared: 'Hazaras are not Muslim, they are Shi'a. They are kafir [infidels]. The Hazaras killed our force here, and now we have to kill Hazaras ... If you do not show your loyalty, we will burn your houses, and we will kill you. You either accept to be Muslims or leave Afghanistan ... wherever you go we will catch you. If you go up, we will pull you down by your feet; if you hide below, we will pull you up by your hair.'

The Taliban also entered the Iranian consulate in Mazar where, to howls of international protest, they murdered eleven diplomats. Tehran responded by massing an army of 200,000 on its eastern border; Ayatollah Khomenei warned of a 'huge war' that could engulf the entire region.[3]

The 1998 massacre is often held up as the worst of several examples of Taliban atrocities during the struggle to subdue the north. According to a United Nations estimate at the time, some 5,000–6,000 Hazaras were put to death. And yet the number of Hazaras killed is still hotly disputed. Like so many incidents during those violent times, the killings were never formally investigated. The headline figure of 6,000 dead was first released to the world by the United Nations in Islamabad, who based it on about half a dozen eyewitness statements taken from refugees who had fled the city for Pakistan. But these had reported seeing handfuls of dead, not thousands; and when Western journalists attempted to verify the UN figure on the ground in Mazar, they found they could not.

'Everyone always exaggerates everything in Afghanistan, and the truth tends to get lost in all the shouting,' one of these reporters told me. 'The Hazaras all said things like, "I didn't see it myself, but if you speak to so-and-so in the street around the corner, they saw hundreds of people being shot: they'll tell you." But when it came down to it there was very little evidence. In my experience, the true figures are usually about a tenth of what gets reported.'

The Taliban, for their part, still deny that they killed any Hazaras at all. Mullah Zaeef insisted that the Hazaras who died were the victims not of Taliban fighters but of rivals in the Northern Alliance. He even claimed that they were killed during the vacuum of power before the Taliban entered the city, and it was in fact the Taliban who had restored the peace.

'There were accusations that our soldiers committed rape. But the very idea is outrageous! I challenge you to find one single woman who says she was treated that way by us . . . it is all Northern Alliance propaganda, and the West goes on using it as justification for the war now.'

He had an explanation, too, for the murders at the Iranian consulate. The victims there were not diplomats at all but Iranian Special Forces trainers who had been flown in to stiffen the Hazara resistance. The diplomats who should have been there had left the week before on a Red Cross plane – a fact later corroborated by the Red Cross themselves, although it went unreported.

Did Zaeef protest too much? For all his insistence that the Taliban were blameless in the field, it was nevertheless Kandahar's determination to subdue the non-Pashtun north that began the terrible violence there – the worst the region had seen in decades, and which initiated a vicious cycle of tit-for-tat killings around Mazar that is still played out today. In Zaeef's view, a great many fighters had died needlessly as a result of the mishandled occupation of Mazar: the Taliban's first and worst mistake. There were some in the movement who thought – privately – that it had been a misjudgement even to try to conquer the north, and that the Taliban should have restricted their mission to the Pashtun heart-lands. Zaeef calculated that as many as 13,000 Taliban were killed in fighting and other kinds of blood-letting across the north. Vindictiveness had inevitably crept into the movement's credo, tainting the idealism that under-pinned it. Their struggle was in danger of turning into one more squalid ethnic vendetta. Zaeef was so troubled that in March 1999, after a year and a half at the Ministry of Defence, he once again resigned.

'Several issues that I had been commanded to look into lay uneasy with me,' he wrote. 'I had been ordered to search through all the files in the ministry's archives to filter out all Afghan communists who had received a medal of honour or other awards for the killing of Afghans during the communists' rule.'

He was also unhappy with the Taliban's tactics on the Shomali plains, a heavily irrigated farming region to the north of Kabul that the Taliban and Ahmed Shah Massoud's forces had fought over for years. In 1997 the Taliban deliberately devastated the area, destroying the irrigation channels and poisoning wells, forcing 180,000 civilians to flee.

In an episode significantly left out of his published autobiography, Zaeef confided to a friend that he had confronted his old comrade Mullah Omar in private one evening, removing his turban and casting it down between them: a powerful gesture of sincerity.

'I said to Omar: 'What are you doing? This fighting is not what we signed up for. Please: it was never supposed to be this way!'

Omar briefly turned away, and when he looked back his eyes were full of tears.

'My hands are tied,' he said. 'What else can I do?'

Omar's hands were indeed tied. The war had by now taken on a momentum of its own, and his revolution was being manipulated by Pakistan. He also had a growing al-Qaida problem. On 7 August 1998, truck bombs blew up outside the US embassies in Kenya and Tanzania, killing 224 people and wounding 4,500, and Osama bin Laden, who had headquartered himself in Afghanistan two years previously, was the main suspect. This was a turning point for the Taliban, the moment when the destinies of Omar and bin Laden became entwined. It spelled the end for the Kabul government's hopes for any sort of normality in their relations with the outside world. In particular, the trans-Afghan pipeline project, the most potent symbol of a different Taliban future, was dead.

'Unocal lost all interest after the embassy attacks,' Thomas Gouttiere recalled. 'They just cut their losses and ran.'

A Unocal official in Turkmenistan told me that his company's policy was dictated not by Washington but by its share-holders, for whom absolute security in Afghanistan was a sine qua non if they were to support a $2-billion investment project.

On 17 August came what Gouttiere called the beginning of 'Lewinsky Weekend', when President Bill Clinton admitted in a national television address that he had indeed had an 'inappropriate' relationship with the White House intern.

'And so tonight,' he said at the end of his address, 'I ask you to turn away from the spectacle of the past seven months, to repair the fabric of our national discourse, and to return our attention to all the challenges and all the promise of the next American century.'

Three days later on 20 August, US warships launched seventy-five cruise missiles at four alleged al-Qaida training camps in the east of the country near Khost and Jalalabad. The camps were mostly empty: the missiles killed thirty-four people, only six of them Arabs, and bin Laden himself was nowhere near at the time.

The Taliban were predictably outraged at this attack on their sovereignty. Demonstrations were organized and several UN offices were attacked by mobs. A mad rumour circulated that Clinton had been tricked into the attack by Mossad, the Israeli secret service – an allegation based solely on the fact that Monica Lewinsky was Jewish, and therefore apparently a Mossad agent.

'If the attack on Afghanistan is Clinton's personal decision,' said Mullah Omar, 'then he has done it to divert the world and the American people's attention from that shameful White House affair that has proved Clinton is a liar and a man devoid of decency and honour.'[4]

Omar had been under pressure for months to hand bin Laden over to the Americans for trial. Now he categorically refused, insisting that bin Laden was his 'guest'. He added: 'America itself is the biggest terrorist in the world.'

The countdown to war between the Taliban and the West had begun.

5

The Al-Qaida Hijack, 1999–2001

It was not the Western public's fault if they made little distinction between al-Qaida and their Taliban hosts. They were led to think this way for many years after 9/11 by politicians on both sides of the Atlantic, but most of all in America, where a conflation of terminology served to justify the new neo-con determination to get rid of Omar's regime. 'The Taliban and al-Qaida are one enterprise,' a senior US diplomat announced at a conference organized by the British Foreign Office in July 2001. 'President Bush is very serious and could declare the Taliban a terrorist group.'[1]

Our leaders still play upon the idea that they are indivisible. The West's principal justification of the war, indeed, is that if the Western military were to leave before the Taliban are defeated, the conditions would soon be ripe for a return of al-Qaida and their terrorist training camps. There has, of course, been no significant al-Qaida presence in Afghanistan since 2002. Even Pakistan now admits that bin Laden's regional base is on their side of the border. Western politicians have adapted their old rhetoric to this inconvenient fact, although not by much. Ex-Prime Minister Gordon Brown used to refer often to 'a chain of terror running from the mountains and plains of southern Afghanistan and Pakistan to the towns and streets of Britain ... People in Britain today are safer because of the courageous sacrifice of British soldiers.'[2]

The Taliban and al-Qaida, however, have always been very different beasts. Mullah Omar's movement was filled with Afghan Pashtuns with an exclusively domestic agenda; bin Laden's was manned by Arabs whose goals were international. He was driven by anger at the American occupation of the Saudi peninsula during and after the First Gulf War, and at the Saudi royal family for inviting them in. Killing Americans and their allies was, for him, 'an individual duty for every Muslim who can do it in any country in which it is possible to'.[3] The Taliban, by contrast, did not want to kill Americans but to build pipelines with them. Omar may have used terror tactics at home, but he never had any interest in exporting terrorism abroad. Indeed he issued many statements declaring that no foreign country should be attacked from Afghan soil – and continues to issue them today. His goal has never gone further than the establishment of the Taliban version of utopia within their own borders. To date there has not been a single

Taliban bomb in 'the towns and streets of Britain' or anywhere else in the West.

Gordon Brown's contention that British people are safer because of the war is highly debatable. Britain is home to at least 1.6 million Muslims[4] and 1,500 mosques, more than half of which are affiliated with the same Deobandi school of thought that the Taliban embrace. The galvanizing effect of the war on such a community can only be guessed at. Since 2006 at least, the British military have detected the occasional 'Midlands accent' while eavesdropping on the Taliban's radio traffic. It is arguable that the Afghan Taliban have shown extraordinary restraint in not attacking targets abroad in the last sixteen years. In April 2010, by grim contrast, the Pakistani Taliban leader Hakimullah Mehsud released a video message warning that 'The time is very near when our fighters will attack the American states in their major cities.' Hours later, they claimed responsibility for a failed car-bomb attack in Times Square in New York.[5]

It is also questionable whether al-Qaida would even want to re-establish themselves in the event of the Taliban's return. Afghanistan is not the hiding place it once was. The West's knowledge of the terrain is of a different order compared even to five years ago, while satellite and drone technology have made concealment vastly more difficult than before. Meanwhile, the focus of al-Qaida's efforts has moved from the 'Af-Pak' region back to Saudi Arabia and the Horn of Africa. In January 2010, al-Qaida fighters were reportedly 'streaming' away from Pakistan towards Yemen.[6]

Even if bin Laden did want to set up shop in Afghanistan again, would Mullah Omar really welcome him back? It seems unlikely – and without some form of sanctuary provided by the Taliban, any attempt to re-establish a serious terrorist operation on Afghan soil would surely fail. Sheltering bin Laden after 1998 ended Omar's most cherished dream, the establishment of a Sharia state. Why would he make the same mistake again? As a Taliban mullah bitterly remarked to me in 2007: 'The West destroyed our government for the sake of just one man.' From 2002 onwards, the Taliban's exiled leaders and the remnants of al-Qaida in Pakistan became allies of convenience in the sense that they were both at war with the West. But their reasons for fighting the foreigners are as different as they ever were. There is also evidence that Omar has deliberately kept his distance from bin Laden since 9/11. In January 2007, Omar told a journalist by email that he had 'neither seen [bin Laden], nor have I made any effort to do so' since December 2001.[7] 'We have never felt the need for a permanent relationship in the present circumstances ... They have set jihad as their goal, whereas we have set the expulsion of American troops from Afghanistan as our target.'

Their relationship was rooted in the Jihad of the 1980s. The son of a Yemeni who had grown rich in the construction business, bin Laden was among thousands of

Arab volunteers who travelled to Afghanistan to fight the infidel Soviets. He settled in Peshawar in 1982, where he became well known as an organizer of the so-called 'Arab-Afghans', as well as a useful source of funds and engineering expertise for the Afghan mujahideen. Many Arab fighters remained in the region after the war. In 1992, several hundred of them fought alongside Hekmatyar against Massoud in the battle for Kabul, although bin Laden was not among them. Disillusioned by the internal squabbles of the mujahideen, he had gone back to Saudi Arabia in 1990, and from there to Sudan in 1992; he returned to Afghanistan in May 1996, arriving in Jalalabad in a chartered jet accompanied by dozens of Arab militants, bodyguards, three wives and thirteen children.[8]

The personal relationship between Omar and bin Laden has been the subject of just as much ill-informed speculation in Afghanistan as it has been in the West. It is widely held by Afghans, for example, that in the 1990s Omar cemented a medieval-style pact with al-Qaida by taking bin Laden's eldest daughter as a wife – and even that bin Laden had also taken one of Omar's daughters as a fourth wife.[9] But according to every single former or present member of the Taliban I have ever met, including Mullah Zaeef, there is no truth in either story. Inter-racial marriage is not unheard of in Pashtun culture – for instance, Jalaluddin Haqqani, the leader of the Taliban-allied Haqqani Network, numbers an Arab among his wives – but it is very rare in practice. Pashtun marriage partners are traditionally restricted to the same creed and class, and often the same tribe, much as they are in Saudi culture. The idea of a simple country mullah like Omar marrying into the wealthy (and royally connected) bin Laden family is socially almost inconceivable.

For all their undoubted prowess as fighters, the Arabs were never popular in Afghanistan. They were richer and more sophisticated than their hosts, whom they tended to treat with lordly disdain. The Afghans, for their part, despised the arrogance with which they drove about in their shiny new 4x4 vehicles, which were conspicuous by their blacked-out windows and the Dubai number plates their owners couldn't be bothered to change for local ones. The Arabs were adherents of Wahhabism, an ultra-conservative offshoot of Salafism, which was viewed with suspicion even in Kandahar. Wahhabis take their name from Muhammad ibn Abd-al-Wahhab, an eighteenth-century Arab scholar who believed in the purification of Islam from heretical 'innovations' through violence; and the Wahhabi interpretation of Sharia most closely follows the Hanbali school of jurisprudence, a tradition alien to the Hanafi Islam embraced by Afghans.

Bin Laden was a liability for the Taliban from the start, for American intelligence had begun to monitor his activities even before his arrival in Jalalabad. In early 1997, a CIA snatch squad convened in Peshawar in a bid to capture bin Laden, although the mission was aborted. Omar, already suspicious of bin Laden's intentions in

Afghanistan, responded by ordering his guest to move his operation down to Kandahar where he could keep a closer eye on him. 'It is beyond justice,' as Omar later complained, 'that today no distinction is drawn between terrorists and mujahideen in the world.'[10]

The West's mistake was to assume that Omar's Afghanistan was a terrorist-sponsoring state, when in reality it was a state sponsored by terrorists. In one close observer's view, the relationship between Omar and bin Laden was always '90 per cent about money, only 10 per cent about shared ideas and ideology'. Bribery was one of the most important weapons in the Taliban's arsenal as they took over the country, and bin Laden provided much of the ammunition for it, reputedly donating $3 million of his own fortune within four months of his return to the country, just for the Taliban's assault on Kabul. He continued to lavish money on his impoverished hosts once he reached Kandahar, where he built a house for Omar's family, imported fleets of Toyota Hi-Lux trucks from Dubai, and promised to build mosques and schools and to repave the road from the airport.

He also became an important conduit for donations from the Gulf States. The sheikhs liked to combine pleasure with business, and the well-connected bin Laden excelled at arranging hawking and hunting trips for them. A quarry particularly prized by falconers was the Houbara Bustard, the provincial bird of Baluchistan, the meat of which is considered an aphrodisiac in Arabia.

The sheikhs would fly in by private jet or military transport, bringing weapons, vehicles and other equipment, which they would leave behind for their hosts. On one such 'hunting trip', the UAE Defence Minister Sheikh Mohammed al-Maktoum flew in from Dubai with a hundred brand-new Toyota Land Cruisers all fitted with field radios.[11]

Despite such largesse, and despite Omar's public protestations of support for bin Laden, the relationship between the two took a turn for the worse after the US embassy bombings in 1998. An intense debate began among the ulema and the leadership over how to deal with their wayward ally – a debate that was still not resolved when al-Qaida attacked New York three years later. One of the main sticking points was the Pashtunwali tenet of *nanawatai*, the offering of sanctuary to anyone who asks for it. Nanawatai also confers an obligation to help the weaker party in a feud by mediating its resolution. This was the principle behind Omar's insistence that bin Laden was his 'guest', and therefore couldn't be touched.

Nanawatai has long baffled the West. According to a Pashtun folk story, the Shah of Afghanistan was out hunting one day when he wounded a stag with an arrow. As the chase neared its inevitable end, the stag bolted into a peasant hut. The shah, delighted, dismounted from his horse and prepared to enter the hut, but his way was blocked by its owner.

'Do you not know who I am?' said the shah.

'Whoever you are,' said the peasant, 'you may not enter my house. This stag has looked for my protection and I must grant it.'

The shah, impressed by the peasant's steadfastness, went on his way empty-handed.

Nanawatai was not just folklore. In 2005 Petty Officer Marcus Luttrell, a sniper in a US Navy SEAL team, was injured during a firefight with the Taliban in eastern Afghanistan. He crawled seven miles – in the course of which he managed to kill six pursuers – before finding shelter with tribesmen from the Pashtun village of Sabri-Minah, who treated his wounds and refused all Taliban demands that they turn him over to them.[12]

There are, however, conditions to nanawatai, the first of which is complete submission to the host. The most obvious act of submission is the giving up of one's weapons; not to do so is to demonstrate distrust of one's host, the gravest insult to a Pashtun's *ghayrat*, a man's honour and personal dignity. In Waziristan in the mid nineteenth century, a tribesman seeking sanctuary would sometimes be required first to humiliate himself by wearing a halter made of grass around his neck.[13] Bin Laden never gave up his weapons, and he wasn't the type to wear a grass necklace. There were many senior ulema who believed that the Saudi had thus breached the terms of nanawatai, and advised Omar that he could hand him over with a clear conscience. Others, however, argued that to do so would breach the forgiving *spirit* of nanawatai – and in the end, Omar agreed with them.

According to one ex-Taliban member who knew him, Omar was 'more Pashtun than Muslim' – by which he meant that it was entirely typical of him to adhere to the moral position that two wrongs do not make a right.

And yet the decision to go on protecting bin Laden was not taken quite as easily as that characterization implies. Omar was astute enough to realize that bin Laden was also his most valuable international bargaining chip. Even as the ulema deliberated, he was exploring the possibility of exchanging his guest for official American recognition of his regime – something the Taliban had craved from the moment they captured Kabul. He spoke to the US State Department by satellite phone several times on this issue, though without result. The US wanted bin Laden handed over unconditionally. Omar countered that they should first show him the evidence of bin Laden's involvement in the Africa bombings – evidence that, as the *New York Times* reported, had so far proved 'difficult to obtain'.[14] In any case, he was not prepared to see bin Laden tried in the US. Instead he offered to try him in an Afghan court if America could produce enough evidence; and if that was unacceptable, he proposed sending him to be tried in another Islamic country. These offers continued right up until 7 October 2001, the day the American and British bombing campaign began.

Washington insisted throughout that bin Laden should be tried in America. Even the possibility of a trial at the International Court in The Hague was ruled out.

As Mullah Zaeef explained: 'America's demands ... implied that there was no justice in the Islamic world, and with it no legal authority of Islam to implement justice and law among the people. This stands in direct opposition to Islam itself.'

It was deadlock – and perhaps one of the great 'what if' moments in history. It could be argued that with just a little more patience, diplomacy and understanding from the US, bin Laden might have ended up in a court-room, al-Qaida might have lost its figurehead, and 9/11 and the entire War on Terror might never have happened.

Omar, to be sure, was no diplomat either. In late August 1998 he appeared to torpedo his own second alternative for bin Laden – trial in another Muslim country – when Prince Turki al-Faisal arrived in Kandahar expecting the Saudi dissident to be delivered to him. Omar bluntly accused him and the Saudi royal family of being American stooges, an insult so grave that, according to legend, Prince Turki returned to Riyadh 'without even staying for lunch'. The Saudis subsequently suspended diplomatic relations with the Taliban – although they did not withdraw recognition of their government.

The civil war did not end with the fall of Mazar, as every Afghan had hoped. The Tajik leader Massoud refused to compromise with the Taliban, who had proposed a power-sharing arrangement, and instead chose to fight on from his base in the impenetrable Panjshir valley. The tide of war swept back and forth across the north-eastern provinces with further devastating consequences for the inhabitants. The rhetoric between Washington and Kandahar became ever more entrenched as America's obsession with bin Laden grew. UN sanctions were tightened in December 1998, and again in October 1999, hurting trade and banning all commercial flights to and from Kabul. The people's suffering was increased in 2000 by a widespread drought. Appeals for international help went largely unanswered since donors were discouraged by the Taliban's refusal to call a ceasefire. Food prices increased by 75 per cent, and the Afghani currency lost half of its value.[15] An earthquake killed 5,000 in Badakhsan, and a plague of locusts descended on Baghlan. It was hardly surprising if the Taliban leader felt embattled. He needed every friend he could get, and the only two he had were very uncertain ones: Pakistan, and bin Laden.

Tariq Osman, who worked as a computer expert in Mullah Omar's 'Special Office' in Kandahar from 1998 to 2001, experienced the regime's growing bunker mentality in these years at first hand. Omar's compound at Chowni, just to the north-west of the city, had been heavily fortified with several feet of sandbags arranged on the roof to protect against air attack; construction workers were said to have been diverted from a giant new mosque in the city centre in order to build it.

'There were two kinds of Taliban,' he recalled. 'Illiterate peasant mullahs from rural areas like Helmand

and Uruzgan who had actually very little knowledge of Islam; and the educated mullahs, mostly former refugees in Pakistan, who tended to be far more tolerant. The mullahs around Omar had very limited knowledge of anything.' Omar himself was 'a low-level scholar and a very poor public speaker – as were most of his spokesmen, because he chose them.'

Despite an immense beard, Osman himself belonged to neither category. I met him not in Afghanistan but in London at the beginning of 2010, when he was preparing to start a short course in international development at Wolverhampton University. Since 2002 he had done a lot of research work for various international organizations – the East–West Institute, the Asia Foundation, the Oslo-based International Peace Research Institute – while privately pursuing Islamic studies. His ambition was to set up his own Islamic education centre in Afghanistan. He believed that the best way to combat Islamic extremism was not less but more, and better, religious education: a strikingly Afghan solution to his country's troubles.

'A lot of what went on in Kabul in the 1990s – beating people for having short beards, or for showing their ankles – was against Islam. The Prophet preached respect for life and property and human dignity. The problem now is that kids are joining the Taliban without any knowledge of Islam at all. A new radicalization is creeping into the cities. People are being branded infidels just for working for an NGO. This is purely down to ignorance of Islam.'

During the Jihad he had fought across seventeen different provinces for Gulbuddin Hekmatyar's Hizb-i-Islami, an experience that had cost him most of his fingers following an accident with a shell detonator. He quit the mujahideen in 1993, went to study English in Peshawar, taught himself how to use a computer, and ended up back in Kabul in 1998 with a job as the Foreign Ministry's website and internet manager with the rank of Third Secretary. When Mullah Omar let it be known that he was establishing a Special Office in Kandahar – effectively an internet and communications hub for the movement – Osman was seconded southwards to help set it up.

His role gave him a unique insight into the tensions within the leadership, as well as the mad contradictions inherent in a system trying to run a modern state according to rules designed for the late seventh century. Even the existence of the Special Office was controversial. It was also hypocritical. In June 2001, Omar issued a decree forbidding Afghans to use the internet – with the specific exception of himself and his Special Office.

'Mullah Abdul Salaam Helmandi told his own brother that he wouldn't let him into his house if he defiled himself by even entering the internet office,' Osman recalled. 'Yet I was ordered to write up the decree banning the internet on a computer so that it could be emailed to Kabul!'

It took sensitive antennae just to survive at Omar's court, a paranoid world where everyone's past was subject to scrutiny, and signals of factional allegiance were spotted in the smallest of things. The hadith one referred to in everyday speech and even a man's choice of tea was important. Black tea, for instance, was associated with Harakat-i-Inqilab-i-Islami, or the Islamic Revolution Movement, the tanzeem Omar had once fought for. Drinking green tea, supposedly the preferred beverage of the Hizb-i-Islami (Khalis faction), or even hot water (Hizb-i-Islami (Gulbuddin)) could be very dangerous for one's career.

'For two or three years,' Osman remarked, 'I didn't drink any tea at all.'

Just as much care had to be taken with one's dress. Afghans all look much the same to Westerners in their ubiquitous uniform of waistcoat and shalwar qamiz. In Kandahar, the shape of a collar or the embroidery on a placket could be highly political; a square-cut rather than a tail-cut hem on a shalwar qamiz was specifically associated with Gulbuddin Hekmatyar.

The inner circle of mullahs were 'companions' in name only, for there was real political power to be derived from proximity to Omar. Although every edict issued from Kandahar had in theory to be signed by the Amir, Osman soon discovered that this was not always the case. Even at its most senior level, the regime's command and control procedure was worryingly slack.

'Every order for Kabul had to pass through the Special Office. They were drafted and sent to the Amir for signature; I was instructed to go each day at a certain time to collect them from a small, locked cupboard in the porch of the mosque next to the Amir's house. I compared the "Mullah Omar" signature on several of these decrees and found there were at least four different ones.'

Who held the key to the cupboard? Was there more than one copy of it? For Osman, the different signatures explained a good deal about the inconsistency of some of the Amir's decisions in those years.

One of the most puzzling, both to Afghans and to the rest of the world, was his apparent approval of the destruction of the Buddhas of Bamiyan in 2001. Recessed into sandstone cliffs 8,000 feet up in the mountains of central Afghanistan, the two Buddhas had been built in the late Kushan era in the early fourth century. The taller of the pair towered 165 feet above the Hazara town of Bamiyan, a staging post on the Silk Route for almost 2,000 years. The statues were one of the wonders of ancient times, and until their destruction were considered the most remarkable representations of the Buddha anywhere in the world.

I visited Bamiyan in 1998, soon before the Taliban's second Hazarajat campaign, and took the narrow staircase carved into the cliff to emerge at last on to the head of the taller Buddha. There was an astounding view over the town to the fields and plains beyond, a giant dusty bowl tightly encircled by the jagged white teeth of the Hindu Kush. The Buddhas had once been painted red, blue and gold, and the recess walls and the dozens of monks' caves along the cliff were covered with rich frescoes. Traces of these could be seen as late as the 1970s. They depicted the Sun God in a golden chariot being pulled by snow-white horses through a dark blue sky, and maroon-robed monks conversing in flower-filled fields.[16]

The Buddhas had been badly treated during the Jihad years. Hezb-i-Wahdat's Hazaras had used the main recesses as an ammunition dump, and the surrounding caves to house families of refugees. In September 1998, Taliban fighters blew off the face of the smaller Buddha with dynamite, and fired rockets at his groin. Conservationist bodies including UNESCO, the United Nations Educational, Scientific and Cultural Organization, begged Omar to issue a decree preserving what remained. In July 1999 he did so. Although the Taliban considered idolatry *haram*, he sensibly argued that because there were no longer any Buddhists in Afghanistan, there was no possibility of anyone worshipping these idols. He added: 'The government considers the Bamiyan statues as an example of a potential major source of income for Afghanistan from international visitors. The Taliban states that Bamiyan shall not be destroyed but protected.'

The Buddhas were destroyed nevertheless, using dynamite, anti-aircraft guns and artillery over several weeks starting in March 2001. It was the most potent symbol of a country in self-destruct mode: the equivalent, perhaps, of Egypt demolishing the pyramids, and an important measure of how far out of control the Taliban revolution had run. An Afghan refugee friend in London wept in despair when he heard the news. 'These people,' he said. 'Do they intend to destroy everything?'

Various spokesmen scrambled to justify the move in the eyes of an outraged world. According to one explanation, the 'Head Council of Scholars' had decided to teach the West a lesson in moral priorities, following a meeting with a single Swedish monuments expert who proposed to restore the statues' heads. Afghanistan was in the grip of a five-year drought, and the scholars were enraged when the Swede rejected their suggestion that the money he wanted to spend on repairing some old stone statues would be better spent on food aid for starving children. They had a point, perhaps. By the end of that year, the World Food Programme country director Khaled Mansur was reporting 'pre-famine' conditions in some areas, where people were surviving by eating animal fodder and grass.[17]

Whatever the reason for the leadership's decision, even some senior Taliban were appalled.

'I was outraged when I heard about it,' said Jalaluddin Shinwari, the Taliban's Minister of Justice at the time. 'There was no justification for destroying them.'

Shinwari argued that Omar's head had been turned by a group of 'infiltrators' who were 'influenced by al-Qaida and extremist mullahs working for the ISI – people who wanted to damage the Taliban's reputation in order to isolate them internationally, to weaken them and to make them more dependent on Pakistan'.

This was a common suspicion in Afghanistan. A susceptibility to 'infiltration' was a kind of Pashtun national characteristic, a recurring tragic theme in their history. The poet Ghani Khan described how the British exploited it in the nineteenth century to implement their policy of divide and rule: 'The Political Service supplied the tribes with divine-looking priests, who put on the uniform of Allah's servants to serve the devil. They perverted the tribesmen's intense devotion to God into an intense hatred of his brother. They used his childish faith and honesty in the service of deceit and corruption. The British succeeded beautifully. The Pashtuns were too busy cutting one another's throats to think of anything else. There was blood and darkness everywhere. The Empire was safe and the Pashtun damned.'

There were indeed people throughout the Taliban who were not true believers. Many 'mullahs' were in fact nothing of the sort but had simply adopted the honorific for a variety of reasons. Some were politically ambitious. Some acted out of prudence and the instinct to survive. Some were opportunists with private scores to settle, and some, no doubt, were on the payroll of the ISI. 'Mullah' Khalil Ahmed Hassani was an accountant before he joined the Taliban, and had received no religious education of any kind. As he explained to the journalist Christina Lamb, he was assigned to the movement's secret police and ended up as one of their torturers.

'Once, in Kandahar jail, I watched the prison

superintendent Mullah Burki beat people so harshly that it was impossible to tell afterwards whether or not they had been wearing clothes ... when they drifted into unconsciousness we put salt on their wounds to make them scream.'[18]

The Taliban was not the kind of organization that vetted its recruits before they joined. Jalaluddin Shinwari tacitly admitted that this had been one of the movement's gravest mistakes.

'All those bad elements have been purged now,' he insisted in 2010. 'They are all living in luxury in Pakistan.'

It is tempting to speculate that one of the 'bad elements' who influenced the decision to destroy the Buddhas was bin Laden himself: a theory also advanced in *The Giant Buddhas*, an award-winning Swiss documentary made in 2005. The intolerance of idolatry is certainly strong in Wahhabism. In the eighteenth century, the movement's founder Abd-al-Wahhab destroyed the graves of the Prophet and his Companions for fear that they might be worshipped; he also considered destroying the house where the Prophet was born.

As an information-technology specialist, Tariq Osman was considered an outsider too lowly to bother with by the Taliban hierarchy, and thus avoided the worst of Kandahar's back-stabbing politics. He rarely left his office, where he slept on the floor at night. Many senior regime figures including the Foreign Minister, Wakil

Ahmad Muttawakil, used to sneak in to watch Hollywood movies with him in the evenings. By day, Osman taught those Taliban who were interested how to configure and edit computer programs. The internet service he set up was provided, remarkably, by the British company Pipex. By Osman's own admission, the Taliban IT operation was never very sophisticated. Internet traffic from the office was 'very slow – we only had a 9.6KB per second landline. We used to send emails to the embassy in Islamabad, but we couldn't to Riyadh. When I was asked to upload some sound files I had to report that it wasn't possible.' When Muttawakil sent him to the phone company to arrange an upgrade, he was told it would cost $130,000: far more than the Taliban could afford to spend on IT.

In the al-Qaida office just down the road in west Kandahar, matters were of course rather different. The staff there had access to as much high-speed internet as they liked, thanks to a 60,000KB per second satellite uplink that cost $25,000 a month. Osman learned this from one of al-Qaida's IT specialists, a Libyan ex-mujahideen fighter known as Al-Makatala, who found Osman acceptable because he had formerly fought for Hekmatyar. Al-Makatala visited the Special Office from time to time, where he would tease Osman for the paltriness of the Taliban operation. The two became friends, of a sort.

'We spoke technology together,' Osman said. 'There were very few people in the Taliban who could do that, and he was pleasant towards me. He wore his black turban a little differently to the others.'

The relationship between Omar and bin Laden became increasingly fraught as US pressure on the Taliban grew. Between 1996 and 2001, there were thirty separate American requests to expel the Saudi dissident. The Taliban tried to rein in their guest in early 1999 by confiscating his satellite phone, and were particularly anxious to control his access to the media. When a Saudi journalist from *Asharq al-Awsat*, the international Arabic newspaper, arrived in Kandahar hoping for an interview with bin Laden, he was told that he would first need permission from the Taliban foreign ministry in Kabul. To Muttawakil's fury, bin Laden tried to side-step the restriction by inviting the journalist to lunch. Osman found himself caught in an escalating war of faxes between the al-Qaida and Taliban offices, west versus north-west Kandahar; the *Asharq* interviewer eventually took fright, abandoned the lunch plan and scuttled back to safety in Quetta.

On the issues that really mattered, though, the Taliban failed to control bin Laden. Perhaps they genuinely could not. As one ex-Taliban told me years later, 'If America could not control bin Laden, what chance did we have?' In October 2000, an al-Qaida attack on the USS *Cole* in the Yemeni port of Aden killed seventeen sailors and injured thirty-nine. Bin Laden was unapologetic, piously informing his hosts that he answered to Allah, not to men. In early 2001, he convened a major international meeting to formalize the establishment on Afghan soil of a new *qaida ul-jihad*: a 'base for jihad'. It was attended by extremists from all over the world and yet Omar, Osman was astonished to discover, was not invited or even consulted on the meeting's agenda. When Osman asked Omar's Director of Media Operations why not, the director replied, with studied neutrality: 'Because he is the Amir ul-Mu'mineen.' It was a devious piece of office politics. The self-appointed Commander of the Faithful had just been kicked upstairs by the world's most notorious Islamic terrorist.

Did Omar have prior knowledge of 9/11? Osman was certain that he did not.

'We would have heard about something so important in the Special Office, and there was nothing. The Director of the Special Office, Mullah Tayeb, was close to bin Laden and he didn't know. I'm sure there was no warning.'

Mullah Zaeef had certainly not known. He cried as he watched the towers burn on television in his embassy in Islamabad. His colleagues were puzzled: was America not their enemy, who had attacked Afghanistan with sanctions and missiles? He reminded them of the price that the Japanese ultimately paid for Pearl Harbor: Hiroshima and Nagasaki, where 'tens of thousands of civilians burned in the hellfire of the bombs. I told them I was sure that America would invade our country with equal vigour.'

In consultation with Mullah Muttawakil, the Foreign

Minister, Zaeef issued a press release that 'strongly condemned' the attacks and called for all those responsible to be brought to justice. 'And we want America to be patient and careful in their actions,' it added.

He set off to Kandahar with a heavy heart soon afterwards, on a final ambassadorial mission to advise his leader what to do next.

6

Surviving the Daisycutters:
2001–2003

America's response to 9/11 was not the nuclear one that Mullah Zaeef feared, although it was certainly vigorous. 'Go massive – sweep it all up, things that are related and not,' Donald Rumsfeld told his aides, just hours after the Pentagon was attacked.[1]

The possibility of a holocaust was on many people's minds at the beginning of the new millennium. 'WMD', Weapons of Mass Destruction, was the new expression on the diplomatic circuit, as Hans Blix's UN inspection team began its fruitless search for them in Iraq, and preparations to invade that country got under way. Pakistan detonated its first nuclear bomb in 1998 in response to India's expansion of its own programme, creating a troubling new dimension to the endless dispute over Kashmir. An opinion poll for *Dawn* newspaper found that over 90 per cent of the Pakistani public favoured a nuclear first strike on Delhi in the event of a conventional land invasion by India. The media was full of stories about stray fissile material turning up in countries like Nigeria and Kazakhstan, presenting the possibility for the first time of a terrorist 'dirty bomb'.

It is often forgotten that the US had decided to topple the Taliban before 9/11. An inter-agency cabinet meeting in Washington a week before the attacks agreed to provide the CIA with $125 million to arm Massoud and the Northern Alliance; the National Security Adviser Condoleezza Rice said the strategy would take three years to work. The seeds of Omar's downfall were thus sown in his inability to finish the war in the north, because after 9/11, any enemy of America's enemy was its friend. The likely consequences of taking sides in a 22-year-old civil war – a conflict that America is still struggling to extract itself from, nine years later on – were hardly considered then. Fury and fear swept reason aside. As Pakistan's President Musharraf put it, America responded like a 'wounded bear'.

The CIA's failure to detect the 9/11 plot was blamed on its director, George Tenet, who tried to make amends by rapidly drawing up a covert invasion plan. In the absence of an alternative, conventional invasion plan from the Pentagon, President Bush accepted Tenet's proposal. He signed an order giving the CIA what amounted to carte blanche in Afghanistan, along with up to another $1 billion in covert-operation funds.

The Taliban collapsed faster than Condoleezza Rice or

anyone else expected. Kandahar itself was captured less than three months after 9/11. Bribery had been an effective military tactic in this part of the world since the fourth century BC at least, when Philip II of Macedonia remarked that 'no fortress was impregnable to whose walls an ass laden with gold could be driven'. It certainly worked for his son, Alexander the Great, whose legacy of conquest includes Kandahar, a city he founded and whose very name is a corruption of 'Alexandria'. The British had used bribery to keep the Khyber Pass open in the nineteenth century. The Taliban had used it, too, in their brilliant northward advance in 1996. But now they were broke and couldn't begin to compete.

One hundred and fifteen CIA operatives backed by three hundred Special Forces personnel fanned out across the country, eventually spending as much as $100 million in bribes to Northern Alliance commanders. Massive amounts of American airpower made sure that the battle was decisive. The campaign opened with a month-long air bombardment, starting with selected strategic targets in the capital – an event that was filmed by more than two hundred foreign journalists attached to the Northern Alliance troops watching from the Shomali plains. Just as it had been for the Soviet Army in 1979, the first US objective was to capture Mazar: a bridgehead for the two thousand American troops waiting across the Uzbek border at Termez, just 40 miles to the north.

With the CIA in a coordinating role, the region's rival power-brokers, Mohammed Atta and Rashid Dostum, mounted a pincer attack on the 8,000 Taliban troops dug in on the city's perimeter. As I had seen in 1998, many of Dostum's Jowzjan militia were mounted on horses, but there was to be no tragic repeat of the Charge of the Light Brigade. American Forward Air Controllers called down ordnance that included the fearsome 15,000-pound 'daisycutter', a bomb so large it has to be dropped by parachute. Daisycutters were designed to create instant helicopter drop zones in the jungles of Vietnam, and detonate with such force that all the oxygen is sucked from the air within a radius of 300 metres. Unlike the carefully choreographed bombardment of Kabul the month before, the press were not invited to witness this horror. But an Afghan journalist in London – a refugee from the fighting in Mazar four years before – was able to telephone Dostum in the middle of the battle for a live update on the liberation of his city. The psychological impact of the daisycutter was evidently not confined to the Taliban trenches. 'He was shouting with excitement,' the journalist recalled. 'I could hear the bombs going off in the background. He said he thought he would be back in Mazar within a few hours.'

Dostum was right. The Taliban survivors abandoned their positions and fled. By 12 November, just three days later, the north, west and centre of the country were in Northern Alliance hands. A British Special Forces officer later described watching the loadmaster of a C-130 Hercules that had landed at Mazar casually tossing out Dostum's reward: four vacuum-packed bricks of

$100 bills, each of them worth $1 million. In Kabul, the Taliban looted the national bank as they escaped southwards in a fleet of stolen cars and taxis. There would be a final stand at Kandahar, the Pashtun spiritual capital; the only other serious pocket of resistance was around Kunduz, a town with a large Pashtun population in the far north-east.

On the face of it, the CIA's strategy had been an extraordinary success. The Taliban, with an estimated 60,000 troops in the field, were overthrown at the cost of just one American soldier killed, and in record time. It was a departmental triumph for President Bush's neo-con wingmen, Donald Rumsfeld and Paul Wolfowitz, who had embraced the CIA plan and taken their country to war without first mustering any of the major land forces that the generals at the Pentagon insisted would be necessary. The combination of covert dollars, Special Forces and airpower was to be tried again, though without the corresponding success, in Iraq. But for now, President Bush could crow about what a bargain the anti-Taliban campaign had been: perhaps the cheapest war America had ever fought.

It was not so cheap for the Afghans. By December there were still no more than 1,300 US troops deployed in the whole country, and these depended heavily on airpower to act as a 'force multiplier'. One study calculated that as many as 4,000 civilians were killed or injured as a result of US bombing over just twelve weeks.[2] The American troop contingent, furthermore, was nowhere near enough to keep order as the Taliban government collapsed. The jubilant Tajik and Uzbek militias were bent on revenge, and took it not just on the Taliban but on all Pashtuns, about a million of whom lived in the north. More than half of these now fled south, as the looting, raping, kidnapping and revenge killings of the early 1990s made an all-too-predictable comeback. Meanwhile, all aid operations to areas affected by drought were halted. According to one estimate, as many as 20,000 people may have died as a result of the intervention, either directly or indirectly through hunger, disease and displacement.[3]

None of this was of much concern to the Americans at the time. 'Operation Enduring Freedom', as the battle-plan was called, was focused on one thing only: the destruction of al-Qaida and the capture of bin Laden. They needed their Northern Alliance allies to help them achieve this, and the quid pro quo was to turn a blind eye to their excesses. From the very beginning, according to the International Crisis Group, 'a culture of impunity was allowed to take root in the name of "stability".'[4] For the next two years, the US's main means of keeping the peace was to go on paying off the warlords who, when the CIA money began to run out, turned straight back to the drug trade. In 2002, 74,000 hectares of poppy were planted: almost ten times the amount in 2001. The villains the Taliban had tried so hard to banish were all reinstalled in their fiefdoms, and the tone for the new Afghanistan was set.

The Northern Alliance's abuse of their position took many forms, though perhaps none was so dreadful as Dostum's treatment of the prisoners who eventually surrendered at Kunduz. Between 5,000 and 7,000 fighters were surrounded there after the fall of Mazar. The great majority were Afghan Taliban, but mixed in with them were hundreds of militants from Pakistan, Chechnya, Central Asia and the Arab countries. In a further sign of the profound difference between al-Qaida and the Taliban, the Arabs wanted to fight to the death, while the Afghans wanted to surrender – preferably to the Americans. There were, of course, no US troops on the ground for the Taliban to surrender to, so they surrendered to Dostum instead, hoping for a degree of leniency from a fellow Afghan that their Arab allies had been told not to expect.

Between three hundred and five hundred of them were taken to the Qala-i-Jangi, the Fort of War, a vast, mud-baked fortress to the west of Mazar. A dozen CIA men were tasked with interrogating the horde, but with typical Afghan laxity the prisoners had not been properly disarmed. A handful of Arabs among them led a suicidal revolt that took six days to put down, one of the bloodiest engagements of the whole campaign. Only eighty-six of them survived, and more than seventy of Dostum's soldiers were killed.

The prisoners had captured the armoury before retreating into a deep basement complex. Dostum's troops struggled to dislodge them from here despite the support of tanks, British and American Special Forces, guided bombs and a pair of Spectre gunships. Oil was poured into the basement and ignited, but still they fought on. Finally, freezing water was diverted in from a nearby irrigation channel. Dozens of the defenders drowned, and the rest at last surrendered. Among them was Sulayman al-Faris, better known as John Walker Lindh, the famous 'American Taliban' who had been born in Washington, DC, and was baptized a Catholic. To many shocked Americans, the complexity and the truly global dimensions of the fight their country had taken on were perhaps revealed for the first time.

I visited the fort several months after the attempted break-out, although it felt as though it had just happened. The basement had an evil atmosphere, reminiscent of a hellish execution cell at Auschwitz I had once been in. The walls were pockmarked with bullet holes and still black from the smoke of the burning oil; here and there I found religious graffiti, the final imprecations of Muslims who had vowed to die. Shell casings and unspent ammunition lay about. The earthen floors had not dried out from the flooding, and an organic, almost metallic odour hung over everything. Gingerly disturbing some rubble with my foot, I uncovered the sodden remains of a keffiyeh, its black and white cotton stained brown with blood. It was as appropriate a symbol as any of the Taliban's terrible defeat. As many as 12,000 Taliban were killed in the campaign as a whole, with perhaps 20,000 wounded and 7,000 captured: well over half of their entire force.

The prisoners who survived the Qala-i-Jangi were shown no mercy by Dostum, who packed them with thousands of others into thirty shipping containers – up to 250 in each – and took them to his base at Shibarghan. Most of them were asphyxiated on the journey. In one container, according to UN officials, only six out of 220 survived. There were reports that when they cried out for air, their Northern Alliance guards obliged by machine-gunning the sides of the container until blood ran from the air holes. A mass grave was later uncovered nearby in the Dasht-i-Leili desert.

American silence in the face of such atrocities naturally fuelled Pashtun anger in the south, and would soon help to revive the Taliban movement. The Americans had formed an evil alliance in pursuit of their al-Qaida goal, and once they had taken sides in this way, the rest of the international community had little choice but to go along with it, including the UN. When Kofi Annan's special envoy Lakhdar Brahimi was questioned about Dasht-i-Leili in August 2002, he replied that his responsibility was to the living, not the dead, and that he didn't have the resources to pursue an investigation.

'I said what I said for those who wanted me to hang Dostum on the first pole,' he told Ahmed Rashid later. 'If we started doing that, where would we end up? My business was to talk to all the wrong people, the murderers and rapists and killers.'

Yet calls for Dostum's role in the Dasht-i-Leili affair to be investigated have not gone away. The role of the US

Special Forces, who apparently did nothing to ensure the prisoners were properly treated, is also in question. In 2009 a documentary by Jamie Doran, *The Convoy of Death*, prompted President Obama to order his officials to look into the matter once again.

The US's reliance on proxy local forces had many other consequences, including the well-documented failure of the primary mission: the capture of bin Laden. Accompanied by several hundred al-Qaida fighters, he had retreated at the end of November to a fortified cave system in the Tora Bora mountains, 25 miles south-west of Jalalabad and close to the Pakistani border. Thousands of US troops were standing by on aircraft carriers waiting off the Makran coast. There were also a thousand battle-ready British marines stationed at Bagram airbase north of Kabul.

Instead of calling upon any of these, General Tommy Franks left matters to three small-time commanders who were in the pay of the CIA. They included Hazrat Ali, a notorious brigand in his native Jalalabad. His role in bin Laden's escape was never quite proved; he later became an MP. But the fact remains that the al-Qaida leader and some eight hundred Arab fighters were escorted to safety in the tribal areas of Pakistan by local Pashtun guides, who reputedly charged $1,200 per head for the service. The CIA argued even at the time that just a few hundred US Rangers deployed along the unguarded border would have prevented bin Laden's escape.

Some of the Arab fighters made their way south

through Pakistan to Karachi, from where they escaped back to the Gulf on board fishing boats. Others found sanctuary with Pakistani extremist groups in Punjab or Peshawar or Lahore. Still others, probably the majority and perhaps including bin Laden himself, melted into North and South Waziristan, where they were left unmolested for another three years. It was not until 2005 that the Pakistanis began to perceive them as agents provocateurs among the unruly tribesmen of the border areas.

The Americans also failed to capture Mullah Omar in Kandahar. The CIA's placeman in the south was none other than Hamid Karzai, who rallied the Pashtuns of Tarin Kot, the tiny capital of Uruzgan province 60 miles to the north. It was the first organized Pashtun resistance in the southern belt, which the Americans always realized would be the key to overthrowing the regime. It was not until this moment that they decided they would back Karzai for the national leadership. On 18 November the Taliban sent a thousand fighters in a hundred Toyotas in a last-ditch effort to kill him. When thirty vehicles were obliterated by guided bombs before they could even reach Tarin Kot, the leadership knew that the game was up. But Karzai waited too long to move on Kandahar. By the time he got there, most of the leadership were in Pakistan. Omar himself escaped on a motorbike under cover of darkness.

In later years, Afghans would often allege that the CIA let their enemies escape deliberately, in order to propagate the war and justify a military occupation of

Afghanistan. America, they theorized darkly, wanted a permanent presence in the region in order to pressurize Iran, as well as to ensure access to the oil and gas reserves of Central Asia; fighting terrorism had very little to do with it. The truth is that the Americans did let many of their enemies escape, although not for such devious geo-political reasons. It was not they who had an interest in propagating the war, but Pakistan.

Before 9/11 Pakistan was an international pariah, castigated for its nuclear programme and for its support for the Taliban, and labouring under US sanctions. After 9/11, President Musharraf was promoted to George Bush's number-one ally in his War on Terror. Musharraf wrote in his autobiography that the US had threatened to 'bomb him back to the stone age' if he did not cooperate. Coerced or not, his eventual decision to side with the US was to be immensely lucrative for his country. In exchange for American military access to Pakistani ports and airbases, all sanctions were instantly waived and replaced by a raft of new loans. The Pakistani Army did particularly well out of the deal. More than half of a $700-million aid package announced by the White House in 2004 was earmarked for the military, compared to just $19 million intended for 'improving democratic participation'.

Musharraf, however, was playing a double game. Alongside the thousands of Taliban in Kunduz in November were dozens of ISI officers and hundreds of soldiers from the Pakistani Frontier Corps who had been sent to assist them. They had had two months to make their escape but had chosen instead to fight on. Now, embarrassingly, they were trapped. Musharraf asked Bush a favour: a pause in the bombing to allow a plane to extract his officers. Bush was desperate not to do anything to upset his new ally, and agreed. The top-secret operation was handled by Vice-President Dick Cheney; most of the US cabinet were not told. But Cheney was hoodwinked. What was supposed to be a minor extraction turned into a major airlift. As many as a thousand people boarded the Pakistani planes, including many Taliban and al-Qaida fighters who were subsequently allowed to vanish into the border areas of Waziristan. Some analysts believe that more foreign terrorists escaped from Kunduz than they did from Tora Bora. Bush was always naive in his dealings with Musharraf. At their first ever meeting, at which the American pledged $1 billion in aid to Pakistan, Musharraf asked: 'How do we know the United States won't abandon us again?'

Bush answered: 'You tell your people that the President looked you in the eye and told you that he would stick with you.'

His underestimation of Pakistani duplicity was to have disastrous consequences for the War on Terror, and was one of the root causes of the Taliban's resurgence in the years to come.

Despite the mauling they received on the battlefields, the Taliban were never quite broken. Thousands found sanctuary in Pakistan, or simply went home to their families and buried their guns. In Peshawar in October 2002, I met a fierce-eyed tribesman from Waziristan who was in no doubt that their time would come again.

'We are waiting for a sign from Allah and then we will launch a war that will amaze the Americans,' he said.

And yet the resurgence was not inevitable. The Waziri's words sounded like bombast then. I had met him in the office of a friend of his, a Pashtun business-man I was also visiting, who raised his eyes to the ceiling and called him a dolt for always wanting to pick a fight. The Taliban were at their lowest ebb in the years after their overthrow, and the truth was that the Afghans, and even most Pashtuns, were delighted that they had gone. The people were desperately weary of the years of cruelty and war, and saw the US as liberators who would usher in a new era of peace and democracy. In many cities – even in Kandahar – the people literally danced in the streets.

The Americans failed miserably to exploit this tide of goodwill towards them. The first draft of the battle-plan Operation Enduring Freedom that George Bush approved contained no commitment whatsoever to rebuilding Afghanistan. 'We are not into nation-building, we are focused on justice,' he said – by which he meant the capture of bin Laden by all possible means. He was later persuaded that 'it would be a useful function for the United Nations to take over the so-called "nation-building" after our military mission is complete' – a policy later referred to by one despairing foreign policy adviser as 'nation-building-lite'. International attention and resources moved on to Iraq almost as soon as the Taliban were toppled. In the crucial first year after 9/11, the international community spent just $75 per capita on reconstruction in Afghanistan, compared to an average of $250 in Bosnia, Kosovo, East Timor and Rwanda.

The best way to make aid dollars count was in the countryside. Eighty per cent of the population lived off the land, and officials at the US Agency for International Development, USAID, were convinced that helping farmers to overcome the effects of five years of drought could cement the American victory by turning the farmers away from the Taliban for ever. But the Pentagon had little interest in fertilizers and irrigation systems in those days. The US military had determined that all American officials should have an armed escort in Afghanistan, but because there were not enough troops available, the few USAID officials at the embassy in Kabul seldom even left the building.

'Volatile, security-risk-prone areas never stopped USAID in the past, so what was so different about Afghanistan post 9/11? Nothing – except that the Department of Defense did not want us around to see how they were aiding the wrong guys,' said one official who later resigned.

When John F. Kennedy established USAID in 1961, he specifically intended to create a humanitarian organization that would operate independently of the political and military interference that had plagued its predecessors. This did not now prevent the CIA from exploiting it as another tool with which to crush al-Qaida. As late as 2003, the agency was deciding which projects USAID should pursue entirely on the basis of the help these would give to the warlords it backed.

A priceless early opportunity to shape post-Taliban Afghanistan was thus wasted. Helping farmers to plant crops was a solution for the long term, while the neo-cons were looking for short-cuts: an approach that sometimes went disastrously wrong. The US Air Force's idea of helping the starving was to bomb them with HDRs, or Humanitarian Daily Rations. Some 37,000 of these bright yellow food packages were dropped on the first night of the assault on Kabul alone. Most unfortunately, they were the same colour as the cluster bomblets the Americans had also dropped against the Taliban, at least 12,000 of which turned out to be duds.[5] The propaganda effect of the HDR drops was thrown into reverse as Afghan public radio issued warnings to keep away from anything American and yellow.

Another critical mistake was the Bonn Agreement. On 27 November, under the auspices of the UN, the Afghan factions gathered at the Petersburg Hotel on the banks of the Rhine to agree upon the deployment of an international peace-keeping force in Kabul, which would later become the Nato-organized ISAF, the International Security Assistance Force. The agreement also called for the setting up of a 'broad-based, gender-sensitive, multi-ethnic and fully representative government'.

The trouble with the Bonn meeting was that the twenty-five delegates who attended it were anything but representative of the Afghan people. None of the so-called Rome Group, who spoke for the long-exiled monarch Zahir Shah, had been in Afghanistan for the last twenty years. The Northern Alliance team almost exclusively comprised Panjshiri Tajiks, while the delegation from Peshawar was dominated by the family members of Pir Gailani, a Pashtun politician and ex-mujahideen fighter of only middling importance. The Uzbeks, Hazaras and Heratis were barely represented. Worse still, there were no Pashtuns from Kandahar or anywhere in the south, apart from Karzai. And the Taliban were not invited.

'The Taliban should have been at Bonn,' the UN envoy Lakhdar Brahimi said later. 'This was our original sin. If . . . we had asked them to come, because they still represented something, maybe they would have come. Even if none came, at least we would have tried.'

Just as the Pashtuns feared, the Transitional Authority cabinet that emerged was heavily weighted towards the Northern Alliance. The Tajiks, accounting for barely a quarter of the population, were granted control of eight ministries, while the Pashtuns, who account for 42 per cent of the population, were given eleven; and of these, only Karzai came from the south.

No wonder the Taliban considered him an American

stooge. The Bonn Agreement was described as a 'roadmap' for Afghanistan until 2005, by when it was hoped all the institutions necessary for a functioning modern democracy would be in place: a justice system, a bureaucracy, a police force, an army. A commission was set up to develop a new national constitution – the country's sixth since the 1920s – which was eventually ratified at a loya jirga (grand council) in Kabul in December 2003. The Constitution – effectively a rewrite of one drawn up in the 1960s under Zahir Shah, but without the monarchy – provided for an elected President and National Assembly; Karzai was formally elected for a five-year term in October 2004.

The greatest problem was that the supposedly vanquished Taliban remained excluded from the process. The constitution's 160 Articles were drafted with the help of several Western experts such as Barnett Rubin, a political scientist at New York University, and Clare Lockhart of the Washington-based Institute for State Effectiveness. Karzai's opponents argued that the new constitution was a foreign imposition – and were thus almost bound to object to the terms of the new government.

There were other mistakes, notably a failure to take into account the trade and security interests of Afghanistan's regional neighbours. Pakistan, Iran, the ex-Soviet states to the north, India and China all had much to gain or lose from whatever emerged from the Bonn process. They should, arguably, have had a direct stake in it via the UN, which might have convened a special regional conference. Instead, the neighbours were never even formally consulted.

Pakistan and the ISI, in particular, were never likely to take the West's empowerment of the non-Pashtuns lying down. The Northern Alliance had always been seen as pro-Indian, and a Kabul government dominated by it was perceived as a disaster for Pakistani interests. Delhi had helped to arm Massoud during the Jihad, and even Karzai had studied political science at the university at Shimla in the early 1980s. Meanwhile, the neo-cons' determination not to commit serious numbers of troops to Afghanistan convinced the ISI that the Americans would not stay there for long. Throughout 2002 there were no more than 4,500 ISAF troops in the country, the bulk of them in and around Kabul. The ISI therefore advised Musharraf that it intended to nurture the remnants of the Taliban, whom they calculated would soon be needed again; and Musharraf, despite his public alliance with Washington on the War on Terror, needed little prodding to support this policy in private. He too was innately suspicious of India, and described the Northern Alliance as 'a bunch of thugs'.

There were a few sacrificial lambs, notably Mullah Zaeef, who by that stage was the Taliban's ambassador in Islamabad. Zaeef had spent the weeks after 9/11 imploring Bush and his Afghan adviser, Zalmay Khalilzad, to pursue dialogue with Mullah Omar instead of war, but to no avail. A senior ISI chief came to ask him to form and lead a faction of 'moderate' Taliban against Omar, but Zaeef distrusted his motives and was not prepared to break his beyat, the oath of spiritual allegiance, to his Amir. The last ISI officer who came to see him was none other than Colonel Imam, Mullah Omar's trainer during the Jihad. They exchanged greetings, and Imam burst into tears.

'Almighty Allah might have decided what is to take place in Afghanistan, but Pakistan is to blame!' he blurted. 'How much cruelty it has done to its neighbour! And how much more will come!'

It was apparent to Zaeef that his ambassadorial days were numbered. He was at home with his family late one evening, still working to secure the release of the Taliban fighters captured by Dostum at Kunduz, when three ISI men came for him. 'Your Excellency, you are no longer an Excellency!' said the senior officer, who according to Zaeef 'looked as if he had been dragged out of hell itself'. He was driven to Peshawar. Even at this late stage he could not believe that 'Pakistani soldiers, the defenders of the Holy Koran' intended to hand him over to the Americans: 'A moment written in my memory like a stain on my soul.' In Peshawar he was stripped and beaten and shackled to the floor of a helicopter that transferred him to the hold of a US aircraft carrier: the start of a long journey that would end in a four-year spell in Guantanamo.

But Zaeef was a high-profile exception. In fact, the Taliban were safe in Pakistan after 9/11. The key to

the movement's regeneration was the Jamiat Ulema-e-
Islam (JUI), the Assembly of Islamic Clergy, which
controlled hundreds of Deobandi madrasahs across the
region, and which had raised funds and provided troops
for the movement ever since its foundation. Their power
and influence was at its peak in 2002, when they swept to
power in provincial elections in the North-West Frontier
and Baluchistan. The JUI Minister of Agriculture in
Baluchistan, Maulana Faizullah, had fought alongside
Mullah Omar in Kandahar.

By 2003 there were at least seven Taliban training
camps in Baluchistan, and more than fifty JUI-run
madrasahs along the 80-mile road between Quetta and
the Afghan border at Chaman. That summer, vehicle
dealers sold the Taliban nine hundred motorbikes.
Mullah Omar, who went into hiding in Helmand and
Uruzgan immediately after 9/11, arrived in Quetta at the
end of 2002. By then the Taliban had effectively taken
over a whole suburb of the city, Pashtunabad, where all
the old rules about television and women and kite-flying
applied, just like in Kabul and Kandahar in the mid-
1990s. The entire region had turned into a mustering
point for a new insurgency – and the ISI, driven on by
reports that India was 'taking over' Kabul with its own
multi-million-dollar reconstruction and military training
programmes, was complicit in every part of it. Between
2002 and 2006, not a single Taliban commander was
handed over to the Americans.

Such an enormous operation could hardly be kept

secret. In April 2003, a month after the US invasion of Iraq, Zalmay Khalilzad visited Islamabad to urge the Pakistanis to do more to rein in the resurgent Taliban, but was told that his concerns were 'totally ridiculous and baseless'. Karzai then visited Musharraf and presented him with a list of the Quetta addresses of several senior Taliban figures. A spokesman for Musharraf subsequently denied the existence of such a list; whereupon the Americans, astonishingly, declined to corroborate Karzai's version of the meeting, even though the list had been drawn up with the help of their embassy in Kabul.

Musharraf was playing Washington like a fish. He knew the Americans wouldn't risk pushing him too hard now that they were committed to Iraq. The primary US mission in the region was to hunt down al-Qaida, not the Taliban – and the ISI made very sure that any Arabs at large in the border areas were kept well away from Quetta. The cadres of Taliban being reconstituted there were primarily an Afghan Pashtun affair – although the ISI made this very difficult to check. For the last seven years, indeed, it has been almost impossible for any Western journalist to obtain official permission to visit Quetta, let alone Pashtunabad. The *New York Times*'s Carlotta Gall, who visited the city without permission in December 2006, was beaten up by a gang of ISI agents who then impounded her notebooks, laptop and camera equipment. She had earlier interviewed a former Taliban commander who said he had been jailed by the ISI for refusing to go back to Afghanistan to fight: an arrest that was naturally presented, locally and to the West, as a part of the crackdown on militants. The truth was that the ISI were not just turning a blind eye to the Taliban's resurgence, but actively promoting it.

The Americans, for their part, seemed at times almost willing to have the wool pulled over their eyes. US intelligence in Islamabad consistently underestimated the extent of ISI involvement with the Taliban, and attributed the problem to a few 'rogue' agents. Then, at the end of April 2003, Donald Rumsfeld came to Kabul to announce 'the end of major combat operations'. One week later President Bush said the same thing about Iraq, on board the USS *Abraham Lincoln* beneath a banner reading 'Mission Accomplished'. It was the height of neo-con hubris. Bloody insurgencies were getting under way in both countries even as they spoke.

7

Like a Jam-jar to a Swarm of Wasps: The Insurgency Explodes, 2003–2009

The Taliban had hidden away large stockpiles of weapons as they retreated, and from the end of 2002 they started moving in additional supplies. The undermanned forces of Operation Enduring Freedom could not hope to prevent all of this traffic. Nor could ISAF be expected to do much, since their jurisdiction was not extended beyond Kabul until October 2003. By November 2002, even so, 475 weapons caches had been discovered, containing 2,000 AK-47 rifles, 70,000 mortar rounds and 43,000 rockets.[1]

Omar's counter-attack began in the spring of 2003 in four southern provinces: Helmand, Kandahar, Uruzgan and Zabul. They were the obvious place to start. Kandahar, the Taliban's birthplace, was the spiritual and historical capital of the Pashtuns. They had successfully defended their home territory many times over the centuries, and their deep knowledge of the terrain would play to their strengths again. The choice was made easier by the almost total absence of American troops, who were focused on the north-east of the country in their bid to root out al-Qaida. When the first Nato troops at last deployed to the south in late 2005, they were to discover that the US had not even been watching the region by satellite. For four years Omar and his commanders were free to come and go as they pleased, entirely un-monitored by US intelligence.

In a warning of things to come, a force of eighty Taliban was intercepted in January 2003 by a US patrol near Spin Boldak. Much to the Americans' surprise, the Taliban stood and fought for twelve hours, and were defeated only with the help of airpower. An American firebase in the east of the country came under mortar and rocket attack, as did the main US airbase at Bagram. Afghan aid workers and other soft targets were assassinated. So was Ricardo Munguia, a Salvadorian engineer working for the International Committee of the Red Cross – a killing that sent a chill through the whole country. Almost alone among Western NGOs, the ICRC had stayed on during the Taliban regime to provide public medical care. Until Munguia's death, the organiz-ation had been considered untouchable.

Meanwhile, Omar was getting organized. In June 2003 he appointed a ten-man Leadership Council and four new committees dedicated to military, political, cultural and economic affairs. It was the birth of the famous 'Quetta shura'. In a conscious attempt to regain the sense of brotherhood that had served the movement so well in its early days, the appointees to the Council were exclusively Pashtun, eight of them from the south. They included Mullah Obaidullah, Mullah Zaeef's former boss at the Ministry of Defence, as well as Mullah Dadullah, a Taliban war hero who had marshalled the defence of Kunduz: 'A brave young man who never knew fear,' according to Zaeef. He was famed for leading his troops from the front despite having only one leg. He was also known for shooting with a pistol anyone who retreated; and he was thought to have approved the murder of the ICRC engineer from El Salvador.

The only two non-southerners on the council, Saifur Rehman Mansur and Jalaluddin Haqqani, were eastern Pashtuns. Haqqani had been Omar's Minister of Tribal Affairs before 9/11, and would go on to found the so-called Haqqani Network, which today operates in six eastern provinces, with headquarters suspected to be over the border at Miranshah in North Waziristan. His operation differs in important respects. Haqqani, who counts a Saudi Arab among his wives, was always ideologically much closer to al-Qaida, and is thought to maintain personal links with bin Laden even now. He – and now his son, Siraj – are less fussy than Omar about who fights for his network, as well as less scrupulous about how his fighters fund themselves. His forces, which numbered perhaps 12,000 in late 2009,[2] have been associated with frequent acts of extortion, kidnapping and other crimes.

However wicked he sounded, Jalaluddin Haqqani was also a genuine hero of the Jihad, famed for his capture in 1991 of the city of Khost: the beginning of the end for President Najibullah's puppet communist regime. The Americans revered him in those days. The US Congressman and fund-raiser for the Jihad, Charlie Wilson, called him 'Goodness Personified'. He is even thought to have met Ronald Reagan at the White House. Perhaps understandably, Karzai's attitude towards Haqqani was ambivalent. In an early attempt at political reconciliation in the spring of 2004, he even suggested Haqqani should become Prime Minister – although the offer was stoutly rebuffed.[3]

By the summer of 2003, Taliban attacks were an almost daily occurrence. On one day, 13 August, fifty people were killed in simultaneous attacks in three different provinces. The date for the all-important Constitutional Loya Jirga envisioned at Bonn was pushed back because of security concerns. The public had begun to deride their new President as 'the mayor of Kabul' for his inability to extend his remit beyond the capital, but there was little he could do to stop the violence. ISAF's peace-keepers were restricted to Kabul until a new UN resolution was passed in October 2003. In the meantime, Karzai had neither a national army nor a police force with which to enforce his jurisdiction. Western nations had offered to train up these crucial institutions at Bonn, but had so far proved astonishingly slow to make good their promise – particularly Germany, which had agreed to take responsibility for the new police. Between 2002 and 2006 they spent just $89 million on the project, and sent out just forty-one trainers to train 3,500 officers over three years.

Critics later argued that if ISAF had moved faster to douse the fire now smouldering in the south, the insurgency might never have taken hold. But the generals were still under-resourced because of Iraq, or else because many Coalition partners were reluctant to commit troops to what was widely perceived as an American fight. Moreover, until ISAF command passed to Nato in August 2003, they were guided by an administration in Washington that kept insisting that the insurgency was not expanding. In December 2005 Rumsfeld, now seriously bogged down and short of manpower in Iraq, actually signed an order reducing the number of US troops in Afghanistan from 19,000 to 16,000. Instead of heading straight for the trouble spot, ISAF unveiled a plan to extend its footprint gradually. ISAF started with the least challenging region – the north – before working its way around the country in four separate phases. It was not until the winter of 2005 that Western troops deployed in any force to Kandahar, and by then they were too late.

'Regional Command South', as the southern ISAF sector was known, was divided up among the three Coalition partners besides the US who were prepared to do any serious fighting: the Dutch, who were assigned to Uruzgan, the Canadians, who went to Kandahar, and the British, who got Helmand. None of them sent enough troops. Britain, the largest contributor of the three, initially sent a task force of just 3,300 men, only about 650 of whom were what the army call 'bayonets', with the rest engaged in the long logistics tail. And yet Helmand, the largest province in the country, was almost three times the size of Wales.

Whitehall did not anticipate the battle that ensued. Nato intelligence had estimated that there were no more than about two thousand Taliban in the whole of the south. In April 2006 the Defence Secretary, John Reid, notoriously remarked that: 'We would be perfectly happy to leave in three years and without firing one shot.' His optimism was wildly misplaced. The British presence was like a jam-jar to a swarm of wasps. By March 2007 the army had fired at least 1.8 million bullets, in fighting described by General David Richards, who took command of all international forces in July 2006, as the fiercest the British had experienced since the Korean War.

There were several factors that ensured the battle for Helmand would be a hot one. The first was the drug trade. Poppy production in the province rose 169 per cent between 2005 and 2006, accounting for almost half of all the opium produced in the world. With so much money at stake it was clearly in the criminals' interests to align themselves with the ideologues from Quetta in resisting the foreign invasion.

Then there was what General Richards called 'the

Maiwand thing': a reference to the Battle of Maiwand of 1880, when a brigade under General George Burrows was driven back from the banks of the Helmand river by a force under Ayub Khan, resulting in almost a thousand British killed. Memory of that battle remains deeply entrenched in local folklore. Every Pashtun in the province claims that his forefather had fought for Ayub Khan. In view of Helmand's history, a task force from almost any other nation in the world would have been a more appropriate choice for a mission intended to conquer hearts and minds. Instead, to the Afghan mind, the return of the Brits in 2006 was an Allah-driven invitation to a punch-up: round four of a conflict between two nations that had been at it intermittently for 170 years. As a Taliban commander told me in 2007: 'Fighting the British feels like unfinished business for many of us.'

Operation Herrick 4 in the summer of 2006 opened a new chapter of violence that has deepened ever since. And yet the conflagration in Helmand was not inevitable – at least in the view of one British SAS officer who spent several months in 2005 reconnoitring the southern provinces in advance of the main deployment. He operated in what were called 'light footprint' patrols that were arguably far more effective in winning Afghan hearts and minds than the gloves-off approach taken later by the conventional military.

'If they'd listened to our advice I don't think we'd have the insurgency problem that we do now,' he told me in 2010.

The Special Forces' secret weapon was a medical civic assistance programme known as MEDCAP: a lightly guarded field hospital that travelled to suspected trouble spots all over the province. Helmand's 1.45 million people only had one proper hospital, in Lashkar Gah, which charged for its services. MEDCAP was of course free.

'We found there was a direct and unambiguous correlation between the number of IEDs [Improvised Explosive Devices] planted and the number of patients we treated, particularly children,' the SAS man recalled. The first field hospital was set up as an experiment near the site of what was to become Camp Bastion, ISAF's town-sized base in Helmand.

'The people would find us through the bush telegraph. Wherever we went, we'd attract a line of burqas two hundred yards long. We treated hundreds of children. We dressed up our intelligence officers as nurses, men and women, and they would chat up the parents who would tell us where the bombs were. Or else the mothers would go home, tell their husbands how we'd saved their child's life, and the bombs would just stop. We had a policy that no patient would go away empty-handed, even when there was nothing wrong with them. Our stocks of Haliborange vitamin pills were enormous.'

The British had other simple tricks, such as distributing wind-up radios with a Union Jack painted on the back, and which could only be tuned to a radio station that broadcast pro-British propaganda in Pashto. But nothing won the locals around as effectively as the MEDCAP programme, which allowed the British to enter communities that were innately suspicious of outsiders, and to meet their elders.

'Softly softly was the only way to do it. We held dozens of shuras across the province. We'd ask if there were any Taliban locally and they would very often tell us.'

British soldiers and doctors were welcome enough to travel about in small numbers. But the elders at these shuras also begged the British not to come back in any force, warning that there would be a big fight if they did because it would be perceived as a threat to their poppy-farming livelihoods.

'That's the thing that bothers me most,' said the SAS officer. 'In 2006 when the fighting started, we called everyone who resisted us "Taliban". But they really weren't, necessarily. They were just the community's warrior class who had always defended their community against outsiders, and were bound to do so again. The "Taliban" in that sense were an enemy of our own creation. That was why, in 2005, we sent a memo to John Reid at the Ministry of Defence saying, "If you want an insurgency here, you can have one."'

The SAS officer later helped in the reconquest of Musa Qala in 2008, an operation celebrated as an 'iconic' victory over the Taliban by John Reid's successor at the MoD, Des Browne. But the SAS officer didn't believe that the 'Taliban' who had resisted and then melted away as the British re-took the town could honestly be defined as such.

'They were just the town mujahideen: they were *literally* the same people who had defended Musa Qala against the Russians in the 1980s. The Russians took the town from the south. That's why we took it from the north – in order to confuse them.'

He recalled a reconnaissance mission to the top of a hulking mountain overlooking Musa Qala that the British nicknamed Mount Doom, a landmark that the locals avoided because it was considered sacred ground; it was also heavily mined.

'We found an old observation post that still had bits of Russian kit lying about in it: even a tin of cigarettes with those long cardboard filters that they smoke. It was very creepy.'

The SAS officer had taken part in covert Taliban-hunting operations all over the country since 2001, and had fought al-Qaida, too, in a celebrated attack on a training camp near Spin Boldak in 2002. In his experience, he said, killing was a way of life for a startling number of Afghans. He had observed that they would pick up a gun for the slightest of reasons, and fight under the flimsiest of flags. As a consequence it was often quite impossible to tell who was who.

'I think of it as a kind of unholy Venn diagram, with "Taliban" on the left and "al-Qaida" on the right, and this huge, shifting mass of people in the middle,' he said.

The foundation of soldiering in the rest of the world – loyalty to a cause and to one's own brothers-in-arms – was often no more than a notional concept in

Afghanistan, despite the likely dire consequences of dis-
loyalty. One reason that Mullah Dadullah's surrounded
forces in Kunduz in 1997 were able to hold out for so
long was that they were resupplied by their own enemy.
'The commanders who fought against the Taliban
during the day would sneak out of their bases to sell us
ammunition at night,' according to Mullah Zaeef. 'It was
cheap to buy bullets and shells in this way, and
guaranteed that our forces in Kunduz had a relatively
regular supply.'

On an operation in the Panjshir region in 2003, the
SAS officer's squadron hired some local fighters at $25 a
day, an ethnic mix of Tajiks and Hazaras who acted as
their guides.

'We came to the top of a hill above a village and one of
them said: "That's a Taliban village. You need to call in
your aircraft to destroy it." I said, "What, all of them?
They are all Taliban?" "All," he insisted. But of course
we didn't. This was about peasant politics: an ancient
tribal feud of some kind, a Sicilian vendetta. They probably didn't even know themselves why they wanted
the village destroyed. Yet they were utterly unscrupulous
about it.'

On another occasion, on a lonely mountain road in the
northern province of Jowzjan, his patrol was surrounded
by a fifty-strong unit of Uzbek horsemen. There was an
uneasy stand-off as the two sides eyed each other's
weapons, until the leader of the Uzbeks laughed and
suggested they all sit down to have some tea. He

explained that they had been planning to rob the party of foreigners.

'And would you have killed us?' said the SAS man.

'No, not necessarily,' he shrugged.

'And what about the Taliban – are there any of them around here?'

'Yes, we see them from time to time.'

'And would you fight for them?'

'Sure, if they paid us – why not?'

It was a reminder, as the SAS man said, that there were 'an awful lot of bandidos' in Afghanistan. Organized banditry, or 'dacoity' as it is still known in India, is so common in some parts of South Asia that it is considered a kind of profession – and not necessarily an unrespectable one. The Pashtun, according to the poet Ghani Khan, 'has a proud head and an empty stomach; that is why he makes a great dacoit. I would rather see a man hang for dacoity than see him crawl along a pavement with outstretched palms, asking for alms from those who have found generous buyers for their souls. The Pathan loves to steal because he hates to beg. That is why I love him, in spite of his thick head and vain heart.'

The UK plan for Helmand in 2006 was based on what was known as the 'comprehensive approach', an adaptation of the 'ink spot' strategy developed during the Malaya Emergency of the 1950s. The idea then had been to use troops to establish secure centres of development furnished with schools and jobs and clean running water.

As the locals got to hear about the good life to be had in these centres, news of them would spread across the country like an ink spot on blotting paper, drawing in grateful civilians and separating them from the Chinese-backed communist insurgents who preyed upon them. The goal, as Chairman Mao once put it, was to 'drain the swamp' of popular support for the rebel cause – and in Malaya it worked brilliantly.

In Helmand, the British intended to create a 'security triangle' between their base at Camp Bastion and the province's two main towns, Lashkar Gah and Gereshk; aid organizations led by the Foreign Office and DfID, the Department for International Development, would then pour into the breach. But the comprehensive approach was a failure. It is questionable whether the British ever had enough troops to secure the triangle in the first place. They had even fewer available when the Taliban began to press down from the north of the province, obliging Brigadier Ed Butler to garrison the towns of Now Zad, Musa Qala and Sangin, and to send others to protect an important hydro-electric dam at Kajaki. These places were all beyond the scope of the original plan. The 'ink spot' envisioned at Whitehall soon resembled an ink splatter. Just as the Special Forces reconnaissance mission had warned, Butler's garrisons were quickly surrounded and besieged – and as the fighting intensified, Lashkar Gah and Gereshk began to fill not with people looking for work but with frightened refugees. Meanwhile, the British development agencies who were supposed to exploit the army's sacrifices were so concerned about their own safety that they never arrived in the numbers necessary to make a difference.

The battle for Helmand in 2006 has since passed into British Army legend. The Gurkhas and then the Fusiliers who defended the platoon house at Now Zad compared the experience to the celebrated defence of Rorke's Drift in 1879, when 139 redcoats held off a Zulu force of four to five thousand. The Now Zad garrison initially contained no more than thirty British soldiers. The Taliban, who knew that their enemy were unlikely to be so vulnerable in future, and who understood the enormous psychological value of defeating them, attempted to force the compound by frontal assault. Hundreds of fighters armed with AK-47s, sniper rifles and other small arms, backed up by mortar fire and barrages of RPGs, were able to get close up to the buildings across the street from the compound: so close that one Gurkha exchanged grenades with them through an air vent in the garrison's latrine wall. The defenders would almost certainly have been over-run were it not for the supporting fire-power of Apache helicopters.

This scene was repeated throughout that summer in small Helmandi towns that no one in the West had previously heard of, but which have since become household names. British soldiers were still giving their lives to defend them, four years later. On almost every occasion in 2006 it was airpower that saved the day for the foreigners. An estimated 1,800 Taliban were killed or wounded between April and June 2006 alone.[4] The frontal assault tactic was abandoned the following year, when the insurgents fell back on a classic hit-and-run guerrilla strategy. This burned more slowly but arguably inflicted more damage on their enemy. Coalition casualties have risen every year since 2003, when fifty-seven were killed, to a record 520 dead in 2009.

The Taliban's newest and most controversial tactic was a suicide-bomb campaign. The hand of al-Qaida is often seen in this sinister development, for there is no strong tradition of martyrdom in Afghan culture. Although the mujahideen occasionally used the technique against major Soviet targets in the 1980s, it is regarded by most Afghans as a kind of Arab perversion and it remains highly controversial, even among the Quetta leadership. It is sometimes said that Jalaluddin Haqqani, with his closer ties to al-Qaida, was responsible for the expansion of its use. Whoever's idea it was, Mullah Obaidullah was certainly keen on it, and announced in November 2005 that he had assembled an army of suicide bombers who were now standing by, ready to deploy. There were just twenty-one suicide attacks in 2005, but 140 in 2006, accounting for over 1,100 dead.[5]

The Taliban sometimes argued that suicide bombs were justified because they had no air force of their own, and they had to respond to Nato airpower somehow. It was hard to dismiss their complaint that the West's aerial munitions – *guided* weapons supposedly designed to avoid collateral damage – had been killing innocent civilians by the hundred from the moment the Americans arrived. And yet the impulse to attack the West through suicide has yet to catch on in the national consciousness. There are no videos or posters glorifying suicide attackers as there are in some Middle Eastern countries. The bombers themselves are often from the outer fringes of Afghan society: the mentally ill, the educationally subnormal, and the many others who are susceptible to manipulation in a country traumatized by decades of war. In 2007, a pathologist's study of the remains of over a hundred suicide attackers revealed that 80 per cent of them were missing limbs before they blew themselves up, or were suffering from leprosy or terminal diseases like cancer.[6] Omar eventually came to understand that suicide bombing, with its unhappy tendency to kill innocent bystanders, was not the best way to win popular support, and reportedly fell out with Mullah Obaidullah over this issue; in 2009 he tried to restrict its use by specifically instructing his fighters to 'do their utmost to avoid civilian deaths'.

United Nations statistics show that the incidence of suicide bombing in Afghanistan is growing nevertheless, with 239 attacks recorded in 2008. Yet it is difficult to say how many of them are now directed by the Quetta shura. Suicide bombers are usually impossible to identify after the event, and a great many attacks are never claimed by anybody. Omar's spokesmen frequently deny they have anything to do with an attack, and it is certain that militant groups not under Omar's control are sometimes responsible. The devastating attack on a CIA base in Khost in December 2009 was carried out by a Jordanian triple-agent who had been radicalized by his experience of violence in Gaza.[7]

But in any case, suicide bombing has never been more than a terrifying adjunct to the Afghan Taliban's new guerrilla strategy. The centrepiece of their campaign has proved to be the IED, the Improvised Explosive Device. The Afghans learned the art of booby-traps in the 1980s and they hadn't forgotten their skills. There was no shortage of materials to make the bombs with, or of targets to choose from. The British, particularly, didn't have enough helicopters, and were increasingly forced to use the roads to get around in Helmand. The vehicles they use have become more and more heavily armoured, but the Taliban always seem to stay one step ahead. The Taliban destroyed their first large British armoured vehicle, an eight-ton Spartan manned by the Household Cavalry, at Musa Qala in August 2006, using the ludicrously simple method of burying two or three Soviet-era anti-tank mines stacked one on top of the other. When the foreigners deployed sappers armed with metal detectors, the Taliban developed IEDs made of plastic and wood; when they brought in sniffer dogs, they learned to urinate around their bomb to mask the scent of explosives.

The statistics showed who was winning this deadly game of cat and mouse. In 2006 there were 2,000 IED attacks which killed seventy-eight Coalition troops, amounting to 30 per cent of the total killed in that year. In 2009 there were 7,000 IED attacks which killed 275 troops: 61 per cent of the total in that year.[8] Attacks of all kinds on US forces and their Nato allies totalled 21,000 in 2009: a 75 per cent increase over 2008.[9] No wonder the insurgents regarded 2009 as their most successful year to date.

As the Taliban well knew, IEDs grind away at the morale of the foreign troops who have to face them each day. 'This is probably the most scared I've ever been,' wrote one British press photographer embedded with a US/Afghan National Army Humvee patrol. 'You literally start shaking as the convoy's engines start up. Even the briefings scare you when they explain what you'll be expected to do if they have to amputate a limb.'[10] But this was only part of the point of IEDs. Equally important was their continuous demonstration, both to ISAF and to the Afghan population, that the Taliban could strike their enemy whenever and wherever they pleased.

This was the propaganda thinking behind the Taliban's regular set-piece attacks that even ISAF describe as 'spectaculars'. Perhaps the most astonishing example came in June 2008 when they orchestrated a mass prison-break from Sarposa jail in Kandahar, less than two miles from Camp Nathan Smith where hundreds of Canadian ISAF troops are based. There had already been unrest at the jail, where conditions were dire even by Afghanistan's low standards: a hunger strike by two hundred prisoners, in the course of which forty-seven of them physically stitched their mouths shut. The break-out began when a tanker truck approached the main entrance and was blown up, killing all the guards and destroying the gates. In the confusion, another suicide bomber made his way to the back of the jail and breached the perimeter wall for a second time. Meanwhile, a squad of sixty fighters mounted on thirty motorbikes poured through the front to attack the remaining guards with machine guns and RPGs, and to open up the cells. It was several hours before any Canadian troops arrived on the scene, by when all 1,200 inmates, who included almost four hundred suspected Taliban fighters, had either slipped away into the surrounding pomegranate groves or else were brazenly loaded on to waiting minibuses. Only a handful of them were recaptured later in the town.

It was an iconic moment for the insurgency. The Taliban had not forgotten the annihilation of their comrades who had tried to break out of the Qala-i-Jangi, six and a half years before. By pulling off an operation of such extraordinary skill and daring at Sarposa, they were able to prove to themselves and to the world that the new Taliban was a force to be taken very seriously indeed – another taste of things to come.

I met a group of Taliban commanders one winter's night in early 2007, in a safe house in a village in Wardak province.[11] Wardak was barely 30 miles from Kabul, yet in much of the province the writ of Karzai's government ran only during the hours of daylight, when the Taliban slept before taking over completely at sundown. Abdullah, the group's leader and the military commander for the province, was a man of about my age as well as a father of young children, although he was frighteningly pessimistic about his prospects of watching them grow up.

'We are against war,' he explained. 'It creates nothing but widows and destruction. But jihad is different. It is our moral obligation to resist you foreigners.'

They could not therefore stop fighting even if they wanted to, and even if there was no chance of success. The object was not necessarily to win, but to resist.

'One year, a hundred years, a million years, ten million years – it is not important. We will never stop fighting. At Judgement Day, Allah will not ask, "What did you do for your country?" He will ask, "Did you fight for your religion?"'

Over the next three years I followed Abdullah's guerrilla career at one remove through an Afghan contact who kept in touch with him from London. By 2008, the shadow administration in Wardak was so well established that it was operating by day as well as by night. In some districts the government had ceded control completely to the insurgency. The official provincial government simply could not compete with the services the Taliban offered – particularly, I was told, when it came to the administration of justice. A villager involved in, say, a local land dispute, used to have to bribe every official and wait months before a resolution could ever be reached. By stark and shameful contrast, the judgements of the Taliban's Sharia councils were instant as well as free.

In 2009 the Wardaki Taliban began to focus their attentions on the Kabul to Kandahar highway that runs through the east of the province, a vital supply route for the growing American counter-insurgency operations in the south. Abdullah, it seemed, had discovered a special talent for attacking ISAF's convoys, a skill that brought him to the special notice of High Command in Quetta, who began to supply him with every resource he required. His bombs were often detonated by buried command wires which were rumoured to stretch for miles on either side of the kill-zones. ISAF had set up a string of fortified checkpoints along the most vulnerable stretch of road, but still the attacks continued. The bombers were so elusive that the American infantrymen guarding the road took to calling them 'ghosts' – which was nothing new. The Russians had used exactly the same nickname, *dukhi*, for their assailants in the 1980s.

At the beginning of 2010, the frustrated Americans launched a series of night raids in the Wardaki interior in a bid to remove this thorn in their side. They succeeded in wounding and capturing Mullah Abdul-Basit, Abdullah's spiritual mentor, a small, scholarly man whom I had also met in 2007. He was taken to the jail at Bagram, but of Abdullah himself there was no sign. I later learned that he was in Quetta, securing weapons and support for yet another counter-offensive against the Americans.

The Western strategy looked more and more like a recipe for endless war, and by the US military's own admission, it wasn't working. In the spring of 2010, according to a Pentagon survey, Afghans supported the Karzai government in only twenty-nine of the 121 districts considered the most strategically important. With government corruption at every level continuing to run out of control, this was hardly surprising. According to the UN, Afghans paid $2.5 billion in bribes in 2009: about a quarter of the country's official Gross Domestic Product.[12] By May 2010, meanwhile, more than 1,780 foreign Coalition troops had given their lives in the effort to prop the regime up.

I had suspected in 2007 that the West's military response to the Taliban was in trouble, and that negotiating with this enemy would be a better option than fighting them. The statistics alone suggested that negotiations had now become an imperative. In 2007 the idea that the West might ever 'talk with terrorists' was still considered a heresy in Washington, but opinion has shifted since the coming of Obama. Even the new US commander in Afghanistan, General Stanley McChrystal, seemed in January 2010 to accept that the West could not sustain this war for much longer, and hinted that reconciliation with the Taliban leadership was the answer.

'I think any Afghans can play a role [in the government] if they focus on the future and not the past,' he said. 'As a soldier, my personal feeling is that there's been enough fighting.'[13]

Everyone could agree with that. For how much longer would the West really go on sacrificing the lives of its young men and women for a cause that looked so lost?

In May 2010 I received an email from Adrian Lucas whose son Alec, an assault engineer in the Royal Marines, became the 126th British soldier to die in Afghanistan when he was killed by an IED during a clearance operation in Helmand in November 2008. Alec was a football-mad 24-year-old, with a young daughter and a fiancée whom he had planned to marry that summer. Eighteen months later his father was still struggling with his loss, still visiting Alec's grave each day in the cemetery near their home in Peebles.

'The thing is . . . you NEVER think that you will outlive your kids,' he wrote.

His feelings about the war were complex. 'It is important that the [bereaved] families have a say, and, believe it or not, most of us can't stand the thought of a pull-out!'

The Taliban's extremism appalled him. He had watched television reports of Sunday afternoon hangings in football stadiums before 2001. He had also heard how in Helmand, the Taliban were so keen to bring down a 'trophy' Chinook helicopter that they would deliberately shoot a little girl in the leg, send her up to an ISAF base, then wait in ambush for the Emergency Response Team which they knew the soft-hearted foreigners would call in to evacuate her.

At the same time, Adrian insisted that he 'got it' that the conflict would not be won by military means alone, and that ISAF's tactics were often counter-productive. He said that Alec, who was killed near the hydro-electric dam at Kajaki, had died believing that it was his mission to restore electricity to Afghanistan.

'I feel your respect for these people, and I feel it too,' Adrian wrote to me. 'Alec always said in every phone call, "Dad, this place is beautiful and these people are wonderful, I really like them."'

This was the tragic paradox: Alec had been killed by a people he liked and wanted to help, for the simple reason that he was wearing a foreign soldier's uniform. In 2007 when I put it to Mullah Abdul-Basit that the Taliban should stop fighting Nato because we were here to help the Kabul government to secure economic development, he replied: 'Then why do you come here with guns and bombs?'

'Are you saying that it would have been different if we had come here unarmed?'

'But of course!' said the mullah. 'In that case you would have been our guests, just as you are our guest now. If your engineers and agriculture experts had come to us and explained what they were trying to do, we would have protected them with our lives.'

The West's intent was good but the method was not. The Taliban were fighting for two things: a return of Sharia law, and the withdrawal of infidel soldiers from Afghanistan's holy soil. Our soldiers were therefore the last people we should have put in charge of the reconstruction, because they were forced by the insurgency in the meantime to do what they were trained and designed to do – which was to fight. Deeds could not possibly match the West's fine words under such circumstances. The whole basis of our engagement was wrong.

The main objection to leaving Afghanistan's future in the hands of civilians was the risk that the country might 'become once again a sanctuary for al-Qaida', as General Petraeus put it. But was this the reason for the West's continued military presence – or a justification for it?

What if the Taliban leadership were prepared and able to guarantee to keep al-Qaida out in the future – would ISAF withdraw then? And what other areas of compromise might the Taliban be willing to consider in order to break the deadlock? In February 2010 I went back to Kabul to try to find out.

Part II

8

The McChrystal Plan:
Sawing Wood with a Hammer

After a long night's journey from London via Dubai, there was no sign of the car I had asked to meet me at Kabul airport – an inauspicious start to my first Afghan visit in three years. The reason soon became apparent. Two hours earlier a pair of hotels, the Safi Landmark and the Euro Guest House, had been attacked by a mixed force of suicide bombers and gunmen, some of whom were still shooting it out with the police. The hotel I was supposed to be staying in was barely a block away from the Safi Landmark. Many foreign guests had been killed, according to one of the few drivers hanging around by the airport, and much of the city centre was still sealed off. It was a sobering reminder that one didn't need to travel to the provinces to find the war any more. These days it was right here in Kabul.

I hitched a ride with a government taxi-driver who

claimed to have a special pass that would allow us into the secure zone. The mud-slicked roads were spookily empty of ordinary people. Everywhere we looked there seemed to be heavily armed men – soldiers in green, policemen in blue, plain-clothed operatives of the National Directorate of Security, the NDS, about whom I was to hear a lot more in the coming days. The driver's pass was useless when we reached the barricades. There was no way they were letting us through when they saw a foreigner in the back. The driver dropped me instead at the Intercontinental, a 1960s behemoth of a hotel that sits on a hill a couple of miles west of the centre. If nothing else this was a safe place to sit out the siege. There were three armed checkpoints on its access road alone, and soldiers patrolling with uncharacteristic alertness in the gardens round about. Kabul was much changed.

The inside of the Intercon, on the other hand, was as depressing as ever: cold, cavernous and under-lit. Porters and waiters mooched about, waiting for guests that never seemed to come. I settled down in the coffee room to wait for the all-clear. There was one other customer, watching pictures of the attack's aftermath on a television in the corner.

'This damn country,' he said as I came in.

The Safi Landmark was a wreck of shattered glass and neon signage hanging in tatters, while the building opposite had collapsed entirely.

'My wife is going crazy. She keeps phoning to ask

when I'm getting out of here. But that's easier said than done, you know?'

He was an Afghan-American called Mirwais, a Dubai-based businessman in town for a series of meetings with the US military. He was hoping to sell them ten armoured vehicles: 'new-generation ones, all carbon-fibre underneath, very strong but very light'. The cost, he revealed, was $200,000 per vehicle; he complained that the Americans were keener on leasing rather than buying them. He laughed in a worldly way when I teased him that $2 million might be better spent on ordinary Afghans rather than protecting Americans.

'You know how it works,' he said.

On the news, the toll from the attack was still climbing. Dozens were injured and at least seventeen dead, including an Italian, a Frenchman and nine Indians. The word at the airport had been that this was another Taliban 'spectacular'. The fact that the attack had happened at 6.30 a.m. on a Friday, the beginning of the weekend when there were fewer people on the streets, suggested that some thought had been given to minimizing 'civilian' casualties, which since 2009 was supposed to be a hallmark of Taliban suicide attacks. A local TV news presenter was now speculating that others could be responsible, however. It all depended on who was intended as the target: foreigners in general, or Indian ones in particular? If the latter – and the high proportion of dead Indians was obviously suggestive – then the attack could have been carried out by one of the

ISI-backed militant organizations with an axe to grind in the long-running Indo-Pakistani border dispute in Kashmir, such as Lashkar-e-Toiba. This was the same terror group that had attacked the Taj Mahal hotel in Mumbai in 2008, going from room to room in a hunt for foreigners to kill, and from the reports on the television, the Safi Landmark attack bore some of the hallmarks of the horror in Mumbai.

No one knew, of course, but it certainly mattered to me if foreigners in general were the target. My hotel, the Gandamak Lodge, was a favourite with visiting British journalists. Its bar was also very popular with the city's swollen community of foreign diplomats, aid workers and contractors: one of perhaps a dozen Western watering-holes in the whole of Kabul. I knew the place well. It was owned and run by Peter Jouvenal, the former cameraman who had married an Afghan and set up the business a decade before. He was a keen collector of the old British weaponry which can still be found in the country's bazaars, the scattered legacy of the wars of the nineteenth century. The entrance was guarded by a rickety old field gun; the hall was lined with racks of Martini-Henry rifles, the standard-issue British rifle of the 1870s. The Flashman theme was carried into the dining room, which was decorated with more guns and maps and other militaria, while up in the storeroom by the bedrooms, piles of vintage bayonets vied for space with camera tripods, bullet-proof vests and other modern bric-a-brac left behind by itinerant war correspondents over the years.

The hotel took its name from Gandamak village, 35 miles west of Jalalabad, where the remnants of a 16,500-strong British army were annihilated in 1842: the worst defeat the Empire had ever known. The redcoats' tragic last stand was commemorated in 1898 by the artist W.B. Wollen, a copy of whose painting naturally hung alongside the Martini-Henrys in the entrance hall. Watching that morning's news, I couldn't help wondering if it was tempting providence to stay in a hotel named after so famous a massacre of the British.

It was mid-afternoon before the cordon was lifted and I was able to complete my journey. Arriving at the hotel at last I found I was not alone in my nervousness about security. The old field gun had been reinforced by a posse of armed guards, an escape route from the compound had been organized in the event of a frontal attack, and one of the guests said she had hidden a Makharov pistol beneath her pillow. Apart from that, British sang-froid seemed intact. It was surreal to hear that a full English breakfast had been served as usual in the restaurant that morning. Even so, there was no escaping the tension in the streets outside. Uncertainty hung in the air like the swirling mist that now obscured the Koh-i-Asmai, a transmitter-topped mountain ridge that separated the city centre from the University district, and an important point of orientation for every Kabuli city-dweller – at least, when it was in view.

The West's war against the Taliban had changed gear

once again as it entered its ninth year. In September 2009, General Stanley McChrystal made public an earlier report to the White House that recommended sending in 40,000 more foreign troops: a 'surge' that would replicate the tactics that helped defeat the insurgency in Iraq. It was a controversial move. Who was in charge of US policy in Afghanistan: the politicians or the military? Congressman Dennis Kucinich thundered – presciently, it would later turn out – that generals were supposed to be 'subordinate to the President, who is the commander-in-chief. He's the boss. And when generals start trying to suggest publicly what the president should do, they shouldn't be generals anymore.'[1]

But McChrystal kept his job. After months of internal debate at the White House, Obama finally agreed to a surge. Critics accused him of dithering, though in fairness the decision was not an easy one. He was in exactly the same position as Mikhail Gorbachev soon after he became leader of the Soviet Union in 1985. Gorbachev, too, had inherited a counter-insurgency that was in danger of stagnating – and he also agreed to his generals' request for a troop surge in order to force a result. Soviet troop levels subsequently rose to 108,800 in 1985 – which turned out to be the bloodiest year of the whole ten-year occupation.

McChrystal's plan was to use the extra US troops, more than 100,000 of whom were expected to be in theatre by the end of 2010, to secure the main population centres at the expense of small villages and the countryside. The logic seemed sound enough. As McChrystal said, 'the people are the prize' in counter-insurgency warfare, not the insurgents, so it made sense to focus on the places where most of them lived. The goal was to drive the Taliban from the main population centres and to re-establish – or in some cases, to establish for the first time – the writ of the central government. In theory, support for the Taliban would drain away when the locals saw the advantages of better services, good governance, proper law and order. Attacks such as that morning's on the Safi Landmark hotel looked designed to challenge ISAF in the places the Americans had declared were most important to them. In the capital, Taliban spectaculars were now being mounted about once every six weeks. Resident foreigners had begun to compare Kabul to Baghdad – a spurious comparison for now, though not entirely far-fetched, particularly if you happened to work for the United Nations. Just four months earlier, a suicide bomb and gun attack on a nearby UN guest house had killed five.

Down in Helmand, even as I arrived in Kabul, the McChrystal theory was being put into practice. Operation Moshtaraq, involving some 15,000 ISAF troops, the biggest offensive of the war, was under way in the farming community of Marjah. 'Clear, hold and build' was the new military mantra. McChrystal boasted that, once the military had done the clearing and holding, he had a 'government in a box, ready to roll in' to do the building bit, the key part of the battle for local 'hearts and minds'. It all looked good on paper: a strategy from the US's new *Counterinsurgency Field Manual* published in 2007 under the direction of David Petraeus, and of which McChrystal was a devoted follower. But there were serious doubts from the outset that it would actually work.

The first one concerned the people selected to man McChrystal's 'government in a box'. The man appointed to run the district council, Abdul Zahir, had lived in Germany for fifteen years before returning in 2000, and was little known locally even though he was a member of the influential Alizai tribe. The subsequent revelation that Zahir had served part of a five-year sentence for the attempted manslaughter of his son in 1998[2] caused derision in Marjah, and acute embarrassment at Nato headquarters in Kabul.

Then there was the question of troop numbers. There was essentially no difference between 'clear, hold and build' and the 'comprehensive approach' adopted by the British in Helmand since 2006. The undermanned British had struggled to hold the territory they cleared, but did McChrystal really have enough men to do the job now? It was well known in Kabul that he had initially asked his President for an additional 80,000 troops, yet had ended up with only half that number. What was worse, the psychological impact of the surge was diluted from the outset by Obama himself, who for domestic political reasons found it necessary to declare that his troops would start coming home again in 2011, even as he announced their deployment. The surge in Iraq had never been time-limited in this way. The State Department, among others, tried hard to row back from Obama's announcement, arguing that any troops returning home in 2011 would be doing so only as a part of the ordinary rotation system, and that America's military commitment would not end until the job was finished. Among ordinary Afghans, however, the damage was already done. 'You may have the watches, but we have the time,' as their old saying went. Once planted, it was impossible to uproot the idea that for the Taliban to win, all they had to do was to wait.

Operation Moshtaraq was supposed to showcase the new McChrystal approach, yet even its codename was bungled. *Moshtaraq* has an Arab root but is essentially a Dari word for 'together'. For a hearts and minds operation in a province where 92 per cent of the population are Pashtuns,[3] this was not a clever choice: 'Like sticking two fingers up at the people of Marjah,' as one Pashtun living in Kabul later told me. Perhaps, he joked, the war-planners had rejected the perfectly good Pashto word for 'together' – *gaad* – on the grounds that it would sound too much like 'God' on the lips of US Marines, and were anxious to avoid any suggestion of a crusade.

The choice of codename was supposed to illustrate ISAF's solidarity with the local military who accompanied them on the mission (and helped to make up the numbers needed to make it a success): the Afghan National Army. Instead, ISAF had inadvertently pointed up the fledgling ANA's greatest drawback: its dire lack of ethnic balance. More than 40 per cent of its rank and file were Dari-speaking Tajiks,[4] who account for about a quarter of the country's population. Worse still, fully 70 per cent of its battalion commanders were Tajiks too.[5] The ANA, therefore, was arguably not a 'national' army at all but a kind of ethnic super-militia, trained and armed by the West. This was the institution that was supposed to keep the peace once ISAF withdrew: the very foundation of the Western exit strategy from Afghanistan. Nato was in the process of rapidly expanding the ANA from 90,000 to a planned 250,000, with the overall security forces of the country, including the police, eventually supposed to number more than 400,000. But without the proper proportion of Pashtuns in its ranks, wasn't there a risk that it would not keep the peace in the event of future conflict, but would take sides?

The loyalty of the army was already worryingly uncertain. Matthew Hoh, the senior US civilian in Zabul province until he resigned in protest against the war in September 2009, recalled attending an Afghan Independence Day event at a military base that was attended by hundreds of ANA and national police. The large photograph beneath which they paraded, he observed, was not of President Karzai but of Ahmed Shah Massoud, the mujahideen leader assassinated by al-Qaida in 2001, and who is still lionized by Tajiks. 'It is already bad now,' Hoh remarked, 'but unless US policy changes we could see a return of the civil war of the 1990s.'[6] ISAF's planners did not repeat their 'moshtaraq' mistake. The next phase of the campaign, the investment of Kandahar city, had already been codenamed Operation Omid, a Pashto word this time, meaning 'hope'. But it would take more than presentational tinkering – and more than wishful thinking – to fix the underlying problems of the ANA. A United Nations report in January 2010 revealed that nine out of ten ANA soldiers were illiterate, three in ten were drug addicts, and that a quarter of them deserted, every year. Bringing such an army up to scratch will likely require foreign troops to train and mentor them for decades to come.[7]

Many reputations had been staked on the success of the surge. In a briefing to journalists at Camp Leatherneck in Helmand, American military officials described Marjah as 'a town of 80,000 people', a crucial cog in Helmand's mighty opium industry, as well as the Taliban's last significant stronghold in the province. But were these claims really true? Few had ever heard of the place before Operation Moshtaraq. And if it was so important, why had they taken so long to get around to tackling it? Marjah was barely 20 miles from the provincial capital, Lashkar Gah, yet high-intensity military operations had been going on in Helmand for four and a half years. The suspicion in Kabul was that ISAF had deliberately exaggerated Marjah's significance to a compliant media for propaganda purposes. Three weeks after the briefing at Camp Leatherneck, the *New*

York Times ran a story with a Marjah dateline describing it as 'a city of 80,000'. The truth was that ISAF had invested tens of thousands of troops in what really amounted to just another Helmandi patchwork of fields and farming villages.

McChrystal brandished a carrot for the insurgents, in the shape of a reintegration programme supported by a special new billion-dollar fund. At a conference arranged by Prime Minister Gordon Brown in London in January 2010, it was announced that any fighter who agreed to lay down his arms and abide by the Constitution of Afghanistan would be entitled to a job, housing assistance, and anything else he might need to return to the fold of civil society. McChrystal was convinced that the great majority of the insurgency's foot soldiers, perhaps as many as 70 per cent, were fighting ISAF not from ideological conviction but because there was no other work available.[8] He reckoned that the easiest and cheapest way to defeat these so-called 'ten-dollar-a-day Taliban' – also sometimes described as 'Tier Three' insurgents – was simply to buy them off. It was true that unemployment was rife: 40 per cent nationally and as high as 70 per cent in parts of the south, including Helmand.

The problem was that the reintegration programme offered nothing to those 'ideological' Taliban who were not fighting for a salary. These obviously included the Quetta leadership, whose preconditions for reconciliation – the withdrawal of foreign troops, a constitution based exclusively on Sharia – had not wavered in eight years. In 2008, ISAF intelligence officers estimated there were a total of 7,000 to 11,000 insurgents, of whom just 5 per cent were what they called 'Tier One Taliban', the 'hard core' of the insurgency who would probably never reconcile.[9] McChrystal was effectively gambling on the accuracy of this assessment, arguing that it would be easy to deal with the Tier One Taliban once their Tier Three foot soldiers had been stripped away. But how accurate were ISAF's figures, and what did they really mean?

The campaign planners had got their numbers wrong in the past. In early 2006, for instance, it was confidently stated by the British that there were 'no more than a thousand' Taliban in the whole of Helmand province. Yet twice that number were killed in the summer of that year alone, since when the insurgency had done nothing but intensify. The distinction between 'irreconcilable' and 'reconcilable', Tier One and Tier Three, also seemed questionable, because to be a Taliban fighter was as much a state of mind as it was to be a member of an army. A fighter could be Tier Three Taliban one day, Tier One the next, Tier Two the day after that. All people change their minds – though few, arguably, are as fickle as Afghans. Changing to the side of whoever seems strongest was a survival tactic learned over centuries.

This, it seemed to me, was the greatest flaw in the Americans' plan: they had misunderstood the nature of the people opposing them. In particular, they had under-estimated how strongly Pashtuns had always felt about infidels meddling in their land – especially armed ones – and on that level, none of them was truly reconcilable. For all McChrystal's brave talk, the number of IEDs laid by the Taliban had increased by 263 per cent in the twelve months to April 2010, according to the Pentagon.[10] Resistance was hard-wired into the Pashtun psyche, and it was almost always successful: two truths brought home to me on a visit to Ustad Rafeh, a professor of Pashtun history at Kabul University.

'Two thousand five hundred years ago, Darius the Great came here from Iran. The Pashtuns resisted and never surrendered. Then Alexander the Great arrived from Macedonia. His advance from the west was like the wind – until he got to Afghanistan. He was stuck here for many years. Then fifteen hundred years ago, the Arabs came. We accepted their religion, but not their traditions, and we refused to be colonized. Nine hundred years ago, it was Genghis Khan. We killed his grandson. Then you British came, 150 years ago. You had 60,000 troops and the best artillery, but it was *Pashtuns* who surrounded Kabul and killed 17,000 of you as you tried to escape. The rulers of your Empire thought this was an accident: they couldn't accept such a defeat, so they attacked again, in 1880. We killed 12,000 of you that time, at Maiwand. The same with the Soviets in 1979: most of their original army was destroyed. What makes you think that it will be any different for America this time?'

The success of the 'clear, hold and build' strategy was predicated on an assumption that Afghans understood they needed foreign assistance, and that they would therefore welcome it. This, after all, was a country where more than one in three subsisted on less than 30p a day, where more than half of all pre-school children were stunted by malnutrition, and one in five died before the age of five.[11] This was why the US military leadership all thought that 'soft power' – the sinking of wells, the building of new roads or schools – would be a more effective battle-winner in the long term than the killing of insurgents.

History showed, however, that such foreign help was not necessarily welcome. The Afghans knew from experience that civic action programmes, however altruistic in appearance, tended to come with strings attached. The Soviets had used soft power as a counter-insurgency tactic, and the Americans were no different. Had General Petraeus not said as much in Iraq with his remark that 'money is my most important ammunition in this war'? The work of Matiullah Tarab, an angry young poet from Jalalabad, expressed the distrust of many Pashtuns. His verse was taken so seriously by the authorities in Kabul that in 2008 he was locked up for sedition for six months. He wrote:

You Americans come here with a stamp
You brand one man Osama
One man Khalilzad
You came here to rebuild this country
You build roads and bridges

You call that rebuilding?
You should go back to your country with all this concrete
May it kick you in the head as you go

Ustad Rafeh's suspicion of American motives was certainly common in Kabul. 'The US did not come here to help or rescue Afghanistan,' he told me. 'They are here for their own strategic reasons. They want a permanent military presence here, to encircle Iran and to gain access to the oilfields of Central Asia. Their talk of peace and stability is just an excuse.' School-burning looked like fundamentalist nihilism to the West, but in such a climate of paranoia and mistrust, it was all too easy for the Taliban to present it to the people as a legitimate act of war.

Perhaps McChrystal was right that some insurgents could be bribed to stop fighting. The technique had a long track record in Afghanistan. But there was also an old saying, often repeated by the British in the nineteenth century, that 'you can't buy an Afghan. You can only rent him for a while.' Afghan attitudes towards foreigners were coloured by the Koran, certain passages of which can be interpreted as actively endorsing such fickleness. Sura 3:28 advises that 'believers should not take the un-believers as friends rather than the believers. Whoever does that has nothing to do with Allah.' It is, however, all right to 'befriend them with the tongue, not in the heart, if you have fear of them' – and there were of course many Afghans with every reason to fear the armed might of

Nato. The effect of offering such people dollars for their weapons was likely to be very temporary; and if Pashtun pride was insulted in the process, it could even make matters worse.

McChrystal himself was not without subtlety. He was well respected by Kabul's diplomatic community, some of whom considered him one of those rare generals who 'got it' in Afghanistan. As a man who runs eight miles every morning and who likes to eat just one meal a day – to avoid 'sluggishness', it is said – he was almost as ascetic as the Taliban who opposed him. In March 2010 he was reported to be reading Winston Churchill's *The Story of the Malakand Field Force*.[12] Although over a hundred years old, some of Churchill's observations on the resident Pathans (the old British word for Pashtuns on 'their' side of the Durand Line) are still relevant: 'Tribe wars with tribe. Every man's hand is against the other and all are against the stranger . . . the state of continual tumult has produced a habit of mind which holds life cheap and embarks on war with careless levity.'

Churchill also laid out three options for dealing with this fractious region: imposing the rule of law at gunpoint, pulling out and leaving them to it, or working through and with the tribal system. McChrystal told the veteran Afghan correspondent Robert Kaplan of *Atlantic* magazine: 'The third choice – Churchill's choice – is really the only one we have.'

His problem was that Washington was still fixated on the first choice. In March 2010 Barack Obama paid a surprise visit to his troops in Afghanistan, his first since becoming President in January 2009. 'We are going to disrupt and dismantle, defeat and destroy al-Qaida and its extremist allies,' he told them. The alliteration might have been fancier, but the message behind it was no different in substance from anything his predecessor George Bush might have said. It seemed that at the leadership level that really counted – and certainly for the cameras and the American public watching at home – it was business as usual for the War on Terror.

In the end it was no good for McChrystal to remind his troops, as he did in his *Counterinsurgency Guidance* advice distributed to them in 2009, that 'this is their country and we are their guests'. As he knew, *melmastia*, the showing of hospitality and respect to all visitors, is a vital part of Pashtunwali. But the quid pro quo of that tradition is that the visitor must come unarmed; and for reasons of Pashtun history, infidels with weapons tend to be seen as enemy invaders rather than as guests. For an American soldier to appeal to melmastia as McChrystal did was a bit like trying to saw a piece of wood with a hammer.

9

'This One, This Is the Big One': Mullah Zaeef and the Prospects for Peace

The prognosis for 2010 seemed gloomy, but there was one ray of light: the prospect of a negotiated settlement with the Quetta leadership that might bring an early end to the war. At the London Conference in January, and again in a speech in Munich in February, President Karzai felt sufficiently confident of Western support for negotiations with what he called his 'disenchanted brothers' that he used his address to appeal publicly to 'my brother the King of Saudi Arabia, His Majesty Abdullah bin Abdul Aziz', to help mediate them.

The Saudis were the best and most obvious choice for this role. As the 'Guardians of the Holy Places', Mecca and Medina, they had a status in the Islamic world that no other country could match. They enjoyed good relations with the Americans, thanks to the oil reserves beneath their feet. And while King Abdullah was circumspect about the Taliban in public, it had hardly been forgotten that Saudi Arabia was one of only three countries – along with Pakistan and the UAE – who had formally recognized their regime in the 1990s. King Abdullah had a strong motive to help mediate a peace, for he had his own troubles with al-Qaida at home. It was also an opportunity to check the regional ambitions of the Saudis' most feared rival, Iran.

Talks with senior Taliban members had in fact been going on intermittently for at least three years. There were so many talking shops in operation, indeed, that one experienced diplomat described them, in a tone between derision and despair, as 'an industry'. At different times and in many different places – Mecca, Dubai, Oman, even on an atoll in the Maldives – senior members of the Taliban had sat down with MPs from Kabul, with United Nations officials, with representatives of Karzai, and of all the main ethnic and political parties in Afghanistan, including Hizb-i-Islami. In addition, private or semi-private initiatives were said to have been organized by the British, the Norwegians, the Swiss.

Trying to keep track of so many concurrent peace plans was a bewildering business, for information on who was saying what to whom was invariably sketchy or inaccurate. Those participating in dialogue did not always admit to it. Many Afghans had a habit of saying one thing and doing another, or of telling whoever it was they were speaking to whatever they thought they wanted to hear. It was the future of their country they were debating, and with the stakes so high there was inevitably much disinformation in circulation. Rivalry between the organizers of the various talking groups, as they jockeyed for power and influence over the outcome and pushed their own agendas and vested interests, was intense. There was so much dialogue going on, one suspected, that the energy and unity of purpose necessary if genuine progress were to be made had been disastrously diluted. There seemed to be willingness for peace on both sides, but the process urgently needed to be grasped.

For all the talking so far, two parties had been conspicuous by their absence from the negotiating tables: any senior US representative, and Mullah Omar himself. The true intentions of both were subject to much speculation in Kabul. From remarks made by the US Defense Secretary Robert Gates in Islamabad in January, it was evident that even he was still in two minds about the Taliban. On one day, Gates publicly described them as a 'scourge' and a 'cancer'; the next, he said that they were clearly 'a part of the political fabric of Afghanistan' these days. Imtiaz Gul, Chairman of the Centre for Research and Security Studies in Islamabad, remarked: 'Herein lie the contradiction and duplicity on the part of US policy. Are they a cancer or part of the political fabric? You can't apply this principle selectively.'[1]

Divining what Omar really thought about a political settlement was no easier. The delegates from Quetta who turned up at the secret meetings never claimed to speak for him; the best they could offer was to go back and speak *to* him. How much influence they really had over their leader was difficult to gauge, not least because they probably didn't know themselves. A contact who had seen the Quetta shura in action described an 'inner circle' and an 'outer circle' of lieutenants whose portfolios were forever being exchanged. They were liable to be brought back from or sent into Afghanistan at any time to fight and organize the war, or to take up civil positions in what now amounted to a shadow government, complete with its own systems of administration and Sharia justice. Even the Pentagon admitted that these alternative administrations existed in most of the country's thirty-four provinces.[2] Omar was virtually the only constant in this organization, the spider in the centre of a ceaselessly evolving web. The lieutenants' closeness to Omar, and hence their status in the movement overall, was always in flux.

Some thought this was a deliberate tactic of Omar's, an astute piece of personnel management designed to prevent the formation of factions and the emergence of challengers to his rule. Others said that he was not so devious, and that he was only trying to copy the distinctly non-hierarchical management style of the Prophet, whose followers in the campaign against the non-believers in the 680s are traditionally described as the *sahabah* – the 'companions'. One of the few journalists who has met Omar, the Peshawar-based BBC correspondent Rahimullah Yusufzai, described an encounter with the leader at his house in Kandahar in 1997, a year after the Taliban had taken Kabul. Omar was 'tall, with a fair complexion for an Afghan and a Grecian nose, prominent above his unkempt black beard'. He sat on a rickety iron bed in a simple room partitioned by a dirty torn curtain, with Taliban coming and going as they pleased. Rahimullah 'sat on the carpet among the Taliban, watching as Omar chatted, joked, signed letters and at one point unlocked the padlock on a box to give some money to two fighters who had arrived in town with nowhere to stay'.[3] Omar may have been the Amir ul-Mu'mineen but he had no throne, no crown, no badge of office of any kind; he wore the same large black turban, shalwar qamiz and a 'cheap, European-style polyester jacket' as all his colleagues.

Such humility is actually not so unusual among the Pashtuns. It is regarded by many as an essential quality, a defining part of the Pashtun identity: a virtue that is practised as well as to be aspired to, and which is mirrored in every Muslim's literal abasement before Allah five times each day in the mosque. It also serves an important practical function, because the principal institution of Pashtun government has long been the shura, an Arabic word meaning 'consultation', and which is twice mentioned in the Koran. For many centuries in Pashtun society, all important community decisions have been taken not by diktat but by consensus among a gathering of the community's elders. For such a system to work, patience, a willingness to listen to others, and above all humility before one's colleagues are all critical.

Omar's modest clothing was thus not a revolutionary rejection of the trappings of power but an affirmation of Pashtun tradition. Humility also helped to define the Taliban, because it stood in such sharp contrast to the cruel arrogance of the warlords they opposed.

My first priority in Kabul was to see Abdul Salam Zaeef again, because if anyone knew what Omar was planning, he did. He had moved home since I had last seen him in the spring of 2007, to a house in the western suburb of Khoshal Khan Mina. It wasn't far but the drive was long thanks to the atrocious traffic, which was back to normal the morning after the Safi Landmark attack. There was ample time to think about that as the car inched past the bomb site. The crater caused by the primary blast, a ten-yard-wide hole in the middle of the street, had already been filled in with gravel. A white-gloved traffic police-man now stood at the epicentre, furiously blowing his whistle at the motorized anarchy of another Kabul rush-hour. There wasn't a window pane intact for a hundred yards about. The shards had been swept into sparkling piles around the bases of every available tree and lamp-post. It had evidently been a big bomb.

The Taliban's former ambassador to Pakistan had spent four and a half years in American military prisons, mostly in Guantanamo, before being released in the summer of 2006 and repatriated. Since then he had lived a strange sort of existence in Kabul. Although never charged with any crime, he was still far from being a free man. Along with 136 others, he remained on the UN Security Council's notorious 'Consolidated List' of individuals who were either still or had once been connected to the Taliban.* This meant that all his financial assets abroad were frozen, he was forbidden to travel, and he was, obviously, banned from involvement in 'the direct or indirect supply, sale, or transfer of arms and related material, including military and paramilitary equipment, technical advice, assistance or training related to military activities'.

These sanctions made Zaeef sound a lot more dangerous than he appeared. He was so good-natured that in the 1990s in Islamabad, where he frequently gave press conferences, he was known as 'the smiling Taliban'. He looked bookish, almost cuddly, with his twinkling eyes behind wire-rimmed glasses and his big bushy beard, and in fact he was clever, as well as fair-minded and curious about others and the world beyond Afghanistan. Some nicknamed him 'the techno-mullah' because of his unconcealed enthusiasm for the internet and all the gadgetry that accompanies it.

He was not smiling so much when I saw him in 2007.

---

* UN Resolution 1267, which established sanctions against the Taliban government as a whole in 1999, also contained a list of specific individuals to whom sanctions applied. Around the same time, the US developed its own 'blacklist' of people it wanted to detain, which overlapped with the UN list but contained more Taliban military leaders and people associated with al-Qaida; the two lists were later 'consolidated'.

Understandably perhaps, he was still smarting at his treatment at the hands of the Americans. Partly as an exercise in catharsis, partly to document the injustice that he had experienced and witnessed, he had written a memoir that would not be published in English for another three years.[4] He gave me a copy of the manuscript, which told the same shameful stories that he often related in person then, when the memory of his incarceration was still fresh and raw.

This was a man who had tried to put a brake on the Taliban's ambitions, who once reduced his close friend Mullah Omar to tears when he accused him of propagating war in the north. At the time of his arrest in 2002 he was not a terrorist but a diplomat in Islamabad, who had tried earnestly to warn Omar what would happen if he did not acquiesce to American demands to do something about Osama bin Laden. Zaeef had a reputation as one of the Taliban's few proper thinkers. As a pronounced moderate by the movement's standards, his potential as a peace negotiator should have been immediately obvious. Yet his captors made no effort to nurture or exploit that potential. Instead, America in general and its military in particular seemed set on the crudest kind of revenge after 9/11. Hundreds, perhaps thousands, of people were swept up in the wake of the invasion. All were branded 'enemy combatants', regardless of their actual role or status, and all were treated the same – which is to say, appallingly.

Zaeef spent six months in prisons at the airbases

at Bagram and Kandahar before being sent to Guantanamo. He was shackled, gagged and hooded, kicked and beaten 'like a drum'. The Americans knew his importance: 'This one, this is the big one,' he heard someone say at one point, before he was thrown to the ground once again and 'stomped on with army boots'. After one such kicking, during which his captors 'behaved like animals for what seemed like hours, [they] sat on top of me and proceeded to have a conversation, as if they were merely sitting on a park bench. I abandoned all hope; the ordeal had been long and I was convinced I would die soon.'

He was interrogated countless times, although there was nothing the Americans could ever hang on him. Zaeef was convinced they knew that he had nothing to do with the terrorist attacks on their interests. Like other Taliban leaders, almost certainly including Omar himself, he had no forewarning of 9/11. The interrogators themselves changed constantly, but the questions were always the same: 'Where is Mullah Omar? Where is bin Laden?' If no distinction was made in the way the prisoners were treated, no distinction was made either between the Taliban and al-Qaida. The questioning itself became a form of abuse, particularly when carried out in conjunction with sleep-deprivation techniques, which was often.

Many prisoners, according to Zaeef, were entirely innocent. One man he saw being roughly dragged into an interrogation tent turned out to be 105 years old. At

Guantanamo he met a man who had been picked up on the grounds that he was '"wearing the clothes of a mujahid" . . . One man was arrested because he was carrying a mirror, another for having a phone, and a third for watching his cattle with binoculars. One of the prisoners said that they had taken him because his only form of identification was a 25-year-old ID card from the time he had been a refugee. These were the facts and the proof of America.'

It seemed a deliberate policy to humiliate the prisoners, who at Guantanamo were kept in factory-farm-style rows of contiguous mesh cages, six foot by four. In an uncomfortable echo of the abuse scandal at Abu Ghraib prison in Iraq, at Kandahar Zaeef was stripped naked and photographed before a group of mockers that included women. Even more damagingly, Islam was routinely insulted as well. The prisoners' heads and, worse, their beards were shaved: 'A sin in the Hanafi faith,' Zaeef commented. 'Every single hair was gone . . . It is better to be killed than to have one's beard shaved.' At Bagram, meanwhile, a soldier urinated on a copy of the Koran and threw it in a bin. 'All over the camp you could hear the men weep . . . We had been given a few copies of the Koran by the Red Cross, but now we asked them to take them back. We could not protect them from the soldiers who often used them to punish us.'

There was more, much more, in the same vein: a woeful catalogue of abuse and suffering. Guantanamo was 'a graveyard of the living'. There were shades of a Second World War concentration camp in Zaeef's descriptions of prisoners who went mad under the appalling pressure of incarceration without apparent hope of release – or else were already mad at the time of their arrest. Camp Five, a solitary-confinement block set apart from the rest of the camps, became notorious. Human-rights monitors were seldom if ever allowed to inspect 'Grave Five', as some prisoners called it. 'Each brother who spent time in Camp Five looked like a skeleton when he was released; it was painful to look at their thin bodies.'

Just as at my last visit in 2007, the entrance to his Kabul house was under permanent police guard, complete with a little hut to provide shelter from the elements. Zaeef had been told that this was for his 'protection'. He had no doubt, however, that the hut's occupants were no ordinary policemen but agents of the National Directorate of Security, Afghanistan's Secret Service, who surreptitiously logged the identity of everyone who came and went. He was effectively living under a form of house arrest.

This did not mean that he lived in isolation. On the contrary, his *hujra* – the public reception room found in every Afghan home – was usually full of visitors. In 2007 I had sat down to lunch on his sunny porch with at least a dozen bearded and turbaned men. Then as now, Zaeef was visibly broke, but hospitality was an obligation among the Pashtuns and there was no economizing on it.

Cross-legged around a vinyl mat on the floor, the diners ate fast and in silence as was customary, attacking the mounds of rice and mutton with the dedication of the semi-starved. There was no doubt they were Taliban supporters – ex-fighters or administrators who had come to pay court to one of the movement's originals. My translator and I had left our driver in the street to guard the car, and I won a murmur of approval when I asked if some food could be taken out to him. Consideration for others, respect for inferiors, disdain for hierarchy: I had accidentally done a Pashtun thing. You could get a long way with the Taliban simply by minding your Ps and Qs.

These days, Zaeef was in so much demand that his house had not one but two hujras. At busy times he shuttled back and forth between them, running two discussions at once. At night, the rooms doubled as sleeping quarters for guests who had often travelled far to see him. It wasn't just Taliban supporters who came to visit now but the emissaries of foreign embassies, officials from the UN, as well as representatives of the government itself. Karzai might not have trusted Zaeef, but the truth was that he also needed him. If Quetta was ever to be brought to the negotiating table, as the President said he wanted, then Zaeef was reckoned by almost everybody to be the likeliest go-between.

Despite his travel ban, Zaeef had flown to Mecca in September 2008 for talks hosted by King Abdullah and which were attended by Karzai's older brother Qayyum. Other senior ex-Taliban figures living under UN sanctions were present, including the former Foreign Minister Wakil Ahmad Muttawakil. Zaeef did not explain how they were able to do this. Either the UN travel ban was not being enforced properly, or else someone at the UN had deliberately looked the other way. At least one newspaper described the meeting as 'historic',[5] although it was far from clear what was achieved in Mecca. The Quetta leadership was not directly represented. Zaeef claimed, to general disbelief, that the war in Afghanistan was not even discussed, and that he had only gone there to celebrate *iftar*, the traditional breaking of the fast during the month of Ramadan. Nevertheless, when the Mecca meeting became public knowledge, it opened the possibility of meaningful Kabul–Quetta dialogue for the first time.

It was mid-morning when we arrived at the house at Khoshal Khan Mina, but Zaeef had been up half the night in a meeting and was still asleep. He was yawning when he eventually appeared in hujra number one, where he curled himself up in a blanket, weary but still twinkly-eyed between his black turban and beard. There was nothing so mild about his words, though. If anything, his anger at the Americans had hardened rather than dissipated with the passage of time.

'In my last days as an ambassador in 2001, I sent an email to the world – to Congress, to all the embassies – warning that if you attack Afghanistan by force, you will lose,' he said. 'Nothing has changed. We are the same people.'

Whatever had been discussed in Mecca in 2008, he was in no mood to help negotiate a peace with the US now.

'Three years ago there was a possibility, but not now. The Americans talk of peace but they are not sincere. They want a long war, and then to force their conditions on us.'

'They don't want a long war,' I countered. 'They want it to end. General McChrystal feels, as a soldier, that there has been enough fighting. He has said a political settlement is inevitable.'

'So why are they still fighting? What are they doing in Marjah?'

'The point of the troop surge is to place the West in a position of strength from which to negotiate their exit.'

'But that makes no sense! The Americans are already in a position of strength. They have everything – the troop numbers, complete control of the air. We can't even move abroad!'

This wasn't quite true, of course, but I let it pass. The UN travel ban was still technically in effect, despite repeated pleas to lift it from many quarters, including from President Karzai himself. That these pleas were still being ignored illustrated Karzai's puppet status in the eyes of his Afghan opponents. To Zaeef and his circle the ban was a clumsy but humiliating symbol of Western power over them, and which proved once again that the US did not want to negotiate. Few believed it was really about the world's security interests. Although the sanction was authorized by the UN Security Council, Zaeef had no doubt that it would only ever be lifted on America's say-so.

'The Americans talk about justice,' he went on, 'but they are killing innocent people here almost every night. Is that justice?' He was leaning forward now, stabbing the coffee table with an index finger for emphasis, his eyes fixed on mine. 'When they make a mistake they offer $200 for each martyr in compensation, yet after the Lockerbie bombing the US demanded $100 million for every American killed! Tell me – is that justice? Are Afghans really so worthless in their eyes?'

I checked these startling figures later and found them to be only broadly correct, although Zaeef's point was still well made. ISAF's 'condolence fund' typically paid out $2,000 per innocent victim, not $200; while in 2003, Libya paid an astonishing $2.16 billion in compensation to the families of the 270 Lockerbie dead, or $8 million each. ISAF, of course, could not afford such generosity even if it wanted to. According to UNAMA (the United Nations Assistance Mission in Afghanistan) figures, 2,139 civilians were accidentally killed by 'pro-government forces' between 2006 and October 2009.[6] What Zaeef didn't say was that, according to the same source, almost twice as many civilians were killed by 'anti-government forces': 3,959 of them. But the fact remains that at Lockerbie rates, ISAF's condolence fund would have had to pay out over $17 billion.

The greatest cause for Afghan fury with Nato in the past had been the misapplication of airpower. With too few troops on the ground, ISAF tended to fall back on air support to get their men out of trouble – and bombs in built-up areas too often meant 'collateral damage'. There had been some truly horrendous incidents. In July 2008 in Herat province, for instance, an air strike killed forty-seven members of a wedding party. These were prone to misinterpretation by Westerners, because Afghans traditionally celebrate a marriage by shooting guns and RPGs into the air. In another high-profile incident in September 2009 in Kunduz, German troops called in US jets to destroy two stolen fuel transporters. The bombs killed at least forty villagers, possibly many more, who had approached the trucks hoping to siphon off some fuel for themselves. The German Defence Minister, Franz Josef Jung, allegedly suppressed this information at first, prompting calls for his resignation and a rethink of the entire German engagement in Afghanistan – which, considering that the Bundeswehr was the third biggest ISAF troop contributor, was significant.

Zaeef, however, was not complaining about Nato air-power but about 'night raids', the intelligence-driven, Special Forces operations designed to capture or kill insurgency leaders as they slept in their beds. This 'decapitation' strategy, as it was known, had been stepped up dramatically in recent months, but it came at a high cost to the hearts and minds campaign. A Pashtun's home is his castle, and for an infidel soldier to violate it, particularly its inner sanctum inhabited by women, is considered the grossest cultural insult. Entire communities had been radicalized as a result, even when the intelligence prompting the raid was accurate – which it all too frequently was not.

The Western press had recently reported a string of disasters. At 3 a.m. on 27 December 2009, for instance, a 'joint assault force' landed by helicopter outside the remote village of Ghazi Khan in Kunar province to destroy an alleged bomb-making cell. Ten people were shot dead, most of them at close range in their beds. A Nato statement initially claimed their forces had come under fire from several buildings as they entered the village, and had found a substantial arms cache and bomb-making equipment in the targeted house. Eight weeks later, a Nato official effectively admitted that this was a lie. The victims turned out to be entirely innocent. Eight of them were school-children, one of them as young as twelve.[7]

In another incident at Khataba village in Paktia on 12 February, two pregnant women, a teenage girl, a police officer and his brother were killed. A spokesman at General McChrystal's office initially said that the women had been 'tied up, gagged and killed' several hours before the raiders arrived. Eight weeks later, Nato officials admitted this was not the case. A senior Afghan investi-gator accused US Special Forces of a cover-up, even alleging that they had removed evidence by digging bullets out of the victims' bodies. 'I think the Special Forces lied to McChrystal,' he said. Nato promised a forensic investigation, but later said this had proved impossible because the bodies had been buried the same day in accordance with Islamic custom.[8]

McChrystal, to his credit, understood the pitfalls of night raids and the damage they could do to the US's reputation, and decreed in early 2010 that there would be no more of them unless absolutely necessary, and that they should be spearheaded by local forces if so: Afghan soldiers would in theory display a greater sense of Islamic propriety. 'Think of how you would expect a foreign army to operate in your neighborhood, among your families and your children, and act accordingly,' the general had told his troops in his *Counterinsurgency Guidance*. The night raids were continuing, however, along with official statements from Nato spokesmen seeking to justify them when they went wrong. I heard how misleading these could be for myself a few days later when I learned of another night raid, this time on a house in a village in Wardak province south of Kabul.* One man was shot and then savagely stabbed through the heart, while three others were arrested. From a distraught relative of the family, a friend of an Afghan friend of mine living in London, I learned (and was certain that it was true) that they were all shopkeepers and farmers, but the US military spokesman I telephoned claimed otherwise. He read from a text that was shocking in its brevity, his tone chillingly bland. The house, he said, had been occupied by a cell of fighters suspected of attacks on Coalition Forces; a substantial arms cache including RPGs was found; in the course of

---

* Makhdoma village, Chak district, Wardak, 01.00, 10 March 2010.

the operation, one man offered resistance and was killed.

The dead man had in fact been armed with a pistol, although this was hardly unusual in Afghanistan where the right to defend one's home is culturally enshrined. Besides, he had apparently offered no resistance at all. The detainees were all released without charge a few days later. Unlike the deadlier incidents in Kunar and Paktia, the affair went wholly unreported even in the local media. Such stories were so common they were no longer considered newsworthy.

Who was responsible? The Wardaki villagers claimed it was US Special Forces, although this was hard to prove. In the dark and confusion, no one had seen a uniform or insignia they could accurately describe later. US Special Forces were certainly involved in the Khataba incident, however. In an extraordinary scene on 8 April – and which proved that McChrystal's approach was having at least some small effect – Vice-Admiral William McRaven of USSOCOM, the US Special Operations Command, went to Khataba to apologize to the bereaved family.

'My heart grieves for you,' he told Hajji Sharabuddin, whose two sons had been killed in the raid. 'I pray today that [God] will show mercy on me and my men for this awful tragedy.' (Some of his address, in which he emphasized that he and Sharabuddin 'shared the same God', might have surprised the southern Baptists of his own country, although he was technically correct: Muslims, Christians and indeed Jews all believe in the god of

Abraham; Allah, Jehovah and Yahweh are the same person.) Then he underlined the point by handing over a carefully wrapped handkerchief that turned out to contain almost $30,000 – triple the usual compensation rate. Outside on Hajji Sharabuddin's doorstep, the Afghan soldiers accompanying McRaven offered to slaughter a sheep, the traditional act of atonement according to the Pashtunwali.

It was a brave effort. For such a senior commander to apologize in person in this way was without precedent. Even so, the ugly suspicion remained in Kabul that the Special Forces were only paying lip service to McChrystal's attempts to rein in the night raiders. An investigation by the *Washington Post* later revealed that upon taking office, President Obama had secretly approved a huge increase in the number of 'black ops' search-and-destroy missions. After September 2009, when General Petraeus signed a Joint Unconventional Warfare Task Force Executive Order, the number of special operations teams in Afghanistan doubled. Out of 13,000 US Special Forces deployed overseas, some 4,500 are in Afghanistan, with a similar number operating in Pakistan; they are now thought to be responsible for more than half of all combat operations in the Afghan warzone.[9]

In a speech in Washington, Vice-Admiral McRaven's boss, Admiral Eric Olson, the head of USSOCOM, revealed that his men were still being instructed in 'direct action' techniques that included 'man-hunting, killing and capturing the enemy' – or as he called it, '*habeas grabus*'.[10] Although Olson also acknowledged the greater importance of soft power, or 'indirect action', to the counter-insurgency, it seemed that McChrystal was struggling to turn the oil-tanker of American military culture – and for many Afghans it was simply a case of too little, too late. Hajji Sharabuddin told a reporter that he was happy McRaven had come, but nothing would bring back his dead sons or the pregnant women who had been killed. 'I don't care about the money,' he told a reporter. What he really wanted was for the 'spy' who had told the Americans his family were Taliban to be brought to justice. 'When they surrender the spy, then I will make a decision. Maybe I will forgive them,' he said.[11]

Another of McChrystal's problems was that not all forces in Afghanistan came under his command: not even all the American ones. Many shadowy 'private contractors' – little more than mercenary units – were known to be at large. The CIA had over eight hundred operatives in the country complete with their own air force, yet they answered not to McChrystal but directly to headquarters in Langley, Virginia. The CIA programme of 'targeted assassinations' using Predator drones armed with Hellfire missiles had been dramatically stepped up since Obama came to office, particularly in Pakistan's tribal areas. In 2009, for the first time, the US Air Force spent more on training drone controllers than it did on conventional aircraft pilots. Leon Panetta, the director of the CIA, called the programme 'the only game in town'. It was no game for those living near the targets, however. For all the technical wizardry of the launch platform, a missile was still a missile and often anything but 'surgical' in what it struck. One respected Washington think-tank calculated that in Pakistan alone since 2004, fully a third of the estimated 800 to 1,200 people killed by drones were innocent civilians.[12]

As the Pakistani lawyer (and the first Pakistani president of the Cambridge Union) Shahpur Kabraji wrote: 'We know that elements of the civilian population in Pakistan and Afghanistan are harbouring militants. It is equally undeniable that this civilian population is unlikely to feel any sympathy whatsoever for the political aims of Washington when the only face of those aims they see is the business end of a Hellfire missile. These populations must be convinced that by harbouring terrorists within their community, they undermine their own chances for peace and prosperity ... but when hundreds are also killed as "collateral damage", it is not surprising that the message is lost. Kill one innocent farmer, create a village of anti-Americans.'[13]

There was another problem with the 'decapitation' policy, even when Nato's intelligence was accurate, which was that it seemed to have no effect on the insurgency. By 2010, half of the ten-man leadership council, or shura, appointed by Omar in Quetta in 2003 were captured or dead, including the Taliban's greatest tactician, Mullah Dadullah, who was killed in fighting in

Helmand in 2007. And yet the level of resistance had done nothing but increase. The Taliban had no shortage of people willing to step into dead men's shoes. Most of them were younger men, a significant number of whom had been radicalized by the experience of Guantanamo – the kind of leaders who were even less likely to agree to the negotiation that McChrystal said he ultimately sought. The policy was therefore self-defeating: an effective tactic in the short term, perhaps, but potentially disastrous for the long-term strategy. Many senior Nato commanders understood this. One British general told me in early 2010: 'Every time I hear about another hit on a Taliban leader, I wonder if we haven't just killed a McGuinness or an Adams.' But if McChrystal could not control the CIA, what chance was there for an officer in the British Army?

Finally, ISAF control over their most useful Afghan allies in the field – the agents of the Tajik-dominated NDS – was loose, at best. In Kabul it was hinted that it was Afghans who had spearheaded the disastrous Kunar night raid.

'Incidents such as this do not reflect any conduct that ISAF would condone, and it is not the way ISAF trains any of our Afghan partners,' a Nato spokesman commented.[14]

That sounded like buck-passing to the average Afghan, however. It was McChrystal's decree, after all, that had just put ISAF's 'partners' in the lead on night raid operations. It seemed the general was damned whatever he did, because in most people's eyes, and certainly in Zaeef's, it was always 'the Americans' who were at fault in the end.

My conversation with Zaeef turned, as it so often did in Afghanistan, to 9/11 and Osama bin Laden.

'The war is all about America's sense of security,' I said. 'If the West could be sure that al-Qaida will not return to Afghanistan, I'm sure we would leave.'

Zaeef nodded his agreement. 'The US has only one right here: to receive a guarantee that no country will ever be attacked from within these borders. Just as we have the right not to be attacked by the US in future. Sovereignty should be respected. If there are to be negotiations, these guarantees should be their focus.'

'And can the Taliban make such a guarantee?'

'Mullah Omar would set it in stone.'

From the way he looked at me I had no doubt that Zaeef really believed this. Perhaps it was true. But it did not answer the West's concern that the Taliban was such a disparate organization these days that Omar was no longer in full control of it. Taliban-allied groups such as the Haqqani Network in the central eastern districts were often said to operate almost autonomously of Quetta. If Omar promised to freeze out al-Qaida, would these groups necessarily follow? In the end, believers like Zaeef could only give their word for it.

'The Taliban are more united than ever,' he said levelly. 'No one has ever disobeyed an order from the

Amir ul-Mu'mineen. We know that the unity among us is our strength.'

This was as may be. There was plenty of evidence that Mullah Omar was concerned that his commanders were sometimes guilty of departing from the Taliban script. The leadership understood just as well as ISAF that the real battlefield was in the hearts and minds of the people, and that cruelty or unIslamic behaviour among its own troops could only damage the Taliban cause.

In July 2009, almost simultaneously with General McChrystal's *Counterinsurgency Guidance*, Quetta published and distributed its own notes on correct comportment in the field. This small blue pocket book, entitled *The Islamic Emirate of Afghanistan's Rules for Mujahideen*, provided a fascinating insight both into how Mullah Omar saw his movement and how he thought the insurgency was going. The cover bore a splendid pictogram, almost a heraldic coat of arms, showing a tower with a staircase leading to a copy of the Koran that radiated light. The tower was flanked by a pair of curved scimitars and – more surprisingly – two large ears of wheat. The rulebook's sixty-seven articles were arranged into thirteen chapters, and dealt with everything from civil administration and dispute resolution to the correct procedure in kidnaps, as well as regulations on dress, haircuts and smoking. It was a document specifically designed to stamp out any 'freelance' interpretation of the Taliban's core values and thus to re-establish Quetta's supreme authority over the movement: a powerful reminder of who was in charge of the insurgency.

While demonstrating that the Taliban certainly had internal problems, this was hardly the work of an organization on the back foot, as ISAF spokesmen so often claimed. Of particular interest was the section on 'Unity', which stated: 'Creating a new mujahideen group or battalion is forbidden. If unofficial groups or irregular battalions refuse to join the formal structure, they should be disbanded.' The section on suicide attacks and civilian casualties was also significant, not least for the similarity of its language to what the Americans were saying: 'Governors, District Chiefs, line commanders, and every member of the mujahideen must do their utmost to avoid civilian deaths, injuries and the destruction of civilian property. Great care must be taken. If they are careless, all persons will be punished.'

Zaeef and I talked for over an hour about what Afghanistan would look like if the Taliban were to have their way again. Their ambitions for government, he confirmed, were unchanged.

'We never had the intention of running the country before, and nor do we now,' he said. 'We have no intention of destroying this government, either – only to *repair* it.' It was a word that he and other Taliban I was to meet used often. 'Mullah Omar issued a press release repeating this last year. First we want to get you foreigners out. Then we want to repair the Constitution.'

I argued that it was impossible for ISAF simply to withdraw as the Russians had done, because that would send a message around the world that Western arms had been defeated here, offering potentially disastrous encouragement to extremists everywhere. A withdrawal would therefore have to be negotiated, phased, carefully orchestrated.

'This is about Western pride! As a Pashtun, surely you understand this. There has to be some kind of face-saving formula.'

'It's not for us to salvage the West's reputation,' he said sourly. 'You started this war, not us.'

Crucially, Zaeef was candid about the 'political mistakes' the regime had made before it was ousted in 2001. 'We didn't know what we were doing then. We learned a great deal. It will be different the next time.'

The way he saw it, the Taliban were still in the process of completing their project, disarming the people and dealing with the warlords, when they were cruelly ejected from power. Far from being oppressors, an army of southern Pashtuns imposing their customs and values on the reluctant minorities, he said the Taliban had diffused ethnic tensions and were the 'uniters' of Afghanistan. Given just a little more time, he argued, even the West would have seen the benefits of their revolution.

'In 1995 the country was falling apart, splitting into mini-kingdoms. Look what Dostum was doing in the north. He was operating a different currency to the rest of the country! And look at all the tension and fighting and human misery then. The reality is that we rescued Afghanistan.'

'But the Taliban committed many atrocities. In the Hazarajat, in Mazar, on the Shomali plains.'

'That is Western justification for their war. It is the blackest propaganda! I challenge you to find a single Hazara in Kabul with proof that we slaughtered any of them.'

'They might complain about Baba Mazari,' I said.

Abdul Ali Mazari had been the revered leader of the Hazara Hizb-i-Wahdat party; a famous mujahideen commander as well as an ardent advocate of a federal solution for Afghanistan. He was popularly held to have been invited to talks with the conquering Taliban in 1995, betrayed, and thrown to his death from a helicopter over Ghazni.

'Mazari was not murdered. We were taking him to Kandahar but he tried to refuse. He grabbed a gun and began shooting! What were our soldiers supposed to do?'

'So would you be willing to share power with the non-Pashtuns next time?'

'But we shared power with them the last time! Our Minister of Education was a Tajik. The Minister of Planning, even our Minister for the Hajj, were Uzbek. The Governors of Paktia and Khost – *Pashtun* provinces – were also Uzbek. The Governor of Wardak was Badakshani! I promise you that we have no problem with other ethnicities, only with certain individuals who abused their own ethnic groups: the criminals, the warlords.'

It was true that the Taliban had never set out to

'ethnically cleanse' the country in the way that, for example, the Serbs had done in Bosnia in the early 1990s. Mullah Omar had in fact attempted to reach a compromise with Massoud and to put an end to the violence. Zaeef represented Omar at two separate meetings with the Tajiks, the first of them in 1998, when he met Massoud personally. The meeting took place in the middle of the night, deep in Tajik-controlled territory north of Bagram.

'We spread out our *patus* with only the light of the moon to guide us, and sat down underneath a tree in the middle of nowhere,' Zaeef recalled in his autobiography.

Omar respected Massoud as a fellow former mujahid from Jihad days, and recognized and was prepared to grant Massoud's right to share political power with the Pashtuns. But this was not enough for Massoud, who wanted to share military power as well, through the setting up of a joint 'military council'. This was a step too far for the Taliban: a recipe, as Zaeef explained, 'for further clashes and bloodshed'. Unity, he told Massoud, 'does not mean who is going to lead – the north or the south – but rather, unity means that the interests of the nation are at the centre of all decisions.' The two sides never surmounted this obstacle, although the possibility of a negotiated peace remained open right up until 2001.

'The most astonishing part of these talks for me was the knowledge that both sides in fact agreed that war was not the solution,' said Zaeef. 'We all knew that the

241

Afghan people were tired of war and wanted peace, but nevertheless war continued and no solution was found.'

Zaeef in the end was a patriot, a believer in the Afghan nation, and his conviction on this point surprised me. The Taliban were often said to be fighting to re-establish Pashtun hegemony in Afghanistan, yet Zaeef was quite unambiguous about the need to share political power.

'Afghanistan cannot be controlled by one group, it belongs to all Afghans,' he said.

Federalism, he maintained, a solution often mooted by minority leaders like the late Baba Mazari, would lead to 'deep chaos', the disintegration of a country with a 5,000-year history, and the weakening and 'enslavement' of its constituent peoples by rapacious regional neighbours like Iran and Pakistan. He also rejected the creation of a separate Pashtun state, the fabled 'Pashtunistan' that would unite the Pashtun lands on either side of the Durand Line. Pashtunistan was a notion that had long terrified Islamabad, because if it ever came to pass, Pakistan's borders would logically be pushed back as far east as the River Indus – a loss of thousands of square kilometres of territory. Zaeef, though, was adamant. The Taliban did not want a new Pashtun state, or even, necessarily, Pashtun domination of the existing one. What they stood for was the establishment of Sharia within the existing borders of their country, and nothing more.

There was, he insisted again, no threat to Western security interests in this ambition. The over-riding problem was Washington's blindness to this fact.

'They should draw a line. They should not be oppressors – they should not ask for so much.'

The war against the Taliban was, to him, entirely an American war. The fact that ISAF contained troops from thirty-seven other nations was merely window-dressing.

'America's partners have been told this is a war of necessity for the international community, when in reality it is a war of choice.'

Everything, in his view, was ultimately the fault of America. The US was not only opposed to Afghan interests directly, by waging war against the Taliban, but also indirectly through its involvement in the three proxy wars going on in his country. These he identified as Pakistan versus India, the US versus Iran, and al-Qaida versus the World. If America carried on in this way, he warned, then the Taliban insurgency could develop into something much more serious for them.

'I wrote to President Obama last year, and to your Gordon Brown. I explained that it wasn't arms that defeated the Soviets, it was the people's sense of foreign oppression – and it will be the same for you.'

Contrary to common belief, the Taliban were not yet fighting an anti-Western jihad – at least, not technically. The correct interpretation of the Koranic concept of *jihad*, literally 'striving' or 'struggle', but often translated as 'Holy War', is still much debated by Islamic scholars. *Al-jihad fi sabil Allah*, 'striving in the way of Allah', can denote an internal struggle of the conscience as well as the external fight against infidels. Either way, it becomes the religious duty of all Muslims once it has been declared in its external sense – as of course it was against the Soviets in the 1980s. A Muslim engaged in it is called a *mujahid*, a 'struggler for freedom'. In Afghanistan, thankfully, jihad can only be declared with the agreement of the ulema, the country's foremost religious scholars – a Pashtun-dominated group number-ing perhaps four thousand, and who traditionally do not take lightly their responsibilities as the nation's ultimate moral arbiters. The criteria for jihad are strict. When Mullah Omar called for one against the Kabul govern-ment in 1995, the ulema refused, principally on the grounds that a jihad should not be waged against other believers, let alone one's fellow countrymen. In the end they compromised and sanctioned a jihad against what the Taliban called *shar-i-fasad* – evil and corruption.

The point was that, according to Zaeef, the 'Taliban' were increasingly abandoning that label in favour of an older one: they were beginning to call themselves 'mujahideen' again, or as the title of the new blue rule-book more accurately had it, 'the Mujahideen' of 'the Islamic Emirate of Afghanistan', with Mullah Omar as the Emir. The very word 'mujahideen' remains a highly emotive term for Afghans, recalling as it instantly does the glory days of the 1980s. Soon, Zaeef was implying, Omar might not need the endorsement of the ulema. Public anger at the West's presence was reaching such a pitch that the insurgency could become a jihad against the Americans almost by osmosis – and if that happened, he said, all the country, not just the Taliban, would unite to eject the infidels, just as they had the Russians. America was in danger of waking a sleeping monster.

'The mood is changing now. The window of opportunity, the last chance for peace, is closing.'

This wasn't just rhetoric. Different types of Afghan were indeed already making common cause against the foreigners. Back in Britain earlier that month, Channel 4's *Dispatches* had aired a remarkable report by the Afghan journalist Najibullah Quraishi, who had embedded himself with a group of insurgents operating in the northern province of Kunduz. He lived with them for days as they planned and then executed an IED attack on an American convoy on the main road that runs south from Tajikistan – an increasingly important supply route for ISAF because it is considered 'safer' than the traditional one from Pakistan through the Khyber Pass.

Quraishi's hosts were not Taliban. They wore the clothes and turbans of northern Pashtuns, and when pressed they professed loyalty not to Mullah Omar but to the fugitive Hizb-i-Islami leader, Gulbuddin Hekmatyar. And yet they shared precisely the same principal motivation for fighting.

'We have to resist,' a commander explained to Quraishi. 'Jihad has become the duty for all Afghans, because the foreigners and unbeliever countries have attacked us.'

The conviction in his eyes was unambiguous. This was

a man fighting what he believed really was a war of necessity, not of choice. And his followers, strikingly, described themselves as mujahideen. An Afghan friend in London, an old refugee from Mazar, also saw the *Dispatches* programme and recognized the commander of the Kunduz group as the son of a friend of his. 'I know that boy!' he told me. 'I knew his father! We fought the Russians together. The son is doing exactly what the father did, liberating Afghanistan from the infidel invaders. There is no difference.'

It wasn't hard to understand why Zaeef felt as he did towards the Americans. The pages of his newly published autobiography burned with righteous anger. And yet there was an odd tendency among some Westerners to dismiss Zaeef's book, as though the emotion he displayed somehow negated the message within it. One senior diplomat told me he thought the power of its arguments had been 'spoiled' by the anti-American 'rant' towards the book's end. Ambassadors, it is true, do not normally describe the most powerful nation on earth as 'dogs' and 'slaves'. But then, ambassadors are not normally treated like Zaeef, who still has trouble walking properly thanks to the beatings he received. So long as President Obama's 2009 election promise to close Guantanamo remains unfulfilled, criticizing Zaeef's intemperate language missed the point.

The tough line taken against 'enemy combatants' at Guantanamo seemed almost designed to crush their spirit of resistance, but if anything it has had the precise opposite effect. Even American intelligence officials estimated that 20 per cent of repatriated prisoners had rejoined the insurgency; they also admitted that the number of ex-inmates in the insurgency was steadily increasing.[15] One Afghan Taliban expert suggested that up to half of the insurgency's mid-level commanders were former Guantanamo inmates. These were members of a younger generation who had not necessarily had anything to do with the movement before 2001: people who, as the expert put it, had 'looked into the belly of the beast', experienced the 'reality' of the American system, and been so appalled by what they had seen that they had come home to take up arms against it.

Among these people was Mullah Zakir, also known as Mullah Abdul Qayyum, who was released from Guantanamo in December 2007.

'I want to go back home and join my family and work in my land and help my family,' Zakir reportedly told his captors.

Two weeks after my meeting with Zaeef, however, Zakir was revealed as the new Taliban military commander in the south of the country, responsible for operations in six provinces. His deputy, former corps commander Abdul Rauf, had also spent time at Guantanamo.

Zakir was a well-known hawk: 'smart and brutal', according to one Helmandi who knew him.[16] It was not insignificant that at the end of 2008, on behalf of Mullah

Omar, Zakir led a delegation to the Tehrik-i-Taliban Pakistan (TTP), the umbrella movement of the Pakistani Taliban, in a bid to persuade them to put aside differences and help the Afghan Taliban to combat the US presence in Afghanistan.[17] Omar had traditionally been wary of the TTP, whose overt anti-Islamabad agenda was not only different, but dangerous to the Afghan Taliban. Omar's headquarters were in Quetta, and his ability to operate there depended on keeping in with the ISI. Now, however, there was renewed speculation that military expediency was driving the TTP and the Afghan Taliban together again – and Zakir's re-emergence in the south tended to confirm that.

The radicalizing experience of Guantanamo was at the root of so many of Afghanistan's troubles. Two days after Zakir's appointment became known, arrest warrants were issued for a number of high-profile ex-Guantanamo inmates living in Kabul – including Zaeef. It was not a subtle response, and Zaeef was predictably enraged. Only the Americans, he thought, were capable of so clunking a reminder of who was really in control. He was saved from being thrown in jail once again by a last-minute intervention from someone high up in the government, perhaps by Karzai himself. Nevertheless, the ambivalence of his status, the tenuousness of his freedom, was once again all too obvious. No wonder he hated the Americans so much.

10

The Trouble with President Karzai

The year 2009 will likely be remembered as a turning point for the West in Afghanistan – or perhaps as a year of opportunities to alter our failing strategy tragically missed. The first of these was the Afghan presidential election in August. Since early 2007 at least, Western leaders such as David Richards, the new head of the British Army, had looked forward to a successful exercise in democracy which would demonstrate, both to Western capitals and to the Afghans themselves, that the Coalition was at last making progress. Better governance and an end to the corruption in Kabul were seen – as they still are – as the key to turning Afghan hearts and minds away from the insurgency. If President Karzai was so bad, the people would surely speak, and remove him from office; the benefits of democracy, the West's great gift to the world, would be proven once and for all.

This totemic election was an almost unmitigated

disaster. The polls, organized at a cost to the international community of at least $300 million,[1] were marred by massive fraud on all sides, though most of all by Karzai, who was definitively revealed as a man far more interested in retaining his position than in the principles of democracy. Nearly a quarter of all votes cast, some 1.26 million of them, were thrown out as fraudulent. Voter turn-out, at about 30 per cent nationally, was low enough to bring Karzai's mandate into question even before adjustments were made for the cheating. In parts of the south, where ISAF mounted a major security operation codenamed Panther's Claw – the pre-stated aim of which was to allow voters to go to the polls unmolested – the turn-out was almost non-existent. In Babaji district in Helmand, four British soldiers died for the sake of just 150 votes.

In any Western democracy, the results would have been scrapped and the voters sent back to the polls. Not in Afghanistan. Security, logistics and credibility considerations ensured that plans to rerun the election were quickly scrapped – and when Karzai's principal challenger, Abdullah Abdullah, declined to enter a run-off, Karzai was returned to power with the West's reluctant support, on condition that he tackled what he called 'the cancer of corruption' within his administration. Six months later, however, Karzai had failed even to form a government, after the nominations for his Cabinet were twice rejected by the Majlis, or Lower House. This at least demonstrated that the country's democratic institutions were functioning, but did not alter the fact that instead of better governance and a programme of reform, the 2009 election brought governmental paralysis.

You can lead a horse to water, but you cannot make it drink. The West handed Karzai the tools to entrench democracy in his country, and he squandered them. Seventy per cent of the electorate also declined, for whatever reason, to take up the offer of a say in how they are governed. If ever there was a moment for the West to admit that its Afghan nation-building strategy was not working and to try a different approach, the failure of the 2009 election was it. Indeed, the world spent much of 2009 waiting for Barack Obama, who at the end of 2008 replaced George Bush and his neo-con administration that had begun the whole sorry saga with their invasion in 2001, to announce exactly that. But the US military had other ideas, and persuaded Obama to go for a troop surge instead. With this decision, a second opportunity for a real change of strategy was missed.

In March 2010, President Obama and the then Chairman of the Joint Chiefs of Staff, Admiral Mike Mullen, flew into Kabul to upbraid President Karzai for his lack of progress in tackling corruption. According to Mullen, the long-term success of the military campaign in the south was entirely dependent on the issue, particularly in Kandahar, ISAF's next publicly announced objective, where the Provincial Council was headed by the President's half-brother Ahmed Wali Karzai.

Ahmed Wali had long been accused of controlling the local heroin trade, as well as of flagrant ballot-rigging to help the re-election of his half-brother in 2009. Since 2006 at least, every Western plea to remove Ahmed Wali from office had been rebuffed by the President, who doggedly demanded 'evidence'. The West seemed unable to produce anything other than anecdotes, however, which naturally gave rise to all sorts of conspiracy theories in Kabul. It certainly did not help the Western case that Ahmed Wali was said to have been on the CIA payroll for years.[2]

In November 2009 the NGO Transparency International published its annual Corruption Perceptions Index, which measures the perceived level of public-sector corruption in 180 countries around the world. Afghanistan came in 179th. This was three places lower than in 2008, lower even than Haiti, Iraq and Myanmar; only Somalia was worse. Everyone agreed that corruption was the disease killing the country. The Taliban argued that they and not the Karzais were the cure, and even their opponents had to concede that they could hardly do any worse.

Eight months into his new term, Karzai had attempted just one reform: the emasculation of the Election Complaints Commission, the one institution that had tried to keep the electoral fraud in check. In the past, three of the five commissioners had been selected by the United Nations. Karzai now proposed, by presidential decree, to appoint all five of them himself.

He needed the endorsement of Parliament to turn his decree into law, however, and his MPs refused to grant this. Karzai's self-interest was too brazen even for them. The presidential response was bizarre. Instead of rounding on his MPs he lashed out at the West, declaring that it was not Afghans but foreigners who had perpetrated the greatest fraud of 2009. In three successive outbursts he specifically accused the US, Britain, the UN, the EU, CNN, the BBC and several Western newspapers of conniving at his removal from power while claiming to uphold the principles of democracy.

The strings controlling this puppet were tangled. Sometimes when an arm was pulled, a leg kicked. It had happened before, as in 2007 when Karzai launched an emotional tirade against misapplied ISAF airpower, and wept on camera for the innocent Afghan children that had been killed. He himself had almost been killed in 2001 when a US Special Forces air controller accidentally guided a 2,000lb bomb on to the spot where he was standing; the nervous tic that appeared in his eye at times of stress was a legacy of his injuries. But this incident was even more serious. By revealing his true feelings towards his American backers, Karzai insulted the memories of the hundreds of foreign soldiers who had died in support of his government, and was in danger of alienating not just the long-suffering State Department but, far graver, American public opinion. On John Stewart's *Daily Show*, the satirical television 'news show with attitude', Karzai was being called a 'turncloak'. Had the

President really 'lost it', as his main rival for the presidency Dr Abdullah claimed?

Not everyone thought Karzai's accusation was unjustified. Even Kai Eide, the former UN envoy, thought there had been undue foreign interference in the 2009 election process – a view that won him few friends among the international community, some of whom took to nicknaming him 'Al Kai-Eide'. He singled out the decision by US Special Representative Richard Holbrooke to urge a large number of Afghans, including senior presidential advisers, to run against Karzai. Holbrooke spoke at the time of creating a 'fair playing field', but it didn't seem very fair to most Afghans, and to the President least of all. 'People should listen to what [Karzai] is saying,' said one of the President's aides. 'These are issues he has had on his mind for a long, long time.'[3]

In his first outburst, Karzai accused the foreigners of 'pursuing their own interests' while claiming to want to help Afghanistan, adding that 'a very thin curtain distinguishes between cooperation and assistance with the invasion'. His terminology was highly provocative. As he well knew, the foreigners were no longer 'invaders' but had stayed on at his government's express invitation, and with a mandate from the UN. In the same speech he warned of the possibility of 'national resistance'. What did that mean: was he talking about the threat of jihad that Mullah Zaeef had spoken of? Later, in a speech to MPs in Kandahar, Karzai offered a clarification of sorts:

'If I come under foreign pressure, I might join the Taliban,' he said.

A Taliban spokesman was quick to scoff at the suggestion. 'If he really wants to join [. . .] he should face justice first,' said Zabiullah Mujahid. 'He should face justice for bringing foreign troops to Afghanistan. He should face justice for all the crime that has happened during his rule, and for the corruption and for what is going on now. Then we'll decide whether we will join with him or not.'[4] This rebuff wasn't of much comfort to Washington, however. A White House spokesman described Karzai's remarks as 'genuinely troubling'.

The Americans could hardly forget that their strategic partner had once been a supporter of their great enemy. In 1995 Mullah Omar even offered him the post of ambassador to the UN, although Karzai turned it down and later broke with the movement, telling friends that he suspected – accurately – that it was being manipulated by the ISI.[5] But this did not necessarily mean he was unsympathetic towards their goals. 'There were many wonderful people in the Taliban,' he told the *Washington Post* in 1998.[6] When Karzai described the Taliban as his 'disenchanted brothers', as he did at the London Conference twelve years later, did he mean the term 'brothers' literally? His own sense of disenchantment was certainly now more than clear.

In 2009 as the world waited for Obama's response to McChrystal's request for more troops, the US Vice-President Joe Biden had argued against the surge precisely because he felt Karzai could not be trusted. He was supported by the US ambassador to Kabul, Karl Eikenberry, a retired general who had served two tours of duty in Afghanistan, and who had warned Hillary Clinton, the Secretary of State, that Karzai was 'not an adequate strategic partner'. In Washington it was beginning to look as if Biden and Eikenberry might have been right.

For all the sophistication of the way Karzai presented himself to the West – the cleverly assembled outfit, his mastery of seven languages, the statesmanlike manner, his looks and his native charm – his was no doubt a case of once a Pashtun, always a Pashtun, whose instincts were perhaps not nearly as liberal or modernizing as some of his backers would like. In April 2008, Karzai remained unaccountably silent when a 23-year-old journalism student, Sayed Parwez Kaambakhsh from Mazar, was sentenced to death by a local court for 'insulting Islam'. Kaambakhsh's only crime was to have circulated an article taken from an Iranian website questioning why Muslim women cannot have multiple husbands in the same way as their menfolk can legally take four wives. He had no legal representation at his trial, which was held in secret. Yet Karzai refused to intervene even when the death sentence was upheld by the Upper House of Parliament.[7] Similarly, just before his re-election, Karzai was accused of backing a con-stitutional amendment that appeared to forbid women from refusing to have sex with their husbands. The *Daily*

Mail, in an article entitled 'As Bad as the Taliban?',[8] quoted a spokesperson for the United Nations Development Fund for Women who described the amendment as 'the legalization of rape in marriage'.

Was the President acting from a need to curry favour with his fundamentalist supporters? Or did he partially or privately agree with this kind of extreme conservatism? Perhaps it was a complex mixture of the two? His signals were never clear. Some suspected that he took pleasure at times in deliberately antagonizing the West. Others looked for clues in his private life. It was often said that his wife, Zenat Qureishi, an experienced gynaecologist before she married, was forbidden in the traditional Pashtun way to leave the Presidential Palace without his permission. Afghanistan's educated First Lady was potentially a valuable asset if the President was serious about improving women's rights, but for whatever reason she remained well out of the media's reach.

It was hard in some respects not to pity Karzai, for his position between West and East, Nato and the Taliban, was an almost impossible balancing act to maintain. Mullah Zaeef described him as an almost tragic figure, a man who woke up every morning 'between the tiger and the precipice, never knowing which way to turn'. The pair had met a number of times since 2006, always at the invitation of the President. 'We sparred verbally, but tried to find a solution together,' he recalled in his book. 'It is quite an enigma, and it is hard to see who can cut this knot.' He certainly did not dislike him personally:

'One can feel that he is not a cruel man. He would not consider killing someone or throwing him in jail.' Nevertheless, he thought Karzai was hopelessly out of his depth as a leader, 'unable to differentiate between friend and enemy, because he did not come to power the way he should have, through slow, difficult steps.' As a consequence he was a man as much sinned against as sinning, a kind of Afghan King Lear: 'He is imprisoned within a circle of people that keeps him far from the truth, and the information he seems to get is very weak and often has nothing to do with reality. But he relies on this information, and it results in inappropriate action.'

In the end, though, Zaeef held Karzai in contempt. Although not a cruel man, the President was still responsible for the cruelties of his 'guests', the foreigners, and was guilty by association. 'He could condemn those actions, but he is caught up in politics. He loves power, and wants to stay where he is.' Or, as the Taliban spokesman Zabiullah Mujahid put it: 'It's just a game he is playing. He is trying to show people he is not under the control of the Americans, but it's completely false.'

11

Getting Rich Quick in Tajik Kabul

Many Kabulis I met complained that they had seen no
benefit from the billions of aid dollars that had
supposedly been spent in their country. Eight years into
the post-Taliban era, it was true that most public buildings, such as the National Library or the Academy of
Science where I had met the Pashtun history professor,
Ustad Rafeh, remained depressingly dilapidated.
Meanwhile, the ever-worsening condition of the city's
traffic-clogged roads provided daily evidence of civic
mismanagement and, it was always cynically inferred,
corruption. As a Kabuli friend muttered: 'If the Taliban
had had as much money as Karzai has, everything round
here would be made of gold by now.' Instead, after rain,
every road surface was covered with a skin of brown
slime that refused to drain away. It was little better when
the sun came out, for then the roads dried and the slime
was turned into clouds of choking dust. Where they

existed at all, pavements were often dug up and completely impassable, even in the prestigious embassy district in Wazir Akhbar Khan, where pedestrians hopped between stepping stones in shirt hems and sandals permanently caked in filth.

Those foreign billions had gone somewhere, however, and the general sense of grievance, which always seemed strongest among the city's Pashtun community, was accentuated by conspicuous pockets of free enterprise that dotted the city and which always seemed to be owned by Tajiks. Kabul had always been dominated by the Persian-speaking Tajiks, the second largest ethnic group in the country. They traditionally worked as merchants, bureaucrats, doctors and teachers – a kind of urban middle class to the rural Pashtun aristocracy. In many cases the new Tajik wealth was shamelessly flaunted, most conspicuously in the concentrations of flashy villas that had sprung up around the city centre.

Allegations of corruption clustered especially thickly around Marshal Fahim, an ethnic Tajik born in the Panjshir valley, from where his friend and co-commander Ahmed Shah Massoud had mounted his famous resistance against the Russians in the 1980s. On Massoud's death and the fall of the Taliban he became the Defence Minister, a position he was soon accused of abusing by packing the army's ranks with Tajik fighters. This may have been the least of his sins. In 2002 the CIA, who had paid Fahim millions of dollars to ensure his support during the invasion period, were shocked to discover that their protégé was still deeply involved in narcotics trafficking, even running a private cargo plane over the border with Tajikistan. He was also accused of treating the Panjshiri emerald-mining industry almost as a private asset, with the profits said to have been stashed in a string of secret Dubai bank accounts. Fahim was removed as Defence Minister in 2004, but he remained a powerful and deeply divisive figure who has survived at least four assassination attempts since 2002. According to Mullah Zaeef, men like him had 'a vested interest in keeping the Taliban out, and perpetuating the war'. His luxurious home in the capital, he added, belonged to a Pashtun businessman evicted after he was accused of supporting the Taliban.

In 1994 as head of the Tajik-dominated KHAD, the hated Soviet-era secret service, Fahim had once arrested and interrogated Hamid Karzai on suspicion of his being a spy for the ISI. Despite this, Karzai chose him as his running mate in the 2009 presidential elections – a choice roundly condemned by the NGO Human Rights Watch.

'To see Fahim back in the heart of government [is] a terrible step backwards for Afghanistan,' said one of its directors, Brad Adams. 'He is one of the most notorious warlords in the country, with the blood of many Afghans on his hands from the civil war.'

Afghanistan often made strange bedfellows of its politicians. Perhaps Karzai calculated that it was better to keep this enemy close than to have him plotting from the outside. At any rate, he was used to vigorously defending his former tormentor in public. In 2006 he described him as his 'dear brother ... No one can ever reduce the respect that Marshal Fahim has earned for himself.'[1]

The new 'Gulbahar Shopping Center', a block of gaudy greens and yellows near the Foreign Ministry, provided a more prosaic illustration of Tajik advantage in Kabul. It was named after a town at the foot of the Panjshir valley, while the American spelling of 'Center' gave a good indication of who and what was really driving the city's wartime economy. The entrance was guarded as heavily as a government ministry – armed policemen in balaclavas, sandbags, a machine-gun-topped Humvee stationed across the street – but beyond the body-friskers and bag-checkers lay a different world. There were four floors of shops arranged around a lofty atrium where fountains and piped music played. There was a children's play area equipped with a dozen penny-rides, and a shoot'em-up games arcade for the teenagers. The floors were all of marble, and a flashing glass elevator glided up and down. At first glance this unlikely vision of the new Afghanistan looked as sharp and clean as any shopping mall in Dubai.

The sparkle, though, was on the surface. The better shop sites near the entrance were occupied, but deeper inside a good third of the retail space had yet to be let. It was Thursday lunchtime, a peak shopping period, yet there were few customers around. There was also a shabbiness to this aspiring temple of consumerism that would have jarred in the Gulf. Bare electric wires protruded here and there, and the plasterwork showed signs of premature decay. It was in the end an Afghan approximation of prosperity, not the real thing. The goods on display – hi-fi equipment, the latest mobile phones, glitzy jewellery, gleaming household appliances – were beyond the means of perhaps 95 per cent of the people of Afghanistan.

Judging by facial shapes and the clean-shaven chins on display, the shoppers here were almost all Tajiks. I suspected that many of them enjoyed the inflated salaries paid by international organizations: members of that small army of interpreters, drivers and junior administrators without whom the foreigners could not operate. Working for ISAF or the UN was punishable by death in some parts of the country, but here it was a status symbol. I spotted more than one man strolling ahead of his wife and children with an ISAF identity card ostentatiously displayed in a transparent pouch on one arm.

It seemed to me that many Tajiks had grown fat on the war – and a visit to my friend Saman one afternoon did nothing to alter that impression. Saman was the epitome of a Panjshiri Tajik: clever, resourceful and tough. As a younger man he had fought for Massoud, including in the bitter battles for control of Kabul in the early 1990s. The last time I had seen him was in 2002 when he accompanied me on a trip to the north of the country. He was flat broke then, a demobbed soldier wondering how on earth he was going to support his family in the unusual period of peace that followed the toppling of the Taliban.

His mujahideen contacts and classic Tajik features made for the smoothest of passages through the checkpoints of the Tajik-dominated areas. He was a charming, good-humoured man, as well as very street-savvy. He paid close attention to every conversation, compulsively chewing a toothpick with his head cocked to one side like a bird, sorting and filing away whatever information he thought might be turned to use in the future.

I wasn't surprised to learn that in the intervening eight years he had become so exceedingly rich that he only went out with a bodyguard these days, for fear of kidnappers. It was foreign aid that had made his fortune. In 2002, just after I'd last seen him, Saman had gone into the concrete business. He was inspired in this choice by a friend who had set up an NGO specializing in reconstruction work. The whole country needed rebuilding, the Americans were desperate for local partners to help them do it, and the friend was naturally rolling in dollars. Saman simply copied him. He began by sitting quietly in his friend's office, watching and learning and chewing his toothpicks until he felt confident enough to register his own construction NGO. This exercise took precisely a fortnight; he won his first foreign contract a week later.

I went to see him in his new headquarters. He came out to greet me from behind a sleek black Sony laptop, which was placed in the centre of an immense desk made of polished Chinese mahogany. He was the same smiling Saman, although clean-shaven now and decidedly paunchier than before. He had abandoned his shalwar qamiz and Chitrali cap for some Western-looking jeans and a natty black jacket. There was a fat turquoise ring on his finger, and he was smoking 'Zest' mentholated cigarettes. Business, he confessed, had never been better. He was making so much money that he had even taken a second wife. He was employing over three hundred people on ten different construction projects, the largest of which involved building a new blast wall around a United Nations accommodation compound out on the Jalalabad road to the east of the city.

A year or two previously he had converted his NGO into a regular tax-paying business – the Paryan Road and Building Construction Co., named after his home village in the Panjshir – because it ticked the box marked 'economic development' for the Americans, who preferred things that way. Apart from that, the business and his core clientele had hardly changed. He had no shame about milking the dollar-cow so brazenly. 'It's good money. Anyone can do it. In fact, why don't you? You are a foreigner, you speak English. It would be so easy for you!'

He had recently returned from Washington – 'a very nice city' – where he had attended a US–Afghan 'matchmaking conference', organized by the Afghanistan Chamber of Commerce and Industries. This mostly involved offering his services to dozens of officials in the US military. In the conference literature which he showed me, the wording of his company profile – if not the atrocious English in which it was written – was designed to make everybody feel good about helping him prosper.

'Propagation of heart-rending circumstances exits [sic] in all Afghanistan, because they have survived decades of war, internal and external displacement,' it read. 'In fact Afghanistan has endured swollen intimidation and divested away from the global world facilitation ... Afghanistan exigencies are beyond the availed preservation, thereby and adhered and insistent concentration is the sole way to hoist Afghanistan from the current scary situation.'

The theory was sound enough: American investment supporting a legitimate Afghan business while creating local jobs and mending the nation's ruined infrastructure. The trouble was that, according to Saman, eight out of the ten construction contracts he was engaged on were for foreign, not Afghan, infrastructure: principally defence reinforcement and road-access work for Nato bases. The UN compound blast-wall project was entirely representative of what he did.

This was hardly a model for a lasting economic recovery. Saman's company was really no more than a parasite on the back of the mighty Nato war machine. Any benefit to Afghans was short term at best, and not even Saman thought the boom would last.

'We've got another year of this, two at the most, and then it will finish,' he said.

The Americans, he was convinced, would leave that soon: hadn't President Obama said as much when he announced the troop surge in 2009? And when that happened he was sure the Taliban would come back into power.

'Nothing will stop them now. In fact they are already here, aren't they? Didn't you hear that bomb the other day?'

The prospect of the Taliban's return didn't seem to bother him.

'They will be a different Taliban this time, like a domesticated cat compared to a tiger,' he said; and if things got really bad he could always retreat to the Panjshir, a region the Taliban had failed to penetrate even in their tiger days. He only smiled and shrugged when I asked him what he might do there, although I was sure he would find something, and survive. Panjshiris like him always did.

The Tajik grip on Karzai and the West was strong. It wasn't just Tajik dominance of the army that threatened to upset the country's ethnic equilibrium, for they also controlled the NDS, the National Directorate of Security; and the baleful influence of Marshal Fahim was still to be seen in both. The NDS was headed by yet another Panjshiri, Amrullah Saleh.

'We continue to allow the key organizations to be dominated by people from a single ethnic minority,' one senior diplomat remarked; 'in fact, by people from a single valley controlled by that minority. Why? We say we are here to support democracy, but we have effectively taken sides in a 35-year-old civil war.'

The NDS was the successor to the KHAD (*Khadamat-e Etela'at-e Dawlati* or state information agency), which occupies a special place in Afghan demonology. A client organization of the KGB, its first director was Mohammed Najibullah, who later became President and was murdered by the Taliban in 1996. Najibullah dealt with the regime's enemies with terrible cruelty. Arbitrary arrest, torture, show trials and executions were all routine. There were eight KHAD detention centres in Kabul alone; some 27,000 political prisoners were said to have been murdered at the most infamous of these, the prison at Pul-i-Charkhi just east of the city. In December 2006, ISAF discovered a mass grave in its grounds that was thought to contain the bodies of some 2,000 victims of the Soviet era. To this day the American military, with scant appreciation for Pul-i-Charkhi's grim symbolism, use it as a transfer jail for prisoners released from Guantanamo.

The NDS was supposed to be different from the KHAD. Its operations were theoretically circumscribed by the new Constitution that it was intended to uphold, but in practice it operated with a good deal of autonomy, just as the KHAD had done – and there were worrying signs that its methods were getting harsher. The human-rights abuses they were suspected of committing during night raids were only a part of this story. Many Afghans complained that although the organization's title had changed, its personnel had not – and nor had their communist mindset. This naturally made them wonder what the point of fighting the jihad had been. The very suggestion that the KHAD was returning under a new, American-backed guise was enough to give anyone the jitters.

Even Karzai's new Minister of Interior, Mohamed Hanif Atmar, had once worked for the KHAD; he lost a leg defending Jalalabad against the mujahideen in 1988. Atmar was perhaps typical of the new breed of politician embraced by the Americans. In the late 1990s he studied information technology and post-war reconstruction at the University of York, reinventing himself as a smooth-talking, English-speaking technocrat. His reformist agenda was so plausible that in March 2009 it was suggested in Washington that he should be installed as Prime Minister as a means of bypassing the wayward Karzai.[2] It made many Afghans wonder: what kind of state was it that the West was really building in Afghanistan?

Soviet-style bureaucracy was inarguably creeping back. It was noticeable in petty things, such as the new requirement for all foreigners to register with the local police – or even in the official from the Ministry of Agriculture who tried to levy a $25 export tax on my tourist carpet when I later left the country through Kabul airport. But the growing totalitarianism of the NDS represented something more serious. They seemed intent on trying to control the way the war against the Taliban was reported; and they were increasingly heavy-handed with anyone, even foreigners, who went off message. In the wake of the Safi Landmark hotel bombing, for instance, the foreign press corps – whose television crews had covered much of the NDS response to the attack live on location – were told by officials from the

Orwellian-sounding Department 33 (Media) that in future they would not be permitted to do so, 'in the interests of security'. This was in apparent contravention of the Constitution, which solemnly upheld the freedom of the press. A week later, when the independent research organization ICOS began interviewing refugees from the fighting in Marjah, the NDS threatened to arrest the organization's head, the Canadian QC Norine Macdonald. The official line was that there were no refugees from Marjah: only smiling citizens grateful to be 'liberated' from the Taliban menace.

'Shaping the narrative' was a legitimate counter-insurgency tactic much practised by the Americans, but there was a big difference between shaping the narrative and suppressing it. Qais Azimi, a local employee of the English-language arm of al-Jazeera television, had a far scarier run-in with the NDS in January 2009, when he went to investigate reports that the Taliban had emerged in the northern province of Kunduz.

'I didn't believe the reports at first,' he recalled. 'There weren't supposed to be any Taliban in Kunduz back then, but I thought I'd check it out anyway. When I got there I met a mullah, Abdul Salaam, who took me on a drive around the province that lasted two hours, with about a hundred Taliban on motorbikes as an escort. I filmed the whole lot.'

Back in Kabul he presented his scoop to his boss at al-Jazeera, David Chater, who ran his footage the same evening. The following afternoon, he was summoned to the offices of the NDS: 'And don't bring a camera,' they told him. At which point, Azimi knew he was in trouble.

To begin with, an NDS officer accused him of faking the footage, and then that he had been duped by the Taliban.

'I realized that they really didn't know there were Taliban in Kunduz. It turned out that the local NDS man did know, but was so afraid of losing his job if headquarters found out that he hadn't told them. He got fired later.'

The NDS men grew increasingly upset and aggressive. After two hours of questioning, Azimi was handcuffed, blindfolded with goggles and a hood, and made to stand in a ditch at the bottom of the garden in the NDS compound.

'I said my prayers. There were three guys around me. One of them cocked a gun next to my head. I heard one of them say, "Let's do it tomorrow." I was convinced I was going to die.'

He was then taken to a dark, wet basement room containing a bottle of dirty drinking water and a battered Koran, annotated with the messages of former inmates proclaiming their innocence. He was shackled to a chair, and the interrogations began again. In the course of seventy-two hours, he was questioned by no fewer than thirty-two people.

'They were all Khalqi ex-communists,' he recalled, referring to the revolutionary Marxist faction of the 1970s, 'big men with fat moustaches. They accused me of being ISI, then of being a British spy. They even accused David Chater of being a British spy.'

Azimi knew he had a constitutional right not to answer these allegations – or thought he did. At one point one of his exasperated interrogators produced the infamous 'Red Book' of rules that had governed KHAD activities in communist times, and pointed to an article stipulating that acts of enemy propaganda were punishable by death.

'I said, but that's an old communist law! Didn't we fight a jihad together to get rid of those people? And this guy wagged a finger at me and said: "That just shows you how little you know. The Red Book might be old but it has never been replaced, and until it is, it remains the law in this country."'

Azimi was eventually released following strenuous protests from al-Jazeera. Karzai, who was on a state visit to Moscow at the time, at first believed the NDS and even issued a statement that Azimi was guilty of 'promoting terrorism'. Four days later, however, four German ISAF soldiers were ambushed and killed in Kunduz, proving the truth of Azimi's story.

'Karzai is a friend now,' he said. 'He asks me for advice; I've had three private meetings with him. I think he's a nice guy, but he's kept in the dark by the people around him. It's a mafia government. His friendship protects me, but I still worry about getting arrested again.'

One of the most troubling aspects of the NDS's excesses was the West's apparent indifference to them.

Indeed, Amrullah Saleh, the NDS chief, enjoyed the respect of Western diplomats who saw him as an effective operator in the difficult and dangerous intelligence war against the Taliban. He had cooperated with American officialdom since at least 1997, when he was sent by Massoud to Dushanbe, the capital of Tajikistan, to act as a liaison officer to the CIA. Although the diplomats privately acknowledged that his methods would be unacceptable in the West, they tended to excuse him on the grounds that the Afghan way of doing things was 'different'; and that anyway, they had no business telling him how to do his job. Saleh himself remarked smoothly that: 'If you want to work in the garden, you sometimes have to get your hands dirty.'

Out on the front lines in the south, ISAF commanders were often equally ready to turn a blind eye. The NDS men who operated alongside the troops, including British ones, were far more effective and trustworthy than their other local allies, the ANA and the Afghan National Police. Major Dan Rex, who commanded a detachment of Gurkhas at the platoon house in Now Zad in Helmand in 2006, recalled an incident when a Taliban company commander was captured and brought in for questioning by the resident NDS chief, whom the Gurkhas nicknamed 'Hazmat'. His idea of interrogation was to fire an 'empty-ish' pistol at the prisoner's head; the Gurkhas hurriedly dispatched their captive to Lashkar Gah for 'more orthodox' questioning.

Whether the prisoner was really treated any better

there, however, was a moot point. In April 2010 a human-rights activist, Maya Evans, launched a High Court action in London alleging that as many as 410 Taliban suspects handed over to the NDS by British troops between 2006 and 2007 had been tortured. There were claims of beatings, electric shocks, sexual abuse, stress positions and sleep deprivation – part of a 'dreadful and continuing story' of abuse, according to Evans.[3] Michael Fordham QC suggested that the MoD and the Foreign Office were seeking to protect their detainee-transfer policy by adopting an approach of 'seeing no evil, hearing no evil and speaking no evil'. Bob Ainsworth, the Defence Secretary, maintained that 'safeguards are in place to prevent mistreatment', yet even the Ministry of Defence admitted that the UK had no jurisdiction to investigate allegations made against the NDS.[4] Similar allegations had been levelled in Canada where a diplomat, Richard Colvin, told a parliamentary inquiry: 'The NDS tortures people. That's what they do. So if we don't want detainees tortured we shouldn't give them to the NDS.'[5]

Western support for Panjshiri Tajiks like Amrullah Saleh had its roots in the Jihad. Of all the mujahideen commanders of the 1980s, Ahmed Shah Massoud was easily the most Western-leaning. The politics of the party he belonged to, Burhanuddin Rabbani's Jamiat-i-Islami, were at the liberal end of the mujahideen spectrum. He spoke a little French thanks to an early education at the progressive Lycée Esteqlal in Kabul, and understood the importance of a strong public image in the West. The journalists who flocked to the Panjshir to report on his genuinely brilliant guerrilla campaign against the Soviets were always made welcome. The Lion of the Panjshir, as he was soon known, seemed the romantic epitome of the charismatic rebel leader. In his famous Chitrali cap, and with looks a little like Bob Marley's, he became a kind of Western poster boy in the style of Che Guevara. In the mid-1990s he was the only ex-mujahideen leader to succeed in resisting the Taliban, which made him the natural choice of ally for the Americans.

When Massoud was assassinated by al-Qaida two days before 9/11, his former lionization turned into a full-blown cult which his heirs in Jamiat-i-Islami were quick to exploit. Post-Taliban Kabul was filled with posters and photographs of the *Amir Sahib-i Shahid* – 'Our Martyred Commander' – with slogans to match, often in question-able English: 'The Charismatic Martyre: Your way move forward!!!' In 2002, Karzai designated Massoud an official 'National Hero', while the date of his death, 9 September, became a national holiday known as 'Massoud Day'. And the West went along with this hero-worship. With funding from the French, plans had been drawn up for a large statue of Massoud in the middle of a major roundabout in central Kabul. He was even nominated for the Nobel Peace Prize.

Not everyone was pleased about this, particularly in Kabul. Massoud's forces were blamed as much as any other faction for the slaughter of civilians during the battle for the capital in the 1990s. For instance, Jamiat fighters were involved in the infamous attack on the Hazara suburb of Afshar in 1993, an operation notorious for the systematic rape and summary executions that took place. Bodies were mutilated and left piled in the street, and decapitated heads were mounted in windows.

'The West has this really strange thing about Massoud,' one experienced Western observer told me. 'He's still seen in one dimension only, as this great anti-Soviet liberator of Afghanistan.'

But history, as he remarked, was constantly being rewritten in Afghanistan, and in 2010 there was little sign that Massoud's reputation or influence were diminishing.

The high priest of the cult was his former aide, Dr Abdullah, the Secretary General of the Massoud Foundation: an 'independent, non-aligned, non-political' organization, according to its website, although there was nothing apolitical about Abdullah himself. In 2009 he emerged as Karzai's main challenger in the presidential election, and might conceivably have won if he had not pulled out of the second round of voting at the last minute.

He was known as Abdullah Abdullah, a name which by itself hinted at his long interaction with the West. Like many Afghans he didn't actually have a second name; Western newspaper editors were reputedly so confused by this that they felt compelled to make one up for him.[6] An ophthalmologist by training, his political career began when he was sent up to the Panjshir in 1985 by the Swedish Committee, a humanitarian organization concerned by the lack of medical care available to the mujahideen. He eventually became one of Massoud's closest advisers; so close, indeed, that he was still dogged by scurrilous rumours about the relationship. He was one of the few educated English-speakers around Massoud. On the latter's death he was appointed spokesman for the Northern Alliance, and then – always just a short hop in Afghanistan – to Foreign Minister, under Karzai.

It was the weekend, so he was at home in the suburbs rather than in his office when I went to meet him, although the surrounding security measures were hardly less relaxed. A platoon of paramilitaries manned a barrier and chicanes of concrete at either end of his street. I was led through a high-walled courtyard set around neat rose-beds and a close-cropped lawn studded with crazy paving, and then into a reception room where I was told to wait. The room was more Hilton hotel than hujra: by some margin, the flashiest interior I had ever seen in Afghanistan. The furniture was repro eighteenth-century French in gilt and red. There were expensive carpets on the polished parquet floor, a large flat-screen television on the wall. Elegant wooden side-tables and a faux-antique writing desk were topped by small modernist knick-knacks and family photographs in silver frames. Abdullah had come a long way since the rebel hideout days, and he wanted everyone to know it.

Most revealingly of all, there was a floor-to-ceiling

mural of Massoud sitting beneath a tree on a rock somewhere high in the Panjshir. In the background a
sun-dappled Arcadia is glimpsed, a mountainside
tumbling to a glinting river and a patchwork of tiny
emerald fields. Massoud, one finger in the pages of a
book he has just been reading, is gesticulating and smiling at five of his Chitrali-capped followers who sit
cross-legged at his feet, gazing up at him like adoring
disciples; and next to Massoud, on his right-hand side, is
Abdullah. The future torch-bearer of the Panjshiri ideal
looks nobly out of the painting with an expression of
ineffable sadness, as if afflicted with a premonition of the
tragedy soon to befall his beloved mentor.

The man himself soon swept into the room. It was the
third time I had met him, though he didn't remember
me. The first time was in 1998 when he was still in the
Panjshir, sitting on a rock as he signed a document
permitting me to travel further up the valley. In those
days he was dressed rather as he was in the mural, in
sandals and a simple shalwar qamiz. The second time,
in Kabul in 2002, he had become the Foreign Minister
and was wearing a pinstripe suit. He looked the part but
seemed to be struggling in his new role, and didn't like it
one bit when I suggested that all the 'Massoud worship'
going on in the capital was unlikely to play well with
non-Tajiks, and the Pashtuns least of all.

'It is *not* Massoud worship. It is not just Panjshiris who
look up to him. His posters are not just in Kabul – I've
seen them everywhere, even in Kandahar!'

Today Abdullah was wearing a rich brown cloak, a heavy gold necklace, and a black and white designer watch the size of a small alarm clock. His sartorial progress alone augured badly for reconciliation with the austere Taliban. He was like a character in a sequence of Hogarth's satirical prints.

'The Quetta leadership haven't changed one bit,' he said. 'Some of the rank and file might be reconciled, but there is no possibility of compromise with the top. They are intimately linked with al-Qaida, there's no doubt about it. And if you ignore the recent arrests in Pakistan, there is no pressure coming from there either.'

He had little sympathy for Mullah Zaeef's suggestion that the Taliban wanted to 'repair' the Constitution rather than to destroy it. Although he conceded that power was over-centralized, and that this had been a mistake of Karzai's, it was clear that he thought the Constitution was fine as it was, a perfectly adequate vehicle for establishing what the Massoud Foundation called 'an Afghan society garnished with moderate Islam'.

He also disagreed with the need to re-open the Bonn Agreement of 2001. The Taliban had not been invited to Bonn, and many Afghans thought the conference had done nothing but re-empower the old warlords. Pashtuns tended to complain that their interests had been particularly under-represented, a suggestion Abdullah flatly dismissed. 'The Pashtuns *were* represented. The Supreme Court Chief Justice, the Attorney-General: all

Pashtuns. The Taliban were not, but the Taliban do not speak for Pashtuns . . . Today we are losing the support of the people in the south, and thus the war, but that is not Bonn's fault. After 2001 we missed an opportunity to isolate the Taliban leadership, but that was because Western attention was turned to Iraq.'

Just as in 2002, he was at pains to present himself as democracy's most passionate advocate in Afghanistan – the antithesis of Karzai, he pointed out, but 'just because Karzai isn't a democrat doesn't mean the people aren't ready for democracy'.

Democracy nevertheless had been 'the big loser' in the stolen elections of 2009.

'I knew there would be corruption, patronage, back-room deals, even before I became a candidate. I hoped an independent body would police the election, but the IEC [Independent Election Commission] was not independent.'

This, he explained, was why he had pulled out of the second round of voting: 'There would have been more fraud, more lives lost, another $200 million wasted. I did it for the good of the country.'

This argument would not do. No one had complained more loudly than Abdullah about Karzai's outrageous ballot-rigging, yet according to Dimitra Ioannou, the EU deputy chief observer, some 300,000 of the votes for Abdullah were equally suspect. In the northern province of Balkh, people were allegedly forced to vote for him at gunpoint.[7] I failed to pin him down on this, though. Our meeting, frustratingly, was more of a lecture than a conversation, and once started, Abdullah never seemed to stop talking. I had many other questions prepared – about Marshal Fahim, about the ethnic imbalance in the ANA, about the Panjshiris' control of the NDS – but he brushed aside every interruption and returned again and again to his main theme: his role as the heroic defender of democracy.

'I was born in this house, right upstairs,' he said at one point, indicating the ceiling. 'My father was a senator. I well remember the day in 1973 when I came down to breakfast – I was a schoolboy then – and found him listening to the radio with a sad face. I was surprised that he hadn't already gone to work. Then he said, "You're not going to school today. There has been a coup d'état! It's the communists . . . Parliament will be dissolved." It made a big impression on me. That is why I joined the Resistance later on. I have always believed – Massoud believed, right up to the day he died – that without a system of one person, one vote, there will never be a solution to this country's problems. When that system arrives, my job here will be done.'

All too soon an aide came in to announce the meeting was over. Abdullah stood, smoothed down his robe and swished off into the interior of his unusual home, while I was shown out by the other door.

12

Not Black and White, But Grey: Hizb-i-Islami and the Afghan Parliament

In the days that followed I criss-crossed Kabul, meeting Afghan officials from across the political spectrum: so-called 'reconciled' Taliban, MPs, government ministers. Some were more outspoken than others, and there were significant differences of opinion about what should happen next, but all of them shared Mullah Zaeef's underlying frustration with Washington – and they all agreed that unless America changed the direction of its policy soon, Afghanistan was heading for disaster.

I went to meet Abdul-Sattar Khawasi, the First Secretary of the Wolesi Jirga, the People's Assembly or Lower House of Parliament, the institution whose recalcitrance over the President's election-commission power grab had sparked the latest row between Karzai and the West. The chamber building was naturally heavily fortified with machine-gun nests on every corner, and it took half an hour to clear the chaotic security screening process at the entrance. The corridors inside, by contrast, were dark and cool and meticulously swept; a few officials scurried about in ill-fitting Western suits, murmuring salaams as they passed each other.

The entrance hall was lined with the photographs of the country's 249 MPs who were elected in 2005, the first democratically elected parliament in decades. The next parliamentary election was supposed to take place in May 2010 but it had been postponed for four months. Foreign donors, appalled by the fraud that marred the 2009 presidential election, feared that the next round could do more harm than good and so had withheld the necessary funding.

The portrait gallery made interesting viewing as I waited for my appointment: a perfect cross-section of the astonishing variety of the Afghan nation. Over sixty of the photographs were of women. The democratization of Afghanistan was a bold experiment in modern governance. The new Constitution, drawn up with the help of Western technical advisers, stipulated that at least 25 per cent of the members of Parliament as well as of the local government assemblies had to be female. It had proved a controversial measure, for in this misogynistic society the Taliban were not the only religious conservatives who objected to it. It was only in 1959, a mere fifty years ago, that Ariana Airlines had ordered its air hostesses out of their burqas: the first Afghan women ever to appear in public without them. The idealism behind the parliamentary quota was no doubt laudable, but the West's insistence on it was always bound to cause trouble. It was also hypocritical. After the 2010 general election in Britain – a parliamentary democracy that has had centuries to mature – female MPs still accounted for just 22 per cent of the total: no better than fiftieth in the world league table for the proportion of women MPs.[1]

Some of the characters in the portrait gallery, I noted, were also out and out rogues. Pacha Khan Zadran, for instance, one of the twenty-six signatories to the Bonn Agreement of 2001 that launched Karzai on the path to the presidency, was also a commander who notoriously shelled Gardez, the capital of Paktia, in a dispute over the governorship of that province in 2002. Once a target for US Special Forces who nicknamed him 'PKZ', he was little more than a bandit who had changed sides at the right time. There were many others with similarly dubious pasts – crooks and warlords, killers and thieves, the very people that Afghans had hoped would be banished from power for ever when the Americans arrived, and whose destruction the Taliban had sought from the start.

Khawasi had something of a firebrand reputation, an MP who was unafraid to speak his mind. A 37-year-old Pashtun from Parwan province in central Afghanistan, he had trained as a lawyer in the early 1990s before finding work as a civil servant, including at the Ministry of Justice under the Taliban. He had never been a hardliner, however – just a junior government official who knew how to keep his head down. He said he had never agreed with the Taliban's war against the Northern Alliance. Violence, he explained piously, was seldom the answer to a problem: it was almost always better to try to bridge differences through dialogue. His past, at any rate, had evidently not impeded a stellar parliamentary career.

'Obama is trying to paint and decorate my house without my permission,' he said, adding that a majority of MPs felt the same, even if they did not all say so in public.

'The international community say they want to help here, but Afghans are very independent-minded. They see armed foreigners as invaders – it is black and white to them, and hatred of them is on the increase.'

The hope of the Afghan people for a national 'rebirth' in 2001 had been traduced, in his opinion. Karzai's proposals for peace talks at the London Conference in January 2010 were welcome, but they had been undermined by America's huge war machine.

'McChrystal pressured him to sign off on the new campaign in Marjah. It was 100 per cent pressure, and the timing was completely wrong! How can you announce a peace deal as you go into an attack? Karzai is more of a puppet than ever. The Taliban will never talk to him now.'

Like Zaeef, Khawasi was full of dire predictions. He said he had recently warned a senior American diplomat that Nato would suffer a defeat 'worse than the USSR' if the US continued with its present policy, and his eyes blazed at the memory of the diplomat's response.

'He told me this was "enemy talk". He said this to me, the First Secretary of the Wolesi Jirga! What a stupid thing to say to any Member of Parliament! Are we supposed to express the will of the Afghan people here, or the will of Washington? The Americans cannot make up their minds. I think they are *mariz*,' he added, touching his turban with a forefinger: psychologically ill.

The American surge in the south, he said, was a 'childish' strategy that would only lengthen the war. The threat of a resurgent al-Qaida that worried the West was 'not real'. The military campaign was not just morally but financially unsustainable. As a technocrat, he was professionally galled by the money being wasted on it.

'ISAF spend $60 million a year on bottled drinking water alone. Each US soldier costs $1 million a year: that is a thousand times more than an ANA one! And still, with all these soldiers, they can't even secure Kabul. The Safi Landmark hotel, the Serena hotel, the Presidential Palace – they are all under attack.'

The solution, he thought, was for ISAF to announce a firm timetable for withdrawal: nothing less would satisfy Quetta now. Responsibility for national security should be handed to the ANA, and the government should in future be empowered to govern. We Westerners would be welcome to stay on as civilian 'partners, helpers, observers', but should have little or no role in the resulting settlement between the Taliban and the Northern Alliance. To avoid a repeat of the bloodshed of the 1990s, he thought, any peace deal should be brokered by the

OIC, the 57-member-state Organization of the Islamic Conference, with the UN and Afghanistan's regional partners sitting on the sidelines. And then fresh elections needed to be held.

'The constitution will need to be changed, but that is a relatively minor thing. Peace must come first.'

His prescription for the future was of some interest. Khawasi, I knew, was one of a dozen MPs who had travelled in January to a hotel in the Maldives, the Bandos Island Resort, for a secret three-day peace conference that included representatives of the Taliban. There was something bizarre and delicious about Mullah Omar's people sitting down to discuss high politics in a hedonistic diving resort. Bandos Island's website displayed a tiny, sun-kissed coral reef of just 180,000 square metres, a Western honeymooners' paradise where, according to the blurb, 'the gentle lull of the sea, the whistling breeze, and the rustling of the palm fronds on the beach will help transcend you from the hurly-burly rigours of daily life'.

I had been trying hard to discover the significance of these talks, which had been organized by Humayun Jarir, a son-in-law of the Hizb-i-Islami leader Gulbuddin Hekmatyar – the famous former mujahideen leader (and former Prime Minister), now a 'specially designated global terrorist' with a bounty of $25 million on his head. In contrast to his earlier openness, however, Khawasi was strangely reluctant to talk about his trip, and indeed seemed put out that I even knew about it.

'Thanks be to Allah for raising such an important issue,' he said, before immediately changing the subject.

I persisted, though. I had spoken by telephone to Jarir, who was keen to publicize the meeting after it had taken place, and had even sent me a list of the participants along with a press release. There had only been two Taliban present, Mohammed Zahir Muslimyar and Fazel Luqman Farooqi, whom another source had identified as members of the Peshawar shura, not the Quetta one that mattered most. But the list was quite impressive nevertheless. Almost every major player in the country had sat down with the people from Hizb-i-Islami, including representatives of two former presidents from mujahideen times, Burhanuddin Rabbani and Sibghatullah Mujadeddi. Kharim Khalili, the Hazara leader, and Rashid Dostum, the Uzbek one, were both spoken for. A UN official called G.M. Gulzai was also listed, suggesting that these talks had enjoyed some measure of international approval, although I was never able to establish who this Gulzai really was. A contact at UNAMA insisted he was not one of theirs. He thought he must have come from headquarters in New York, and that 'G.M. Gulzai' was most likely a pseudonym anyway.

The Jarir talks were interesting because they presented the possibility of a bridge between Karzai and the Taliban. Hekmatyar shared the Taliban agenda of getting rid of the foreigners and re-establishing Sharia, but disagreed with them on how the latter should be achieved. Unlike Mullah Omar, he was a deeply political animal who instinctively understood what could be gained through negotiation. He had been Prime Minister twice, and craved that kind of power for himself again; some said that he had made common cause with the Taliban's insurgency entirely in pursuit of that end. Khawasi was evasive, however, when I suggested that Karzai planned to draw in Hekmatyar as a first step towards reconciliation with the Taliban.

'It is possible, although the President has no such strategy that I am aware of,' he said.

All he would say about the Maldives meeting was that it was a 'first step towards a negotiated settlement', for which 'the establishment of intra-Afghan dialogue' was 'essential'. I was sure he was right about that: peace could never be imposed from outside Afghanistan, and would only grow from internal consensus. But this was really no more than Jarir's press release had said, a statement of the very obvious. I wondered who had funded such an expensive conference. Khawasi claimed the delegates had paid their expenses themselves. He had gone to the Maldives, he said, 'not as an MP, but as an individual'. Then he let slip that he had in fact been the leader of the dozen-strong parliamentary delegation, who had charged him with approaching Karzai and asking him for a meeting to discuss the Maldives talks.

'And what did Karzai say?'

'We haven't found a time to meet up yet.'

'But the Maldives meeting was six weeks ago! Isn't the peace process a priority?'

'Well,' said Khawasi, shifting uncomfortably in his seat, 'the President is a very busy man. I'm not suspicious of him. You shouldn't . . . read anything into that.'

And then he changed the subject again.

I read two things into that. The first was that it showed how broken the President's relationship with his Parliament was. It did not seem credible that his diary was so full that he had no time for the Wolesi Jirga's First Secretary. Karzai was commonly portrayed as an isolated leader, aloof and paranoid in his Presidential Palace, and Khawasi, who clearly *was* suspicious of him, seemed to confirm that view. The second was that it sounded as though Karzai was not properly interested in the Maldives talks at all – and one likely reason for that, it seemed to me, was the man who organized them, Humayun Jarir.

Being his son-in-law did not necessarily mean that he was authorized to speak for Hekmatyar. Indeed, Jarir had fallen out badly with him when he was accused of going abroad with a large amount of Hizb-i-Islami party funding in his suitcase. He claimed the row was based on a misunderstanding and had been patched over, but others I spoke to told me that the pair were still estranged. Without rapprochement, Jarir was effectively a nobody and the Maldives meeting was almost pointless – unless, as a delegate, you happened to fancy spending three days in a top-class diving resort. 'Afghans love to talk, and they will do anything for a free lunch,' as one

Kabuli contact cynically remarked. 'The Maldives was just punching in the air.'

There was, in addition, a question mark over Jarir's relationship with Karzai, who once threatened to have him arrested should he ever set foot in Kabul again – which was one reason why his conferences never took place in Afghanistan. All this meant that Khawasi would need to tread very carefully if he was to succeed in selling the Maldives talks to his President – who in any case had just publicly backed a different horse at the London Conference with his appeal to King Abdullah of Saudi Arabia to act as peace-broker.

The Maldives meeting was the third such conference arranged by Jarir. The usual venue was Dubai, but this time the delegates had run into 'visa trouble' with the Emirate and been forced to find an alternative at the last minute; the advantage of the Maldives was that it was one of the few countries in the world that did not require a visa to enter it. The reason for Dubai's sudden change of heart was unclear. Either they were genuinely worried about the security implications, or they feared US disapproval. According to Jarir, both the Americans and the British had been forewarned of the meeting via 'diplomatic channels', although he had received no response from either. He complained that the US and the UK consistently 'looked the other way' while people like him tried their best to make reconciliation a reality. But had they looked the other way?

Although the delegates were prevented from holding

their meeting in Dubai, they still had to change planes there to reach the Maldives; and as an intelligence source told me, 'Nobody moves through that airport without the CIA knowing about it.' If this was true then maybe the Americans approved of the meeting after all, and were deliberately keeping out of the process in order not to taint it. The weight of public US endorsement could easily kill something as delicate as a round of exploratory peace talks. On the other hand, Jarir's talks looked an outside bet compared to the Saudi-brokered ones that Karzai apparently favoured; and with General McChrystal's campaign in the south under way, there was no obvious reason why the CIA would want to promote reconciliation with Hekmatyar. Who knew? These waters were deep, and Khawasi had done little to help me fathom them.

A month later, however, some evidence emerged that Karzai was indeed interested in striking a deal with Hekmatyar. On 28 March, for the first time, he met a delegation led by Ghairat Bahir, commonly described as Hekmatyar's 'favourite' son-in-law, and an altogether more serious Hizb-i-Islami personality than Jarir. Bahir, who served as ambassador to Islamabad during the Rabbani presidency, was arrested by the ISI in 2004 and handed over to the Americans, who detained him at Bagram. He was transferred to Kabul's infamous Pul-i-Charkhi jail, before being released on Karzai's orders in June 2008. Karzai offered Hizb-i-Islami control of some key ministries if Bahir agreed to act as a power-broker between him, Hekmatyar and the Taliban leader Jalaluddin Haqqani, although nothing then came of the proposal.[2] Had Karzai's gambit finally paid off? When Obama flew in to rebuke him for his failure to tackle corruption, Karzai reportedly tried to turn the conversation to a less awkward topic by offering a briefing on his recent meeting with Bahir. Obama, unhappily for Karzai, was less than impressed.

'In talks with militants,' Obama replied, 'we need to proceed from a position of strength. In my judgement we're not there yet.'[3]

He might almost have been reading from General Petraeus's *Counterinsurgency Field Manual*. But what did that catch-all word 'militant' really mean in the Afghan context? Washington had a long habit of dividing the world into goodies and baddies – 'You're either with us or against us in the fight against terror,' as President Bush famously remarked in 2001 – but in a country with a history like Afghanistan's, few politicians could be described as truly 'clean'. Hekmatyar was no doubt an unsavoury character with a reputation for appalling violence, but was everyone who had come into contact with him to be tarred with the same brush? As Karzai well understood, the Afghan political landscape was not black and white but grey. I had yet to meet an Afghan who rejected *everything* the Taliban stood for. There was good and bad in all people, and unless America found a way to focus on the good in the people who might be able to help them, there was a risk that the war would never end.

Hizb-i-Islami's status was certainly grey. The party founded by Hekmatyar had split into factions in 2003. His one, known as Hizb-i-Islami Gulbuddin or HIG, was soon designated a 'group of concern' on the US State Department's list of Foreign Terrorist Organizations. The other, Hizb-i-Islami Afghanistan or HIA, was led by the new Minister of Economy Abdul Hadi Arghandiwal, and was not just legal but arguably the most powerful grouping in Parliament. As the non-violent wing of Hizb-i-Islami, HIA was to HIG what Sinn Fein was to the IRA in the 1990s. As in Northern Ireland, the precise relationship between the two factions was obscure, although it was assumed by most Afghans that it was privately a lot friendlier than either would, or could, publicly admit.

Arghandiwal himself objected to the Sinn Fein parallel when I put it to him later – so quickly, in fact, that you could tell he was sick of hearing it drawn by the countless British and American diplomats and journalists who had interviewed him in the past.

'No!' he said. 'We are entirely separate organizations. Hekmatyar was a friend of mine, but we are not following his orders – and 90 per cent of Hizb-i-Islami agrees with that and think as we do. It is not necessary that the party is led by the same man for ever. He is not happy about the HIA. He never wanted a strong Hizb-i-Islami party here in Kabul, and he fights because he does not agree with my approach.'

He spoke excellent English, the result of a higher

education in the US in the mid-1970s. Cynics sometimes suggested that English-language skills had become the main criterion for membership of this Western-backed government, but that criticism didn't seem quite fair in this case. Arghandiwal was qualified for his job. His career had begun in the Planning Ministry more than thirty years before, and he had briefly served as Finance Minister in pre-Taliban Afghanistan. He looked comfortable in his office, which was sunny and large, in keeping with his new ministerial status, and his arguments were sophisticated and refreshingly clear. On election to the chairmanship of his faction in 2008, he had spoken unambiguously about wanting to bring security to the country by negotiating with all armed opposition groups. Everything about him seemed calculated to project the idea that here was a man with whom the West could do business.

Hizb-i-Islami, the 'Party of Islam', had long been a part of the country's political mainstream. It had grown out of the Muslim Youth organization, which was founded by students and teachers at Kabul University to counter Afghan communism in the late 1960s. Hekmatyar was among those students, and had an evil reputation even then for hot-headed extremism. The most infamous allegation was that he ordered his followers to throw acid in the faces of female students who were not wearing the hijab. He founded his party in 1975 in Pakistan. During the Jihad, Hizb-i-Islami became the West's favourite proxy mujahideen group. At least $600 million was channelled directly to Hekmatyar through the CIA and their ISI counterparts in Pakistan. The party became the main rallying point for Pashtun resistance, and its members still regarded themselves as the mujahideen elite, the natural inheritors of political power.

While acknowledging that they didn't control the country yet, Arghandiwal argued that their time was coming again, and that they were already the 'king-makers' in the current parliament.

'It is difficult for Karzai to appoint any minister without our support,' he said.

In local elections the previous year, Hizb-i-Islami candidates had won 75 of the country's 420 Provincial Council seats: enough, he claimed, to have exerted serious influence in the presidential election that took place at the same time. Of the two million votes for Karzai that were counted as valid, he estimated that half had been delivered by Hizb-i-Islami through the Provincial Councils. It might not have been pretty, but democracy was at least functioning in Afghanistan. Westerners often argued that it was pointless as well as foolish to try to impose such a system on a country that had no tradition in it. Arghandiwal perhaps provided ammunition for optimists.

Ideologically, he explained, there was little to separate Hizb-i-Islami from the Taliban: 'They are Muslims like us. All Muslims are the same before Allah. Islam must be taken as a whole – it cannot be broken into bits. We all believe in the Muslim way of life.'

Both Hizb-i-Islami and the Taliban saw the foreign troops as 'invaders', and wanted them out. They just disagreed on how their goals should be achieved.

'The way the Taliban implemented their plans was not entirely in accord with Islam,' he said. 'Islam is a peaceful religion. Hekmatyar believes in the implementation of Islamic law, but he also believes strongly in democracy for Afghanistan – although not necessarily under the present constitution and Karzai.'

A more accurate definition of Hekmatyar's ideology was 'theo-democracy', a term coined by one of his political heroes, Syed Abul A'ala Maududi, who founded the vanguard Islamic Revivalist Party (Jamiat-i-Islami) in Lahore in 1941. However peaceful Islam was as a religion, there was nothing notably non-violent about Maududi, whose pursuit of a 'pure' Islamic Sharia society was uncompromising, and whose rejection of Western ideologies was absolute.

Arghandiwal didn't think that Hekmatyar was about to lay down arms any time soon. Nor did he see much prospect of Hizb-i-Islami reaching a political accommodation with the Taliban, whom he regarded as incorrigible.

'They say they have changed their position on women and so on, but do you believe them? I do not. We can't go back to all that. A clever man does not get bitten by a snake from the same hole twice.'

This was a well-known Afghan aphorism; I had last

heard it on the lips of a Taliban mullah who was puzzled by the British Army's return to Helmand, a place where, after all, they had been defeated before, at Maiwand in 1880.

The Taliban, Arghandiwal said, had 'a plan, but not the wisdom to distinguish between what is in Afghanistan's interests and what is in our enemies' interests. They kill educated people. They burn schools. We Pashtuns allow ourselves to be the hostages of the Taliban, but the Taliban are themselves the hostages of our regional neighbours. That's why I always tell youngsters not to let themselves be tools. They must learn to think for themselves.'

He was in despair in that respect about the state of higher education among Pashtuns. Last year, he said, just twenty-six students from the four main provinces around the capital had enrolled for courses at Kabul University. By contrast, 1,200 Hazaras had signed up at the university in Bamiyan, the capital of the Hazarajat.

'If this goes on, we won't have enough people to fill high office!'

His complaint had an edge to it. Like others I spoke to he was deeply troubled by the growing influence of Iran in Afghan affairs. Iranian financial support to their brother Shi'a, the Hazaras, was undoubtedly on the increase. They had channelled money into the Hazarajat for years, building hospitals, the university, even an airport. Now there were reports that Hazaras had been offering to buy up Pashtun land and property in the north of the country at ten times the market rate. To Pashtuns this was an affront to the natural social order, for they were the country's traditional rulers while the Hazaras, the 'wrong' kind of Muslims, had historically comprised its peasantry. It was a clever form of proxy warfare by Iran that threatened to upset Afghanistan's delicate ethnic status quo, which in turn raised the possibility of renewed ethnic civil war in the future.

'The Pashtuns are stupid. They are only interested in fighting and smuggling, and are satisfied with anyone who provides them with guns and bombs, while Iran gives the Hazaras roads and schools and libraries. Yet when the Pashtuns are given schools, the Taliban destroy them.'

While unsympathetic to the Taliban, Arghandiwal was still in favour of finding a way to negotiate with them. He was encouraged by Karzai's approach to the Saudis, the 'obvious choice' of peace-broker – although the US would have to take the Taliban's potential mediators off the UN Consolidated List before dialogue could begin. Intriguingly, he did not hold America exclusively responsible for the lack of progress on that front, for in his eyes the British were equally to blame.

'I'm sorry, but I won't make that distinction,' he said. 'The US implements Western policy in Afghanistan, but it is the UK that formulates it.'

There was something in what he said. The ongoing reconciliation and reintegration programme espoused by General McChrystal was originally a British idea, as was the 'comprehensive approach' to counter-insurgency, now being applied under a different name in the south. At the same time, the idea that Britain and America were secret partners in some Machiavellian compact – brains and brawn, the clever servant to a powerful master – was also typical of the way Hekmatyar viewed the Special Relationship. This was a sharp reminder that there wasn't necessarily as much difference between HIG and HIA as Arghandiwal claimed. There were those in Kabul who suspected that, far from disapproving of the setting up of a purely political wing, Hekmatyar secretly saw it as a Trojan horse, a means of seizing political control again when the military ousting of the West was complete.

'Hekmatyar looks irrelevant now, but you should never write him off,' one seasoned observer told me. 'He's a consummate politician, and he's very clever.'

Was Hekmatyar playing the long game? It was a scary thought. There were many Afghans who considered him a psychopath. Arghandiwal insisted that his (supposedly former) friend was a passionate advocate of women's rights and education, though I had my doubts that such a fierce leopard could ever change its spots. His alleged crimes went far beyond throwing acid in the faces of liberated students. During and after the Jihad, he had allied himself and fought against almost every other group in the country in his ruthless quest for power, bringing death and misery to thousands. He was accused of helping bin Laden escape from Tora Bora in 2002, and of trying to assassinate Karzai in 2003. No wonder the news that Karzai was talking to his son-in-law Ghairat Bahir had caused such a stir. An amnesty extended to such a treacherous man would have to be a profoundly generous one.

It would, however, be necessary eventually if Afghanistan was ever to find peace. Bahir, it emerged later, had presented Karzai with a fifteen-point peace plan on behalf of his father-in-law. He told reporters that while Hekmatyar had no formal ties to Mullah Omar, they still 'influenced each other'. Bahir's main argument was that the US's attempts to reconcile junior insurgency commanders were pointless, and that if they were serious about reaching a political settlement they needed to speak to the leadership.

'In our culture if you are talking to anyone and ignore the head of the party, whoever it is, you will get nothing,' Bahir told reporters. 'Hizb-i-Islami minus Hekmatyar means nothing. The Taliban without Mullah Omar means nothing. They have no option. This is the reality of our culture, it's not something to like or dislike.'[4]

His argument, interestingly, mirrored that of the former UN envoy, Kai Eide, who remarked shortly before the 2009 presidential election: 'If you want significant results [from the reconciliation programme], you have to talk to important people.'

Talking directly to Hekmatyar, a 'global terrorist' with $25 million on his head, was next to impossible these days. But I had interviewed him before, for the London

Times in Mazar-i-Sharif in February 1998. It was some-thing of a scoop even then: the first interview he had given to any Western journalist in over two years. After his capitulation to the Taliban in Kabul he had fled into exile in Iran, and had hardly been seen or heard of since.

Mazar was a tense place in early 1998. It was the only city in the country that had not yet fallen to the Taliban, who had captured and then been ejected from it twice the previous year at the cost of thousands of lives. Truckloads of heavily armed men cruised the muddy streets by day, and enforced a shoot-on-sight curfew by night. Burhanuddin Rabbani, still the nominal President of Afghanistan, was planning a new coalition cabinet, an alternative administration to the new regime in Kandahar and Kabul. He had met the Alliance's leaders in an abandoned hotel just west of the town centre on the day of my arrival, but I had been unable to get any nearer to the actual meeting than the street outside. This was dangerously filled with fighters belonging to one faction or another, eye-balling their rivals from the tops of trucks that bristled with guns and RPGs. The atmosphere was tense and aggressive and I didn't linger.

A few days later I went for a walk around the city centre, principally in order to warm myself up, since it was sleeting in Mazar and the hotel I was staying in, the Bharat, had sporadic electricity and no hot water. Passing the famous Blue Mosque, I noticed a crowd of people outside the main entrance, and stopped to study the amazing range of headgear on display: a classic indicator of the ethnic hodge-podge the Mazaris comprised. There were tribal turbans, kufi caps, Uzbeki lamb's-wool *karakuls*, rolled-up Chitrali *pakuls*, fur hats with ear flaps, Red Army crap-hats, even a Russian officer's cap with a glittering badge and red and white braid. Others wore grubby anoraks with the hoods up, or swathed their heads and shoulders in woollen *patous* so tightly that only their eyes showed, dark and narrowed against the cold. Soon the guards began to clear a path through the crowd, levering them back with the stocks of their Kalashnikovs: a VIP had come to pray at the shrine, and he and his entourage were making their exit.

From the photographs I surreptitiously took that day there is no mistaking Gulbuddin Hekmatyar: the slightly hooded eyes, the convex beak of a nose, the long face accentuated by a sculpted black beard that was greying at the cheeks. He was tall and stately, and wore a black turban with a long tail and a heavy overcoat to match. A television camera appeared as he salaamed briefly to the crowd, his right hand over his heart, the cameraman swivelling as Hekmatyar was bundled into a waiting Toyota and rapidly driven away.

Whatever the reason behind Hekmatyar's public appearance here, the TV camera proved that he wanted it publicized, because the press did not materialize without permission in Afghanistan. I hurried back to the hotel to try to arrange an interview. Late that afternoon, three Hi-Lux trucks roared to a halt outside, each of them carrying three or four swaggering gunmen. The receptionist looked frightened as I climbed into the middle vehicle, but I was glad of the heavy escort, which would speed our way through any checkpoint. Hekmatyar, I learned, was installed in a compound in the desert scrubland a few miles east of the city. He had only been there a few days: his first time on Afghan soil for over a year.

From the compound's fortifications it was clear that he didn't feel very secure here. Guards patrolled a parapet by the reinforced main gate; a fleet of machine-gun-topped Toyotas was parked inside with their fronts pointed towards the exit. I was led across freezing slush to a building in the corner where I was patted down for weapons – or suicide bombs – before being shown into a guest room. Hekmatyar was waiting at the end amongst an entourage of surprising size, perhaps twenty or so men. I didn't know then that Hizb-i-Islami modelled themselves on the Ikhwan ('brothers' in Arabic), an Islamic tribal militia noted for the merciless throat-cutting of their enemies, and who helped their leader Ibn Saud to unite the Arabian peninsula and then found modern Saudi Arabia in 1926.

The overstuffed faux-leather armchairs lining the sides of the room were all taken, apart from one in the centre. I sat down in awkward silence. It was going to be a more formal interview than I had anticipated, even though I knew Afghan dignitaries often arranged such encounters this way. Diplomats and journalists were treated much the same: we were all spokesmen and emissaries of a foreign power. Hekmatyar, and indeed his attendants, were more smartly turned out than was customary in this part of Afghanistan, in pressed white shirts and black turbans with the tails smoothed carefully across their chests. I suspected the Ikhwan had been subtly citified by a year of exile in Meshed or Tehran. There was something positively Ayatollah-ish about Hekmatyar himself.

The substance of his message, delivered in faltering English learned long before in Pakistan, was remarkably similar to what his son-in-law was now telling Karzai, twelve years on. Only the enemy had changed.

'A military solution is not the answer. I propose dialogue, a ceasefire, an interim government leading to proper elections. We need to find an *Afghan* solution.'

He was in Mazar, he said, at the repeated invitations of the Northern Alliance, although he had made it clear to President Rabbani that he wanted no part in the proposed coalition cabinet.

'A coalition is not the answer. Hizb-i-Islami is the only party that can unite Afghanistan. It is the only national party: we have support in both north and south. If Hizb-i-Islami were to show partiality, there could never be peace.'

He claimed to want nothing more than to serve his country: 'I want the people to know that. I want the West to know that.' But he had also calculated – entirely accurately, as it turned out – that the Northern Alliance ranged against the Taliban was too shaky to last for long.

Rabbani's meeting had not been a success. The Tajik leader, Ahmed Shah Massoud, had scented a trap and refused to attend at all. Without either him or Hekmatyar, the coalition idea was already dead. Were the alliance to collapse completely, Hekmatyar must have reasoned, Mazar and the north would fall, the country would belong to the Taliban, and his Iranian exile could become indefinite. He was a supreme opportunist who saw a chance instead to broker a deal with the Taliban, which he no doubt hoped would return him to what he really craved: the prime ministership in Kabul.

'And the Taliban – what do you really think of them?'

'Their methods are . . . incorrect. But we all want the same thing, finally: to live in an Islamic state, and to live in peace.'

I thought this was a bit much coming from him.

'But do you think the people would welcome your return to power? I mean, after so many died in the bombardment of Kabul. Don't you regret that?'

For the first time I caught a flash of anger in his eyes. I had put the question too directly; he was offended by my impertinence, and there was an ominous pause before he answered.

'The martyrdom of innocents is always unfortunate,' he said eventually. 'The fighting in Kabul was not of our choosing.'

A braver journalist might have pressed him further. He had taken a leading part in the four-year battle for the capital, which had 'unfortunately' killed tens of thousands of civilians. On the other hand I knew it was not a good idea to push him too far. In 1994, notoriously, the BBC Pashto Service's Mirwais Jalil was murdered immediately after an interview with Hekmatyar that had displeased him. In 1987, Hekmatyar was also said to have rewarded the killers of a BBC cameraman, Andy Skrzypkowiak, whose only crime was to have taken some footage of a battle against the Soviets won by a rival mujahideen leader.

I suddenly remembered how alone and exposed I was – and scuttled for the safer ground of softer questions.

Later, as the interview began to wind down, he remarked that it was 'good to be conversing again with the Great Satan'.

It was a relief to learn that his equanimity was restored.

'Excuse me, but I think you mean Little Satan?' I replied with a mock show of offended Britishness. Hekmatyar actually laughed.

'You may be smaller, but you are also quicker and cleverer,' said an aide at his elbow, to knowing smiles all round.

The winter sun was beginning to set through a grubby window. Hekmatyar, as though bored, suddenly signalled that he wanted to pray. Everyone stood, a gunman appeared at my side, and I wondered how on earth I was to get back to my hotel.

'Er, Mr Hekmatyar. The curfew ... I wonder if I could ask your men to take me back?'

An imperious flick of his beard at his aide was all it took, and soon our convoy was thundering back down the frozen road to town, the muffled machine-gunner on the lead truck silhouetted against a western sky heavy with the promise of another snowstorm.

13

How to Talk to the Taliban

Whether or not Hekmatyar would ever give up his guns, the establishment of HIA, the non-violent wing of his movement, surely held promise for the future. However much Arghandiwal objected to his faction being compared to Sinn Fein, the Northern Irish model resulted in the eventual disarmament of the IRA and a working political settlement. HIA offered Hizb-i-Islami supporters an alternative to violent resistance, and many thousands of former fighters who might otherwise have taken to the hills with Hekmatyar had almost certainly chosen it since 2002.

Michael Semple, the former head of the EU mission, argued that HIA's political engagement with Kabul offered 'a case study of what reconciliation might have been like had the Taliban opted to develop a political organization parallel to its insurgency ... [Karzai's] handling of Hizb-i-Islami arguably constitutes the most successful example of a reconciliation strategy so far pursued since Bonn.'[1] Semple, an Irishman who grew up in Northern Ireland during the Troubles, understood better than most how difficult the process of reconciliation could be. In a bizarre diplomatic incident in 2007, he was expelled from the country following entirely false allegations that he had tried to broker a deal with the Taliban behind President Karzai's back.

Not all Taliban were 'No Surrender' die-hards. Some of its leading members did in fact try to establish an HIA-style political wing after Omar's regime collapsed. It was called Khadim ul Furqan, the 'Servants of the Koran', and was set up in Islamabad in 2002 with the specific aim of bridging the gap between Quetta and Kabul. Its founder was another former mujahideen commander, Arsala Rahmani, the Taliban's one-time Minister of Higher Education; he had previously served as Deputy Prime Minister under Hekmatyar. Rahmani sought permission to set up a Khadim office in Kabul, but the Karzai government blocked his request for almost three years. Meanwhile in Quetta the hardliners were in the ascendant, and fixated on ridding Afghanistan of its foreign invaders through armed struggle. They did nothing to encourage his project either. Rahmani's big idea for peace was effectively still-born – although the man himself is very much alive.

Born in 1937, Rahmani was an old man by this country's standards, with eyes that swam behind a big square pair of bi-focal glasses. He wore a striped, long-sleeved *chapan* over his shoulders, a garment favoured by rich northern wool-traders, and which Karzai has made famous. His teeth were bad and when he smiled, which was often, his hand flew to his mouth to hide them. He was one of the dozen senior Taliban figures who had reconciled with the Karzai government since 2002, and was perhaps the most statesmanlike Afghan politician I had ever met, with the clever trick of exuding gravitas and humility at the same time. In his present political incarnation he sat as a Senator in the Upper House, the Mashrano Jirga, where he headed the Education and Religious Affairs Committee, with special responsibility for organizing the Hajj. As he well knew, these portfolios would be critical in any future settlement with the insurgents: 'A key bridge to the Taliban,' as he put it.

He thought the Taliban's policy on girls' education in the 1990s had been badly misrepresented by the West.

'The Taliban were never against building girls' schools. It was a problem of infrastructure. There was no ban; it was just that we couldn't afford to build them then. I remember discussing with Omar a plan to allow trainee female doctors and nurses to return to work. It was no problem for him.'

'So what about the burning of girls' schools? If the Taliban returned, would that continue?' I persisted.

Rahmani worked a set of prayer-beads with his fingers as he marshalled his response.

'Those who burn down schools are not true Taliban.

Everyone should know that education is the key to our future. It is not possible for a country to cut itself off from the rest of the world.'

Internal reconciliation with the Taliban, he acknowledged, would probably lead to a period of international isolation for the country, but that would pass eventually. 'This country is ready to be a good international partner to the world, and it deserves that chance.'

Rahmani knew everybody that mattered: Mullah Omar, even bin Laden in the old days. As a native of Paktika province, he still had significant Taliban connections within the strategically critical south-east of the country. He had also met often with senior religious leaders in Pakistan such as Sami ul-Haq, the director of the famous Dar-u-Uloom Haqqania madrasah near Peshawar. Ul-Haq was more than just a headmaster: he was also one of the founders of Pakistan's Muttahida Majlis-i-Amal, the MMA, the coalition of six Islamic parties that held the balance of power in the North-West Frontier province. Rahmani was convinced that any peace process would fail if the interests of such people, and those of the ISI who stood behind them, were not taken into account. His emphasis on the need for a *regional* solution to the war was rare among Afghan politicians, but it was surely correct. Washington acknowledged the importance of the broader approach in January 2009 when Richard Holbrooke, a diplomat famed for brokering peace in Bosnia in 1995, was appointed as the Administration's first ever Special

Representative for Afghanistan and Pakistan. Britain quickly followed the American lead when its ambassador to Kabul, Sir Sherard Cowper-Coles, was recast in an equivalent role for Whitehall.

It was hard to think of a more useful adviser to both countries in the search for peace than Rahmani. And yet the senator, extraordinarily, had remained on the UN's Consolidated List since 2001. Of the 142 'associates of the Taliban' originally placed on the list, just twelve of any significance had agreed to a formal reconciliation with the Kabul government; and of those twelve, Rahmani, as a senator, was easily the most senior within the Karzai administration. It was a bizarre state of affairs: a statesman who was also an official pariah, lumped together with insurgents and terrorists, formally banned from foreign travel and from holding any assets abroad. Why?

'Only the UN Security Council can answer that,' he smiled. 'I gave them all the documents proving that I was a member of Harakat, not the Taliban.'

Perhaps this distinction had been lost on the Security Councillors in New York. Harakat-i-Inqilab-i-Islami was one of the so-called 'Peshawar Seven' mujahideen organizations that had enjoyed American backing during the 1980s Jihad; the name Khadim ul Furqan was in fact a revival of the 1970s forerunner of Harakat. It was a traditionalist group from the south that had all but dissolved after the Soviet retreat, but the party had been reborn with the emergence of the Taliban in the mid-1990s, when many Harakat fighters came out of retirement to join the new movement. Even Mullah Omar had been a member of Harakat once.

Rahmani was more sanguine than Mullah Zaeef had been about living under the Security Council's shadow – 'I really don't have that many foreign bank accounts for them to freeze,' he shrugged – and it also seemed that the travel ban was not always enforced in his case. With the UN's permission he had in fact visited several countries: Saudi Arabia, France, Britain – even Kenya.

'I went to Ireland once, with that strange airline of yours . . . Ryanair.' He laughed, hand over mouth again. 'Can you believe they charged me one pound for a cup of tea?'

He hadn't lost his sense of humour, but deep down he minded very much that he remained on the Consolidated List, however laxly its attendant sanctions were applied, and he was still lobbying to have his name removed. His inclusion was a symbolic insult, a sign that America was still not sincere about wanting peace.

'They will fight for another eighteen months, and they are building up the ANA and the ANP to continue their fight when they stop,' he said.

Rahmani, I knew, had accompanied Mullah Zaeef on the first, fabled peace-talks trip to Mecca in September 2008. Was it not possible for the Saudis to drive peace talks forward while America took a back seat?

'No. Only the Americans have the weight to make talks happen. It is they who are fighting the Taliban. I remember a group of Pakistanis came here to talk peace in 2004. I told Karzai then that it was useless, and that if he really wanted peace he should make the Americans commit to the process. But nothing has changed.'

'But would the Taliban ever accept a peace brokered by the Americans?'

'I am not speaking for the Taliban here – I am speaking for the Afghan people. But if the conditions were right, then why not?'

The main condition, he confirmed, was the withdrawal of foreign troops.

'The foreigners won't stay here for ever. They never do. But there will be no peace here until they go.'

Rahmani's old party, Harakat-i-Inqilab-i-Islami, was a shadow of what it had been during the Jihad, but it still existed as a political entity and I was keen to discover what role, if any, it had to play in a future peace deal. The following day I visited its leader, Hajji Musa Hotak, at his run-down headquarters in a south-western suburb of the capital. He was yet another ex-mujahideen commander, and as his name indicated, a member of the same tribe as Mullah Omar, the Hotaki Ghilzai. These days he was an MP for his native Wardak province, and another 'reconciled' former associate of the Taliban who, unlike Zaeef and Rahmani, had just succeeded in having his name removed from the UN Consolidated List. He was, I noted, a cigarette smoker: a sign that he considered himself more ex-mujahideen than ex-Taliban, a movement that had banned the habit as a symbol of moral decay. It was cold in his office – he said it had been snowing in the passes that morning as he commuted in from Wardak – and we huddled around a small sputtering gas heater on the floor as he told his story.

Harakat, he confirmed, had been one of the two original mujahideen parties favoured by the ulema and other religious conservatives, with a powerbase in the Pashtun south. Hotak had served Harakat loyally for years, but it had gone into decline after the Soviet withdrawal in 1989. Harakat's leader in those days, Mullah Mohammed Nabi, was offered the vice-presidency under President Rabbani, but declined on the grounds that he had not fought the Russians simply to take power himself. He did, however, encourage some of his commanders to take up political positions, Hajji Hotak among them. He worked in the Rabbani government Finance Ministry for two years but, disillusioned by the growing internecine violence, he quit in 1993 and returned to Wardak.

Harakat enjoyed a rebirth with the emergence of the Taliban. The movements shared the same constituency; they made a 'natural alliance'. Hotak joined Omar's revolt. As a former employee of the government, he proved a useful go-between in negotiations between the two sides, if not an ultimately successful one.

'I really didn't want the war to come to Kabul. The city had suffered enough bloodshed under the mujahideen. When the Taliban reached Wardak I *ran* between Omar and Rabbani to try to stop the fighting.'

The negotiations of 1996, he said, might have led to a coalition government being formed, and peace. But the Taliban demanded that the pro-government forces disarm before any talks – which Ahmed Shah Massoud refused to do.

Hotak was appointed Deputy Minister of Planning in the new Taliban government, with responsibility for the civil development budget. His budget, he said, was drawn from customs revenues, *zakat* (the Islamic alms tax) and *'ushr* (the Islamic tax on farm produce). The tax collection system, however, was in a terrible state. The sums at his disposal were consequently tiny: $11 million in the first year, $18 million in the second, rising to a high of $75 million in the last year, 2000–2001.

'$75 million for a country as big as Afghanistan – can you imagine? That is what it costs to keep seventy-five American soldiers in Helmand for a year. But a little went a long way then, because there was no corruption: as different as land and sky today.'

This was a common enough perception in Kabul. Hotak was clearly proud of what he had achieved at the Planning Ministry. The capital's electricity grid and road system had been fixed during his tenure. 'And just look at the roads now,' he added. In Mazar, piped gas was restored to every home, although the system had since fallen into disrepair and there had been 'no domestic gas in Mazar for the past eight years'. He also took credit for securing two major joint-venture contracts with foreigners, one with a Pakistani company to extract granite, another with the Chinese to explore natural gas deposits in Jowzjan province – although the arrival of the *Amriki* had brought a swift end to both.

His memories of the Taliban times were mixed.

'They brought security and there was no corruption. At the beginning, there was a wonderful atmosphere of trust. But the Taliban were also too extreme in some aspects: the Office of Vice and Virtue, the television thing, the way they treated women. And then their idealism was corrupted. The movement was infiltrated by all the mujahideen parties – twenty-nine of them! – and there was foreign interference, and the Northern Alliance, and the communists. They gave the Taliban a bad name. The same thing is happening now, to Karzai.'

Hotak did not flee to Pakistan when the Taliban were overthrown, or take up arms with the insurgency.

'I was tired of the fighting. Enough was enough.'

He also had a strong survivor's instinct. Throughout the Taliban campaign to take over the country, he had maintained discreet contacts with Karim Khalili, the Hazara leader, even during the period of the latter's resistance towards the Taliban. As the regime collapsed, he sought safe haven in the Hazarajat.[2] With a leader as powerful as Khalili behind him, he was safe from American retribution – at least for a while. In December 2003 he was even among the 502 delegates who endorsed the new Constitution at President Karzai's Loya Jirga in Kabul. But then, disaster came.

Under the Taliban, Hotak had been the kind of

government minister who double-hatted as a military commander. Hundreds of fighters remained loyal to him even in 2003, and he maintained a significant arsenal of heavy weaponry in Wardak. He judged that the time had now come to surrender his weapons, and he did so in good faith under DDR, the new government's Disarmament, Demobilization and Reintegration programme. This was no small matter for him, for his arsenal included as many as thirty-five Stinger missiles – a potent status symbol in Afghanistan as well as a valuable one. The Stinger, a shoulder-held anti-aircraft weapon, had been supplied to the mujahideen by the CIA in the 1980s to take down Soviet helicopters, and was widely credited with turning the tide of that war. The US subsequently tried to buy back any unused ones, offering more than \$180,000 for each,[3] and yet Hotak had given them up for free.

He was promptly rewarded for his gesture with a US Special Forces night raid on his home. 'I still get flashbacks,' he said. 'They broke down doors, smashed every window. I was clubbed, and bitten by dogs. My sons and nephews were hooded and shackled. My aged father was dragged out. No human being would do the things those animals did.'

Hotak would have ended up in Bagram, but the Americans were prevented from taking him there by his neighbours, who surrounded their Humvees and refused to move out of the way.

'Even they couldn't drive over the people. So they took

my brother to Bagram instead. They kept him there for two and a half years.'

Despite that bitter memory, Hotak's greatest hope was that a peace could be negotiated. Harakat these days, he insisted, was a 'neutral' political party which could have a vital broking role to play in a settlement. This, he explained, was because it was still the party of the ulema, the religious scholars, just as it had been in the 1980s.

'It was us who set the Jihad against the Soviets,' he said. 'The ulema are silent now, but if they were to endorse Mullah Omar's war against America as a true jihad, the whole country would rise.'

This was another version of Mullah Zaeef's Cassandra-like warning. The ulema, it was true, had dictated the spiritual direction of the country often enough in the past. The modernizing King Amanullah had tried to push through his reforms without their support, and ended up paying for his presumption with his throne when, in 1928, Pashtun tribesmen from Jalalabad marched on the capital with the support of the ulema; Amanullah's army chose to desert rather than to resist. Mullah Omar knew he could not afford to alienate the ulema. When, for example, they declined to endorse his call for jihad against the Rabbani government in 1995, he did not insist on the point. President Karzai also understood the impossibility of ruling Afghanistan without at least their tacit approval. This was why, according to Hotak, Karzai had come to Harakat-i-Inqilab-i-Islami

Taliban fighters who
surrendered to the
Northern Alliance await
their fate in a cell in
Shibarghan, northern
Afghanistan, in
December 2001.

Above: September 2001: in the wake of 9/11, the *ulema* again debated whether to hand Osama bin Laden over to the US – but too late to prevent the start of a major American bombing campaign (*below*, on the front line north of Kabul).

Above: Unable to defend the capital, the Taliban were driven southwards by Northern Alliance troops, who reoccupied the city in November.

Right: Northern Alliance troops check the bodies of Taliban fighters killed during an attempted prison break at Qala-i-Jangi that took six days to suppress.

Above: Serious questions remain about the treatment of prisoners by the Uzbek leader, General Rashid Dostum. President Obama ordered a fresh investigation into alleged atrocities in 2009.

Left: US Defense Secretary Donald Rumsfeld (*far left*) announced 'the end of major combat operations' in April 2003 – just as the insurgency began to heat up.

Below: US troops continued their hunt for terrorists – although telling friend from foe has never been easy in Afghanistan.

Bottom: Mullah Dadullah, a one-legged Taliban icon, was killed in fighting in Helmand in 2007 and exhibited to the press in Kandahar.

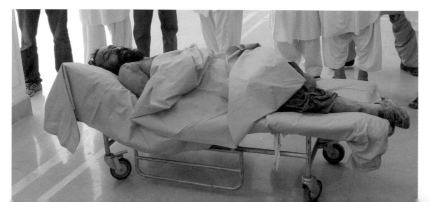

Left: Low-level insurgency developed into full-scale war in Helmand in 2006: the fiercest fighting experienced by British troops in half a century.

Above: The Taliban later switched to a deadly roadside bombing campaign (a wrecked ANA Humvee).

Above: US Special Forces were granted new search and destroy powers in 2009 – but at what cost to the campaign to win local 'hearts and minds'?

Above: General Stanley McChrystal was supposed to reinvigorate the counter-insurgency. But the West's exit strategy still depends on newly trained local forces, such as Sergeant Abdullah of the Afghan National Police (*top right*).

Below: Meanwhile, the insurgency is strengthening. In 2008, suicide bombers and gunmen on motorbikes sprang 400 suspected Taliban from Sarposa jail in Kandahar; in 2009, Mullah Omar published a book of rules designed to regulate Taliban behaviour (*right*).

Below: At a conference in London in January 2010, Karzai renewed the call for negotiations with his 'disenchanted brothers' – who responded with attacks in Kabul that killed at least ten (*right*). In June, Obama replaced McChrystal with General David Petraeus (*bottom*). But can the hero of Iraq repeat his success?

A *shura* of tribal elders in Sangin, Helmand, in 2007. The tradition of reaching consensus through dialogue remains strong among the Pashtuns: the likely key to any negotiated Afghan settlement.

before the presidential election, asking to be appointed the party's official candidate.

'And what did you say?'

'We agreed, on two conditions. First, we told him he had to make peace with the Taliban, and second, to stop killing our Muslim brothers.'

'And now?'

'And now he is trying to start talks, as he promised. His appeal to the Saudis at the London Conference was all about this.'

'But the killing of your Muslim brothers has not stopped.'

'It is the Americans who are doing that. Karzai has tried to stop them, but his government has no power. He was forced to agree to the Marjah campaign.'

Hotak offered the same solution as the others I had spoken to: empower the government, tear up the UN Consolidated List, close Guantanamo, 'and stop asking us to disarm – we are not crazy!' Just like Mullah Zaeef, he insisted that the Taliban did not want to destroy the government or the Constitution; they only wanted to repair it. As one of the original Loya Jirga delegates of 2003 he knew something about this. The wrangling over the new Constitution's 160 articles was so intense at times that the public took to describing the gathering as a loya *jagra* – 'a big fight'. Nevertheless, the document that emerged from the process was by no means a uniformly bad one.

'There are no more than eleven articles that need to be

changed – that were put in by the international community, and are not in Afghanistan's interests. These are not mountains. The Taliban wants to discuss them in a reasonable way.'

Hotak was despondent, however, about the recent arrest of Mullah Abdul Ghani Baradar, who had been picked up by the ISI in Karachi at the beginning of February and, along with his two teenage sons, reportedly subjected to severe torture. Baradar was Omar's number two and a founding member of the Taliban. The ISI's motive for the arrest was not yet clear. Nato officials in Kabul initially heralded the event as a 'turning point' in the war – evidence, perhaps, that Pakistan was at last bending to US pressure to crack down on the Taliban leaders known to be hiding there. Hotak, however, thought the opposite. Baradar, he claimed, was at the dove's end of the spectrum of views within the Taliban leadership. He had spent almost two years trying to persuade Baradar to come to the negotiating table, and now all his efforts were wasted. He suspected the ISI had targeted Baradar because they were not consulted on his secret communications with Kabul, and did not approve of freelancers within what they still saw as 'their' organization. Like Arsala Rahmani, Hotak was certain that there would never be peace in Afghanistan unless the ISI's interests were taken into account. The ISI's continuing manipulation of the movement for their own ends was just an unfortunate fact of life.

'The ISI could arrest Mullah Omar tomorrow if they wanted to,' Hotak insisted.

He said the main block to progress, as ever, was the Americans. The people no longer trusted them; they were not sincere about peace; the renewed military campaign in the south proved it. Their actions shaped everything that happened in the region – even, he implied, the arrest of Mullah Baradar – and it was their fault if progress on reconciliation had stalled. Karzai, according to Hotak, had 'given up' on getting the Americans to agree to talks. But he was undecided about the British, whose true attitude towards reconciliation was something of a mystery to him – as indeed it was to Hotak.

In late 2008, he claimed, a British embassy official had approached him asking if they could arrange a meeting with the Taliban – and requested that this be done without the knowledge of either Karzai or the US.

'I told him that would be difficult, but I did as he asked.'

Three meetings eventually took place in the spring and autumn of 2009, all of them in Dubai, involving 'input from MI6 in London' and 'ministry-level Taliban'. Among the latter, he revealed, was Maulawi Delawar Shahabuddin, a former High Court Chief Justice for the Taliban. The British, however, refused to entertain the idea of a fourth meeting, and Hotak was at a loss to explain why.

'My reputation with the Taliban suffered because of this. Maulawi Shahabuddin said to me, "Where are your British friends now?"'

A British intelligence official later disclosed that the Dubai meetings had been stopped because the main Taliban interlocutor had turned out to be 'the wrong man'; and it was true that Shahabuddin – current whereabouts unknown, according to the UN Consolidated List, but 'believed to be in the Afghanistan–Pakistan border area' – was not the influential figure in Omar's circle that he had been in the early days of the movement. Nevertheless, a promising negotiating back-channel had been closed off, and that seemed a great pity. For reasons of history, there was a level of understanding between the British and the Afghans – including at least some Taliban – that the Americans could never hope to achieve.

'The British are special to us,' Hotak confirmed. 'Our relationship with you was so good during the Jihad. You have been coming here for 170 years. We feel we *know* you.'

And yet by closing down the Dubai track, MI6 had surely weakened this British advantage. The distance between the sides was left a little wider than before; trust, that rarest of precious commodities in Afghanistan, had been wasted.

Hotak understood that Britain could not by itself dictate international policy, but he still could not understand our silence. Did we not sit on the UN Security Council? Were we not the second largest foreign troop contributor to ISAF? And were we not one of America's most important allies, her truest friend in Europe, the beneficiaries of a famous Special Relationship? In short, what country in the world was better placed than Britain to influence Washington's strategy in Afghanistan?

'The British should encourage talks, not block them,' Hajji Hotak concluded. 'The ulema will back you if you do. And the reputation of your country will not just be left intact – it will be enhanced.'

14

In the Jalalabad Fief of Shirzai

Kabul was a bubble, divorced from the reality of life in the rest of Afghanistan, and I was anxious to find out what was happening beyond the capital. Jalalabad, ninety miles to the east, seemed a good place to look. It was only the country's sixth city by size, but it was the capital of the important eastern Pashtun belt, while its position on the main road between Peshawar and Kabul, a crucial artery for armies and international traders alike, lent it a strategic and economic significance out of proportion to its size.

Even the drive there revealed something about the state of the country. In 2002 on my last visit to Jalalabad, the road from Kabul was in a disastrous state. The tarmac had been destroyed by a decade of passing Soviet armour, and hardly a single bridge was intact, so that what should have been a two-hour drive took a full day to complete. The bridges had since been rebuilt and the road repaved, yet my journey still took almost five hours. Beyond the awesome gorges that guarded Kabul, my car ran into a traffic jam that blocked the road in both directions for a distance of ten miles. There were many tunnels on this mountain road, most of them too narrow to allow two heavy trucks to pass each other. The policemen who were supposed to control the traffic instead took bribes from the truckers, who were always in a hurry and wanted to go first. When the trucks met in the middle of a tunnel, they were each prevented from reversing out again by the weight of traffic behind. The result was an entirely avoidable impasse that my driver said happened almost every day: an object lesson in social stupidity and short-sightedness, as well as in the corrosive effect of petty corruption among policemen.

In October 2002 I had stayed with two Pashtun businessmen, Aziz and Basir, in an abandoned ice factory that one of them owned.[1] Omar's regime had been gone for less than a year. They had shaved their beards and were glad to have their television back. On the other hand, they were nostalgic for the days when they could go out of their house without locking the front door, for there was no security in post-Taliban Jalalabad. Karzai's initial appointee to the governorship of Nangarhar province of which Jalalabad was the capital, Hajji Abdul Kadir, had been in office for less than eight months when he was assassinated in Kabul. The resulting power vacuum had been filled by the militiaman Hazrat Ali, whose men had begun to run amok, shooting and looting almost at will. Of the many stories from that time, one of the most infamous concerned a town centre bureau-de-change, which contained a large night safe reputedly stuffed with rupees. Hazrat Ali decided to burgle it, but was unable to crack the lock by conventional means. So he returned with a tank, drove through the shop front, tied the safe to the back of the vehicle and towed it off down the street, wall and all, until the safe burst.

To the dismay of Aziz and Basir, the American military had repeatedly turned a blind eye to this gang-sterish behaviour, probably because Hazrat Ali had assisted the US Special Forces in the fight against al-Qaida at Tora Bora in December 2001. Or so they suspected. In 2003, astonishingly, Karzai appointed him as Jalalabad's Chief of Police, before sacking him the following year over allegations that he was in league with the Taliban. Hazrat then became an MP. He still was one in 2010.

I was keen to see how, or indeed whether, matters had improved for the people of Jalalabad since 2002. The provincial governorship had passed in 2004 to another strongman with a dubious history, Gul Agha Shirzai. In his previous role as governor of Kandahar province, Shirzai by his own admission had received a million dollars a week in kickbacks from the opium trade, amassing an alleged private fortune of $300 million.[2] The son of a champion dog-fighter, Shirzai was a powerful, rough man with a communist-era moustache and a reputation for ruthless ambition. He revelled in his best-known nickname, 'the Bulldozer', though probably less so in another one, 'Jabba the Hutt', the obese and sadistic crime lord in *Star Wars*.

Shirzai had been appointed the governor of Nangarhar because he was a Karzai loyalist, who with ISI assistance had led the military campaign to oust the Taliban from Kandahar in 2002. He was also widely considered a darling of the Americans, who had even mooted his name as a contender for the presidency in 2009, even though it was Western pressure that had forced Karzai to remove him from his post in Kandahar. For all his alleged villainy, Shirzai was far from being a bad provincial governor. However imperfect, he was seen by Western diplomats as a man who could get things done, and he operated with a certain cheeky style. He had even proposed building a luxury tourist hotel with US funding near the caves of Tora Bora, the site of bin Laden's last stand in Afghanistan. Ironically, considering the allegations that he had profited from the drug trade in Kandahar, he was credited with dramatically reducing Nangarhar's once formidable poppy harvest. Jalalabad's infrastructure, particularly its roads, had also seen great improvements during his tenure, and he was popular among the poor, to whom he was a generous and sometimes wildly spontaneous donor. He ran the place like the overlord of a fief, and although this was an affront to democracy, his dictatorship was at least a relatively benign one.

Beneath the surface, however, not all was well in

Jalalabad. Violence was on the increase in the city. A council official had been killed by a suicide bomber just ten days before. 'It's like 1994 all over again,' said Mufti Mohin Shah, the Deputy Leader of the Provincial Council. 'Warlordism and insecurity have returned, and the people are fed up. They are ready to welcome the Taliban back again. In fact, it is a reality now: they are already coming. And I'm not worried about that.'

The mufti – a title denoting an expounder of Sharia law, the equivalent of a canon lawyer in Chaucerian times – was thirty-three years old, a member of that generation of Afghans just too young to have fought in the Jihad. His family had returned from refugee exile in Pakistan when Karzai was elected, full of hope for their country's future. A radio producer by training, he had found his way into politics by accident when he helped to set up a local station, Radio Spinghar, which was dedicated to religious programming. Its Sharia law discussion slot, he said proudly, had been so popular that it had been rolled out nationally. Radio Spinghar had even won an award.

I was speaking to him in the Provincial Council assembly hall, the main entrance to which bore a plaque proclaiming that it had been built with funding from the People of the United States in 2006. Under the new constitution, power was supposed to have devolved to local assemblies like this one. The trouble, explained the mufti, was that there had been no such shift of power in practice. Karzai was anxious, and indeed under pressure from the West, to strengthen the authority of central government. He had therefore altered the constitution so that he – or his placeman in the province, Gul Agha Shirzai – retained the power of political appointment, even down to the level of the district councils. The result was outrageous local government corruption everywhere.

'Until we are properly empowered, there is nothing we can do. We are just observers,' said the mufti sadly. 'We did a survey of the district councils recently and we were shocked by what we found. Our business people are regularly paying bribes of $100,000 or more to get things done. You even have to pay something in order to pay: for a building licence, for car tax, for domestic telephone bills – everything!'

I asked him if Kabul was fully aware of what was going on in Nangarhar.

'Of course they are! I named all the corrupt district governors in the local newspaper recently. Look,' he said, producing a copy from under his seat. It was called *Narai*, the 'Globe'. The front page carried a large photograph of the mufti, surrounded by Arabic script that I couldn't read.

'Shirzai went mad when he saw this. He telephoned Karzai to say he wanted the Provincial Council arrested! Then Karzai called us. He told us not to worry, that we should just keep quiet for the next three months because he was planning to send Shirzai to govern another province then. But I think he was lying.'

His stand against corruption must have taken courage. The chair-lined chamber where we were speaking was filled with officials and members of the public on business, and it was clear that not all of them could be trusted. When I asked if the influence of Hazrat Ali was still being felt in the city, he briefly broke into English to explain that they 'still had some problems' with him. Two men connected to Hazrat Ali, I learned later, were sitting twenty feet away and listening to every word of our conversation.

'The Provincial Council has been infiltrated by criminal networks, and Shirzai does nothing to stop them,' he explained when the pair had moved off.

No wonder he 'wasn't worried' by the prospect of a Taliban comeback. Nothing and no one else seemed willing or able to offer him the protection he needed.

I recalled the three-wheeled tuk-tuk taxis I had seen in the town centre on my way to the Provincial Council. There were none of these vehicles in Kabul but they were common here – a reminder of how close we were to Pakistan, where every city swarmed with them. Some of these tuk-tuks carried portraits of matinee idols from 'Pollywood', Peshawar's homegrown cinema industry. The archetypal Pollywood hero is a hunky Pashtun warrior, while the villains – because this is the Raj's former North-West Frontier province – are always perfidious Brits. The films are cartoonishly bloodthirsty, the kind where the machine guns never seem to need reloading. One tuk-tuk I saw displayed a gunman in a

Rambo-style bandanna sipping a wineglass full of blood. The faces on several other tuk-tuks, however, had been scratched out. Had idolatry-hating Taliban supporters wielded the penknife? Or had the tuk-tuk owners themselves been sniffing the wind and taken precautionary measures? It was equally hard to tell if the iconoclasm was fresh or whether it dated back to the *ancien regime*. Still, tuk-tuk artwork provided an unusual barometer of religious opinion in Jalalabad that I thought would be worth keeping an eye on in future.

I went across town to the government guesthouse to meet my fifth 'reconciled' Taliban official on the UN Consolidated List, Jalaluddin Shinwari, who had been the regime's Deputy Minister of Religious Affairs and ultimately its Minister of Justice, a position that in those days incorporated the role of Supreme Attorney-General. I presumed Mullah Omar had filled such an important post with yet another madrasah-educated Koran-basher, but I couldn't have been more wrong. Shinwari was a mild-mannered, quizzical man with a Puckish smile, a diabetic who tired easily and who walked with a hobble that made him seem older than his forty-three years. He looked like a scholar with his glasses and sparse beard, and in fact he was a senior judge who had trained in secular as well as Sharia law at the elite Sharia Academy in Kabul. This automatically made him a leading voice among the country's ulema, as well as one of the former regime's rare intellectuals.

'The foreign perception that the Taliban are all

terrorists like al-Qaida is quite wrong. It has been fed by a handful of Northern Alliance leaders – Fahim, Atta, Dostum, Mohaqeq. But the Taliban are not monsters. Yes, we made lots of mistakes, and I pointed some of these out to Omar. He said he was busy with the war, but he promised on God's word that he would sort it all out when the war was over. Even so, we made progress in government, and the people appreciated that. If you held a ballot today amongst the civil servants at the Ministry of Justice or the Attorney-General's office, I would win 90 per cent of their votes, I swear. This government is just abusing power for its own ends.'

His line was familiar by now. The Taliban deserved the benefit of the doubt and should be given a second chance. The mistakes of the past were the result of inexperience and 'bad influences' on the movement, which had now been purged. It would not be the same the next time – particularly when it came to women's rights, which he acknowledged were 'the most emotive issue' in the West. 'Afghan women have no rights now, under Karzai,' he said. 'The government pays lip service to the idea – just look at all the sloganeering on Women's Day – but the reality is that women are still treated as sex objects. Under Sharia, by contrast, women will be genuinely respected. They will have the right to an education, and to work. But,' he added, holding up a finger, 'they must also wear the hijab. You shouldn't let your fear of cultural traditions get in the way of the main strategy! We must be allowed to do things our way – not Hillary Clinton's way.'

For all his objections to foreign interference, Shinwari was no xenophobe. He said that the Taliban's greatest mistake, the one thing he would have changed had he been in charge before 2001, was the international isolation embraced by its leadership.

'International partnership is the key to prosperity. Afghanistan needs to be more outward-looking, to engage with the outside world. The Europeans are more willing listeners than the Americans . . . Learning foreign languages is very important. Learning English is very important.'

He regretted that his own English was so bad, a fault he was determined to rectify in his children. I met his son, a diffident 25-year-old who greeted his father with a respectful kiss of his hand. He was dressed in Western-style jeans and jacket, an outfit explained when he revealed that he was on a short visit from South Yorkshire where he had been living and studying for the last eight years. He hadn't learned as much as his father might reasonably have expected after such a time – 'My English not so well,' he admitted – but he was fluent enough to explain that he found the town he lived in 'a bit small', and that he liked to go into Sheffield for big city action at weekends. I asked him what he thought of the Taliban. He said he thought there were 'good and bad people in every village'. I wondered if his father's background had ever caused him trouble with the authorities but he said not: 'I don't mention his job with the Taliban, and no one has ever asked me.'

Politically, Shinwari had always been a monarchist who hoped for the restoration of the Afghan King, Zahir Shah, who had been deposed by his republican cousin in 1973 and had gone into exile in Rome. Shinwari had fled Afghanistan during the Jihad, and was still living in Peshawar in 1994 when the Taliban emerged. Zahir Shah's Chief of Staff asked him to join the movement as a kind of ambassador of the court-in-exile. 'I became influential because I was educated in a modern academy, not a madrasah. Omar loved me for that, and needed me.' He was even invited to address the thousand ulema who gathered in Kandahar in 1996 to endorse the war against the Rabbani regime.

Omar had nothing against the idea of a restoration per se. King Zahir was the scion of the Pashtun Barakzai dynasty who had ruled the country since the 1820s. His reign had lasted for forty years, and was remembered by all Afghans, not just Pashtuns, as a golden era of peace – which it was, compared to the mayhem that followed it. What Afghanistan desperately needed to end thirty-five years of civil war was a unity candidate, and even Mullah Omar could see that none was more plausible than Zahir Shah. When Kabul fell to the Taliban, Shinwari followed on, fully expecting to assist at the restitution of the King. 'But there was no restitution. Instead I was invited to join their government. They insisted, so I stayed.' Omar calculated that the Taliban's purification mission was incomplete in 1996, and that the country was therefore not ready for the King's return.

When the Taliban fell, however, Zahir rushed back to Kabul amidst renewed talk that he could regain his throne. At the Loya Jirga in June 2002, he actually won more votes than Hamid Karzai to become the new head of state, but was forced by Zalmay Khalilzad, who was then George Bush's Special Envoy, to withdraw his candidature at the last minute. The Europeans, Shinwari recalled, had been quite keen on Zahir's candidacy, but were silenced by the Americans who ultimately insisted on Karzai and democracy instead. The Americans' past experience of supporting monarchies in the region, he noted, had not been good – a reference to the overthrow of the Shah of Iran in 1979 and the Islamic revolution that followed. Zahir was demoted to a figurehead role – he opened the Loya Jirga of December 2003, for instance – but his health was beginning to fail, and when he died in 2007 the possibility of a monarchist solution receded – although it had not entirely faded from view. Zahir's heir, Crown Prince Mustafa, was running the country's Environmental Protection Agency in 2010, a government appointment that kept the King's Party close to the Karzai administration as a kind of insurance policy against the future; and even Mullah Omar is said still to consult with the Prince from time to time.

If Shinwari's technical expertise had once been useful to Mullah Omar, his status as a leading member of the ulema was now just as important to Karzai. With the President's blessing he was on the point of announcing a new ulema party; even during our meeting, a secretary kept reappearing with different drafts of a press release for his boss's inspection. It sounded like competition for Hajji Hotak, who claimed that his Harakat party already spoke for the ulema. The difference, Shinwari explained, was that his organization would be genuinely independent; Harakat, being an old mujahideen party, had military associations and was seen by many ulema as politically 'tainted'. This was not the first time Shinwari had attempted to launch an ulema party. When he tried in 2007, he was picked up by the NDS and placed under house arrest for a month.

'They put me in a very beautiful apartment in Kabul,' he remembered, 'but it was still house arrest. We were going to name the corrupt within the government, and they felt threatened. This time we have persuaded Karzai that it is a good thing. The ulema already meet every three to six months. This will simply formalize the movement.'

Like Hajji Hotak, Shinwari thought the ulema were the 'key to peace in this Islamic society'. But he also argued that they were powerless to influence anything without the support of the international community, and even of Nato.

'Our movement will not oppose the foreign presence. We will work as partners with you, so long as there is no interference with our cultural and religious traditions.'

As he acknowledged, this was a very different line from the one commonly heard in Quetta.

'We do want the foreign troops to go, but not before

we can defend ourselves, most of all against the intelligence agencies of our neighbours,' he said. 'Our country has a five-thousand-year-old culture. Pakistan has a sixty-year-old culture, and they are trying to colonize us ... If the foreigners left now, the ANA would become the promoters of civil war, just like the Soviet Union's National Army did.'

Omar, he was convinced, was ready to negotiate with the Karzai government. There had been no progress whatsoever on that front, however, whatever Karzai might have claimed in the past.

'[Omar] has $25 million on his head. He cannot move, or meet anybody, or express himself directly. Nothing will happen until his name is removed from the UN list – and without him, all dialogue is fruitless.'

The ulema, he thought, were the most likely intermediaries for talks in the future.

'Every negotiation needs a middleman, a guarantor. They must be knowledgeable and neutral, with nothing to gain from one outcome or another. The problem with the Saudis is that they had conditions: they wanted a guarantee that the Taliban would split with al-Qaida. That was never going to work.'

His point was that it wasn't in Mullah Omar's gift to guarantee such a thing, however willing he might be. America had accused the Taliban of sponsoring terrorism in 2001, when in reality it was al-Qaida who had sponsored the Taliban.

'If the US couldn't control al-Qaida, how do you

expect the Taliban to? The leadership told bin Laden forcefully and repeatedly not to attack any foreign country from Afghan soil, but bin Laden wouldn't listen: he said he obeyed the Koran, not men.'

Although Shinwari had no formal role in the Karzai administration, the President had sent him a few days before to mediate in a local tribal dispute over grazing rights that was still ongoing and, indeed, intensifying. Eighteen people had so far been killed, three of them that morning. The land in question, 10,000 acres of it, was in Shinwar district to the south-east of Jalalabad, and was contested by two Shinwari Pashtun sub-tribes, the Ali Sher Khel and the Mohmand. As the Chief of the district's first family, Jalaluddin Shinwari was an obvious choice of peace-broker. He wanted me to accompany him to see how a traditional tribal dispute resolution worked in practice: a jirga, a long lunch with the elders of both tribes, ending with an agreement symbolized by a ritual known as 'the placing of the stone' between them. We never made it to Shinwar, though. Instead we sat waiting in the guesthouse for two days as reports came in that the feud was going from bad to worse. The Mohmand accused the Ali Sher Khel of starting the fighting with weapons supplied by local policemen, many of whom were members of the Ali Sher Khel – and Shinwari suspected they were right.

'Our police are supposed to be a national police force, but in this case it seems they have been partisan. All too typical these days, sadly,' he said.

With no other means of defending themselves, the Mohmand had complained to the local Taliban, who had counter-armed them. A small dispute that should have ended bloodlessly was thus threatening to turn into a new flashpoint for the insurgency.

Shinwari was desperate to get out on to the ground, but was prevented by the interference of Governor Shirzai and a delegation of government officials who kept flying in from Kabul by military helicopter, intent on trying to fix things their way. This wasn't working, not only because the government were responsible for the local police – and so were not seen as neutral by the Mohmand – but also because both sides considered the dispute to be the government's fault in the first place. Some months before, the government, hoping to curry favour with both the Ali Sher Khel and the Mohmand, had short-sightedly granted both tribes the grazing rights to the same disputed patch of land. The Shinwari Pashtuns were a powerful group numbering perhaps 2.5 million people across six eastern provinces whose support, or at least passivity, had always been important to Kabul. It was the Shinwari, indeed, who led the march on Kabul that ultimately toppled Amanullah Khan in 1929. The fact that they occupied a region straddling the border with Pakistan added to their modern strategic significance.

On day two of my stay, it emerged that the government officials had travelled to Shinwar for lunch with the elders, just as tribal custom dictated – but had only sat down with the elders of the Ali Sher Khel. The Mohmand elders inevitably suspected that the government was taking sides and, incensed by this insult, had ordered their fighters to return to their gun positions. Shinwari was naturally furious, most of all with Governor Shirzai who arrogantly refused to even answer his phone calls, but he hid his indignation well: he knew better than to challenge the authority of the Governor or the officials from Kabul. Impatience would only make matters worse, and he resigned himself to a long wait.

The affair amply illustrated the tensions beneath the surface of Pashtun society, and how quickly they could boil over into blood-letting. It was also a lesson in the failings of the central government system, its tangled line of command and control and the roughshod way it trampled on tribal tradition. The cost to Karzai was potentially disastrous. The only beneficiaries of the confusion were the Taliban, who knew better than anyone how to exploit the Mohmands' sense of injustice.

The dispute would never have escalated if the local police had not armed the Ali Sher Khel – and it was the West, ironically, who bore the ultimate responsibility for that, since it was they who armed and trained the ANP. A detachment of forty policemen had been ordered to escort Shinwari on his peace-broking mission, and they were all waiting in the guesthouse too. They were easy to approach as they lounged about on the sofas, smoking, joshing each other, desperately bored. The new ANP were just as important to the West's exit strategy as the

ANA was, but these policemen's lack of discipline did not fill me with confidence. At one point, one of them accidentally directed his Kalashnikov at me.

'So why do *you* point your guns at people whenever you come out of your bases?' he glowered when I asked him nicely not to.

Another young policeman – and they were all very young – confided that he and three of his friends had already decided they would 'disappear' if there was any trouble on the mission to Shinwar. He was not a local but a Tajik, from Jebal os Seraj. He said they had no faith in their American-supplied weapons, which were cheap, East European copies of Kalashnikovs that were always jamming at the wrong moment. His training, he said, had lasted just three months.

They all agreed that they were in the job only for the money. The ID card sported on the Tajik's chest turned out, on close inspection, to be a bank card. On the second day of my stay, a Thursday, the policemen were suddenly nowhere to be seen. When Shinwari asked why, he was told that Thursday was payday and that they had all gone to collect their salaries. Their pay didn't amount to much, however keen they were to collect it: $300 a month for the officers, $200 for the juniors, or less than seven dollars a day. This was far more than it had been – in 2003, junior policemen were paid just $30 a month – but it was still nowhere near enough if the West seriously expected them to stand in future against an enemy like the Taliban, a force that in any case paid its conscripts more.

Even General McChrystal described the movement's foot soldiers as 'ten-dollar-a-day Taliban'. The US had so far spent some $4 billion on the police-training programme. Where were those billions going, if not on salaries? Underpaid policemen were more likely to turn to extortion and other crime to top up their income. They also had a worrying tendency to sell their equipment. According to one report, 87,000 weapons delivered to the new security forces by the US since 2001 could no longer be accounted for.[3]

The young policemen at the guesthouse were all livid at the recent news reports of botched night raids. Cover-ups, they said, had become very common, and they gave many examples.

'They plant a few weapons and call it a cache,' said one. 'Or if they accidentally kill a driver, they drop a bomb on his vehicle to destroy the evidence and they call him a suicide-bomber. Such things have become a trade-mark now.'

I asked him if he felt comfortable, operating alongside allies who behaved in this way.

'What, do you think we are not human? Are we to go on doing this until Doomsday? If they kill fifty people, they create five hundred Taliban. If they did something to my family, I wouldn't stand by, I'd take revenge. I hate the Americans.'

The US military, he thought, were playing a very dangerous game that risked alienating all the ANA and ANP. Two American soldiers had been killed by a rogue policeman in Wardak a few months previously, as had five British ones in Helmand in November 2009.

'Najibullah Zazi was caught in the US trying to detonate a suicide bomb. He admitted it. He said he was avenging his family who the Americans killed.'

He made it sound as though Zazi was another dis-affected Afghan policeman, but in reality his empathy was disturbingly misplaced. Zazi, arrested in 2009 for attempting to blow up the New York subway, had been radicalized by a jihadist imam, and was trained and armed by al-Qaida in Pakistan. There was no evidence that the US military or any other American had ever harmed his family, who emigrated to New York in 1999 when he was fourteen.

I wondered how much if any distinction they made between the British and the Americans.

'You are cousins: the same. We hate you all,' said one.

'The black Americans are the worst. They have no manners. They are like animals,' said a second.

'English very gooood!' said the third. 'The black dogs have white cousins, ha ha ha!'

'There are good and bad,' said their sergeant, more thoughtfully, 'like the fingers of the hand: some long, some short.'

The sergeant's name was Sahil. He was twenty-one and he came from Laghman province between Jalalabad and Kabul.

'What can I tell you about the Taliban? You know more than I do. All I can say for certain is that the more you oppress the people, the more the Taliban will emerge. But if you are kind and humble, they will go away.'

At every meal in the guesthouse, about sixty of us sat down at a single long table in the Afghan style, the policemen in their blue serge uniforms and kepis at one end, everyone else at the other. The guesthouse was a busy gathering point for lobbyists seeking an audience with Shirzai in his governor's residence around the corner. One breakfast time, a meal of hot milk, stale bread and a carton of long-life cream each, I found myself sitting with a delegation of elders in full tribal regalia: beautiful dark robes decorated with complex needlework, and immense broad turbans in a variety of pastel hues. They were from Zabul province, the northern neighbour of Kandahar province, 250 miles to the south. It was interesting that Shirzai's connections were considered powerful enough to risk such a long and dangerous journey. Some of them stared at me with open hostility, something I had rarely encountered in Afghanistan in the past. They thought I was American, and I had a hard job persuading them otherwise.

'You Americans and English are all the same.'

'But I'm from Scotland.'

'Scotland? Never heard of it.'

'It's near England.'

'England? You *are* American!'

'England and Scotland are as different as Panjshiri Tajiks and Kandahari Pashtuns.'

'No!' protested a Tajik voice from down the table. 'You are all cousins, all the same!'

The Zabul Pashtuns thought this was very funny. And yet the more hostile among them remained sullen towards me and soon left the table. Only one stayed behind to talk, as sociable and curious as Afghans normally were. 'If you've been bitten by a snake, you'll be scared of a rope,' he shrugged, by way of explaining the behaviour of his friends.

His name was Hajji Noor Gul. They had come to beg Shirzai to intercede with the Americans on behalf of another elder, who had been arrested and detained by US Special Forces during a night raid – the result, once again, of false information passed to them by an aggrieved party in yet another land dispute.

'It's running out of control in Zabul. I have never seen the situation so bad. I've sent my whole family abroad, and many Zabulis have run to the tribal areas [of Pakistan] . . . Some of them have joined the Taliban. The situation is intolerable.'

Hajji Noor had recently met the Police Chief of Wardak province, where he had previously lived.

'I said to him: aren't you ashamed of bringing the Americans here? But he had no shame. He is a communist – a brutal man. The whole government is communist, and they hate us for destroying communism. The Americans don't seem to realize the danger of allying themselves with the communists. Many people have changed sides because of this.'

All his talk was driven by the past, the memory of the Jihad. Although ideologically inconceivable in the West, it did not seem strange to him that America appeared to have embraced communism since the end of the Cold War. 'Changing sides' was a routine tactic in Afghanistan, the way things had always been. As a motive for fighting, ideology came a distant second to the imperative of survival for traditionalists like Hajji Noor. Such men were the backbone of Pashtun society and, now, the bedrock of Taliban support.

In his resignation letter in 2009, Matthew Hoh, the senior American administrator in Zabul province, wrote: 'In both Regional Command East and South, I have observed that the bulk of the insurgency fights not for the white banner of the Taliban, but rather against the presence of foreign soldiers and taxes imposed by an unrepresentative government in Kabul . . . Our support for this kind of government, coupled with a misunderstanding of the insurgency's true nature, reminds me horribly of our involvement with South Vietnam; an unpopular and corrupt government we backed at the expense of our Nation's own internal peace, against an insurgency whose nationalism we arrogantly and ignorantly mistook as a rival to our own Cold War ideology.'

Later I was approached by another man, the young mullah of a mosque on the road that led to Torkham, the border with Pakistan. His robes and his turban were daffodil yellow, and his beard and the ends of his moustache had been sculpted into tidy points beneath his huge hooked nose. He looked more like a Turkish Grand Vizier than an Afghan from Nangarhar.

'My name is Mullah Allah Mohammed,' he began, with a splendid twist of his hand above his head, 'like "God Jesus". Yes!'

He was humorous, but I was wary of his eyes which glittered with a manic intensity. I thought at first that he was merely an eccentric, passing the time by practising his English on me, but it turned out that he too had an important story to tell. He was another victim of a Special Forces night raid, and was the clearest example I had ever met of a man radicalized by the experience.

'I am Taliban. Yes, yes! Genghis Khan was more brutal than the Americans. The Russians were more brutal than the Americans. And look what happened to them!'

One night in January 2009, US Special Forces blew up the gates of his house, dragged him from his bed, beat, handcuffed and blindfolded him and hauled him off to the local base.

'I run a madrasah as well as a mosque – but only for students, not for fighters. Everyone knows it. It is in Marko district, right beside the main road. As if anyone could train fighters there! But the Americans do not understand.'

Until that moment he had been entirely apolitical: a well-known figure in his community, an educated man of the cloth like his father before him. He was more than a simple mullah. He was a bright and highly charismatic member of the ulema, who had come to the guesthouse to offer Shinwari advice on the new party he was setting up.

His arrest was only the beginning of an experience that, he wanted me to know, had left him deeply traumatized. He showed me his watch, the ceramic strap of which was shattered: the result, he said, of a blow from the butt of an American gun. He kept it in this state of disrepair as a memento of that night, a talisman of injustice. (The watch was a remarkably fancy one, a Swiss-made Rado 'Sintra Jubilé', the sort one saw on sale in the duty-free shops at Dubai airport for thousands of dollars. Watches are important status symbols among Afghans, who like to wear them even when they are old or no longer tell the right time.) The strap was only an outward sign of damage. He also produced a little plastic bag full of pills, Alprazolam, Flunarizine and Inderal: medication, he said, for the psychological problems he still experienced, depression, panic attacks and flashbacks. He also suffered recurrent back problems from his maltreatment.

In the local army base, and later when he was transferred to the US headquarters at Bagram, north of Kabul, Mullah Mohammed was interrogated by 'a US general called John'.

'He said, "Why are you fighting a jihad against us when we are here to help build this country?" but I didn't answer. I said, "Where are you from?" He said,

"California." So I said, "OK. California is far from here. Why are you really helping this country?" He said, "I'm here to keep my kids safe." So I said, "OK. Now imagine if I came to California and put my foot on *your* head, and shackled and blindfolded *you*, and shot up your house and terrified your children – what would you do?" He said, "I would seek revenge." So I said, "OK! We are the same – except that we call revenge jihad."'

General John, whoever he was, was not used to captives who argued back. The fact that Mohammed spoke English, combined with his fighting spirit and, no doubt, his unusually grand appearance, convinced the Americans that they had landed a big fish – although they had no idea from what tribe or terrorist organization.

'They were scared of my turban. They pointed at it and said, "What is the meaning of this?" I looked them in the eye and said: "It's called *a turban*."'

The questioning became more intense as the Americans' frustration grew.

'I was asked my name ten times by ten different people. They said, "You say you are a mullah, but mullahs don't speak English. Who are you really?" I could not understand this. I speak Pashto, Persian, Urdu and Arabic as well as English. Do they think all Afghans are stupid? I told them, "You are like kids! And yet you have so much money, so much technology. Kids should not be permitted to play with such expensive toys."'

The interrogators gave up in the end, unable to pin anything on their captive. No specific allegation was ever made. Instead of releasing him, however, they decided to send him to Guantanamo. He was stripped of his clothes and ordered into an orange jumpsuit in preparation for the long flight. He was sitting shackled to a chair when General John brought 'a big pastor' to see him – presumably the senior army chaplain at Bagram.

'I said to the big pastor, "Are you fighting the Taliban and al-Qaida, or are you an enemy of Islam?" And the big pastor said, "No, no, we mean your religion no harm!" But I said, "Why are you lying? Our Koran, for example: has it attacked you in any way? And yet your people have burned it, and shot it, and peed on it, here at Bagram and elsewhere. And there were cartoons of the Prophet, Peace Be Upon Him, in that Danish newspaper . . . You *know* this."'

Mohammed had been speaking at this point through a local interpreter, a young woman, who protested in a Pashto aside that the Americans couldn't possibly have done such things to the Koran at Bagram.

'I said to her, "Why are you defending them, you slave-girl? You probably shagged some white guy in a night club." And then General John admitted that these things *had* happened to the Koran at Bagram! I said to him, "I see you have great respect for your big pastor. But I too am an imam of a mosque, yet you treat me with disrespect. How do you think this will look, in the eyes of the people?"'

General John had his answer soon afterwards, when a large group of armed Shinwaris protested against

Mohammed's arrest by blocking the main road to Torkham. Governor Shirzai, according to Mohammed, telephoned Karzai in a panic, warning him that Jalalabad could fall if Mohammed was not released.

'But Karzai has no influence with the US military. So he called Bush, in Washington!'

This was in President Bush's last month in office, and although it was hard to imagine that the White House really had been involved, Mohammed was nevertheless released from Bagram the same day.

'They were going to fly me home, but a doctor inspected me and said my blood pressure was too high to get on a helicopter. That was true. I had been wearing a hood for twelve hours, and the straps were so tight I thought my eyes were going to pop out of my head. So they brought me back to Jalalabad in a tank. And then Shirzai drove me back to the village personally.'

Mullah Mohammed finished his story with a warning that I had heard again and again in Afghanistan.

'I just can't understand the Americans,' he said. 'What they are doing makes no sense – and if they go on as they are, the whole country will rise against them.'

15

The Taliban of Chak

After Jalalabad I had intended to visit the district of Chak to interview some gun-carrying Taliban – the same group, in fact, that I had met in early 2007. Their leader, Commander Abdullah, had told me I was welcome to come back at any time, and I was keen to take advantage of his Pashtun hospitality in order to see for myself how things had changed for him. But Afghanistan has a habit of frustrating even the best-laid plans, and it was another eight months before I was finally able to make the trip.

Back in 2007 the Taliban's control over Chak, and the 112,000 Pashtuns who live there, was restricted to the hours of darkness – although Abdullah vowed to me he would soon be in full control. Since then, sure enough, the district had been so thoroughly Talibanized that Abdullah's men now collected taxes. They even issued receipts using stolen government stationery headed 'Islamic Republic of Afghanistan'; with commendable parsimony they crossed out the word 'Republic' and inserted the word 'Emirate' in obeisance to Mullah Omar.

The most astonishing thing about Chak is that it is not in one of the war-torn provinces of the south or east but in Wardak, a province abutting Kabul itself. Its strategic importance is no secret: when the Taliban took control of it in 1996, the fall of the capital soon followed. And yet Abdullah, operating less than an hour's drive from the city, had managed to consolidate his rule while evading Coalition forces for over four years. Nato claimed throughout the autumn of 2010 that the Taliban were on the back foot following the US troop surge. Mid-level insurgency commanders were said to have been removed from the battlefield in such 'industrial' quantities that their leadership was struggling to find replacements.[1] But the ground truth (as the British Army calls reality) was different in Chak. If what was happening there was in any way typical of other Afghan districts – and all I had heard in Jalalabad suggested just that – then the outlook for Nato's exit strategy looked bleak indeed.

Abdullah's reputation as a demon Nato truck-destroyer appeared well deserved as my fixer and I drove south along the main road to Kandahar towards our rendezvous. Every mile or so we passed another new 'COP' – a heavily sandbagged combat outpost, each manned by a couple of young and frightened-looking ANA – although the security they provided was evidently cosmetic. In places the tarmac, laid by the

Americans just seven years previously at a cost of $190 million, had been blown up so regularly that the surface had almost vanished and the dust and gravel track beneath was taking over again like a manicured garden reverting to jungle and weeds. There seemed something inevitable about this, for nothing man-made ever lasts for long in Afghanistan.

There was at least little traffic to slow us down out here beyond the suburbs of Kabul. When the newly-paved highway re-opened in 2003, the 300-mile journey to Kandahar was theoretically cut from two days to six hours, representing a giant boost for the economic re-generation of the country – or so it was claimed at the time. But seven years on, the threat from the Taliban, or from bandits, or from corrupt policemen or militiamen has become so great that Afghans tended not to use the highway at all if they could help it. You needed a low profile, chutzpah and a certain amount of luck to travel it unscathed. The old white Toyota we were in was care-fully chosen for its anonymity; I was wearing local dress, a waistcoat and a shalwar qamiz, with my head swathed in a keffiyeh and my European profile at least partly dis-guised by a bushy beard specifically grown for this trip.

The road to Chak was marked by a painted sign so small that Hafiz, our generously paid driver, almost overshot it. We were supposed to have reached the turn-off before dark, but we were late starting out and dusk had already fallen as we left the false reassurance of the tarmac. We bumped along a track for a mile until our headlights picked out a beaten-up Toyota waiting on the verge. As we slowed to walking pace, a hooded figure with a Kalashnikov over his shoulder dashed out from behind the parked car and came bundling through the passenger door of ours in a tangle of cloth and rifle strap. The first car had already shot off in a cloud of dust and the new arrival, anxious not to hang around, tersely ordered us to speed up and follow it.

The track wound gently upwards among low, dimly-seen hills. Soon we came to a fork. Our guide directed us to the left. Almost immediately we came to another fork. This time we went to the right and rejoined the same track as before. We went on like this, weaving rapidly between inconsequential, gravelly hillocks in a way that I suddenly realized was anything but random. One look at the concentration on Hafiz's face confirmed it: we were in a Taliban minefield. There were dozens and dozens of possible routes to the valley entrance ahead and each of them, I learned, was coded with a letter and a number. On some routes an IED could be deactivated by punching a certain number into a mobile phone, and reactivated in the same way once the vehicle was safely past: a twenty-first-century version of a medieval drawbridge.

The sides of the valley closed in as we entered Chak proper, a place that epitomized the rural Pashtun ideal. The farmers lived as they had always done, in houses built of rocks and mud behind high compound walls, all organized into densely packed villages. The district is famous for its apples and apricots that grow in tidy orchards along the river banks, or higher up on artfully canalized terraces cut into the spectacularly steep valley sides.

We stopped at last in one of the villages and climbed out, stiff from the bumpy journey. The sound of a propeller engine was audible the moment Hafiz switched off the ignition, causing us new arrivals from the city to glance sharply upwards at the cold October sky. I had never heard a military drone before, and it was too dark to spot it now, but there was no doubting what it was. Our guide, laughing at our nervousness, explained that there was no danger. The drone was just a *ringay*, the local, onomatopoeic nickname for a small camera drone. It was the armed versions, the larger-engined Predators and Reapers known as *buzbuzak*, that we needed to worry about – and this definitely wasn't one of those. I imagined some CIA analyst in Langley, freeze-framing a close-up of my face and filing it under 'Insurgent'. In this valley, no one but the Taliban moved about in vehicles after dark.

A group of men materialized from the darkness beyond the road, swathed in patous and the swirling vapour of their breath. At their centre was Abdullah, who seemed hugely amused to see me again.

'You came back,' he laughed, clasping my hand. 'You really came back!'

He led us along the bank of a stream and across a small field to the side door of a mud-brick farmhouse. A steep, narrow staircase let into a perimeter wall of astonishing thickness led to a cell-like hujra that was lit by a pair of flickering hurricane lamps.

Abdullah grinned as we settled on to the floor cushions. 'So, which of us would you say has aged the most since the last time?'

I had to admit that there was grey on my chin that hadn't been there four years previously, while he, in his late thirties, seemed almost entirely unchanged: the same intelligent, darting eyes set in a handsome, weathered face above a thicker than average black beard.

'You're using the same notepads, I see,' he went on, nodding at the pocket-sized reporter's pad I like to use. 'Things must be going badly for you if you still can't afford bigger ones.'

It was a good joke, but also a reminder that Western journalists rarely if ever visited Chak – and almost never interviewed the Taliban face-to-face. Some of his subordinates were staring in outright fascination; Abdullah confirmed that the last Westerner he had spoken to anywhere was me. I had published a photograph of myself at that meeting, sitting cross-legged between two masked and heavily-armed fighters, in my book *A Million Bullets*, a copy of which I had brought along as potentially useful proof that I was the author I claimed to be. I need hardly have bothered: Abdullah knew all about the book, and had even seen the photograph reproduced online.

'On a Danish website,' he specified. 'You, with two of my boys. It was very good!'

I hadn't planned on presenting Abdullah with the

book. It felt a little too fraternal; a bit *Hanoi Jane*. Now, nevertheless, I found myself writing a dedication in the flyleaf.

'To Commander Abdullah,' I wrote. 'In the hope of a better future for Afghanistan.'

Over tea, the pattern of Abdullah's busy guerrilla life began to emerge. He spent his winters over the border in Pakistan, recuperating and rearming for the next arduous fighting season that began again each spring. He had carried out twenty 'operations' in 2010, most of them military in nature and mostly in Wardak, although not all. Taliban High Command had taken to using Abdullah, a rising star in the organization, as a kind of strategic enforcer in the country's hotspots. That summer, for instance, he had been posted to the Jalalabad region; in 2008, he had spent three months in the south. But it was his achievements in Chak, the valley where he was born, that he really wanted to discuss.

The devastation his men had wrought on Nato convoys on the Kabul–Kandahar highway had not been exaggerated. Abdullah claimed to have destroyed 'hundreds' of vehicles in the last three years, using ambush techniques that sounded childishly simple.

'Using IEDs or just RPGs, you destroy the first and last vehicles in the convoy so that the road is blocked,' he told me. 'The first thing that happens is that the escorts – three or four ANA Humvees, usually – always run away. Then the truck-drivers panic. They either jump down from their cabs and run for it, or else they try to steer their trucks off the road. They often crash into each other, and if they are carrying fuel, they blow up by themselves.'

As a former student of engineering at a polytechnic in Kabul, Abdullah had a natural talent for this kind of work. Later, for fun, he threw a pinch of salt into a glass of Fanta I was drinking, causing the sticky orange contents to fizz violently and bubble out onto the floor: the nerdish trick, it occurred to me, of a successful amateur bomb-maker. His personal record, he said, was eighty-one trucks destroyed in a single, memorable night. Not for nothing did the Americans call his stretch of road 'the Highway of Death'.

He made ambushing Nato convoys sound so much like a computer game that I had to remind myself it was real people's lives we were talking about here, not points on an electronic scoreboard. The truckers were cannon fodder. Not for the first time, I marvelled at the appalling risks they took to supply the forces of the Coalition in Kandahar. There was a kind of madness to this war. I was reminded of an old *Lucky Luke* cartoon in which the US Cavalry goes on patrols entirely unnecessarily, through the same Wild West canyon each month – and is duly ambushed there by Indians, as though both sides were keeping an appointment.

Abdullah confirmed that the new combat outposts along the highway merely offered his men more targets. The conscripts sent to man them seldom ventured beyond their sandbags. In many cases they had learned to survive by deliberately looking the other way when the Taliban were around – or else they could easily be bribed to do so. Abdullah recounted how, in 2009, a group of some thirty ANP came over to the Taliban, together with two trucks of guns and heavy weapons.

'They could see that they were following the wrong path, and that the people supported us,' he said.

The majority of the policemen were from the north of the country and were given a set of civilian clothes and sent home, although the leader of the unit opted to join the Taliban and was now a commander for them in the Jalalabad area.

Nothing seemed to impede Abdullah's IED-laying teams – not even the buzbuzak drones that, these days, patrolled the highway around the clock.

'We were scared of the Americans at first,' said our guide from the journey here, and who had followed us into the hujra. 'We heard they had technology so powerful that they could see a mouse blink from space. But none of that turned out to be true.'

I had presumed he was an ordinary Taliban foot soldier, but he turned out to be one of Abdullah's most trusted officers as well as the group's *qari*, or Koran-reciter – the rough equivalent of a regimental chaplain. Abdul-Basit, his predecessor whom I had met in 2007, and who had since been wounded, captured and released by the Americans, was now dead: the victim, apparently, of a freak accident with an RPG. His replacement was twenty-eight, and his name was Mullah Naim.

'In the old days it only took one man with a shovel to plant an IED,' he explained. 'Nowadays we never go out with less than three: one to dig and two to watch the sky.'

It seemed that the Hellfire missiles slung beneath the wings of the drones had a serious weakness. When a missile was launched at night – which was when the IED teams almost always went to work – it was possible, with keen eyes, to spot fuel-burn shooting from its tail during the ignition sequence.

'If a sentry shouts "Missile!" we drop everything and run for it,' Naim went on. 'Depending on the range and missile type, we have between fifteen and forty-five seconds to take cover.'

Once launched, a Hellfire is committed to its programmed target co-ordinates; it cannot deviate like a heat-seeking missile. No Talib, according to Naim, had been lost to a Hellfire in the course of an IED-laying operation in well over a year.

The Taliban cocked a snook at American technology in other ways. They had learned not to speak for more than about a minute on their mobile phones to prevent the call being traced and their location triangulated. For this reason they all carried at least three mobiles each, and frequently replaced the sim-cards. In combat or during ambushes, meanwhile, they tended to abandon their mobiles in favour of variable frequency field radios which, they had discovered, were immune to electronic jamming equipment.

ISAF had undoubtedly woken up late to the threat

posed by these insurgents. Until 2009 there was no more than a single battalion of US troops assigned to Wardak and the next-door province, Logar. Then, however, the Americans sent an entire brigade: as many as 4,000 troops from the 10th Mountain Division based at Fort Drum, New York. They had originally been slated to deploy to Baghdad; a last-minute diversion that spoke volumes about the US's changing military priorities. Their main base was in the south of Wardak, at Sayed Abad, from where they would periodically probe northwards towards Chak: a mission few of them looked forward to.

'Chak for the Americans was the place where the bad-asses lived,' recalled a British journalist who was embedded on one of these missions.[2] 'They spoke with grudging admiration of Taliban bravery. Everyone remembered a six-hour gunfight in Chak where they'd run black on ammo and the insurgents kept fighting, hours after the Apaches turned up . . . Chak was certainly in a league of its own. It was one of those places you were guaranteed to get hit.'

I struggled to think of Abdullah as a 'bad-ass'. Now, as in 2007, he showed me nothing but charm and courtesy. Over dinner – a large Kabuli pilau on a communal PVC picnic rug – he plunged his fingers into the mountain of steaming rice and nudged the knuckle of mutton buried within it towards me. According to Pashtun tradition, the best cut of meat on the plate always goes to the most important guest. On the other hand, his rigid attention to etiquette was perhaps a good indicator of his ideological beliefs, which were just as uncompromising. Not for him the nuanced offers and promises I had heard from Jalaluddin Shinwari or Musa Hotak. Abdullah saw fighting the foreign invader as a religious obligation.

'It is important that you understand that the people here will never stop fighting you,' he said. 'Does Obama truly understand that? Does your Prime Minister?'

In 2007 Abdullah had told me of his ambition to become a *ghazi*, an Islamic honorific denoting a killer of infidels – an ambition that had now been fulfilled, although that in itself was no reason to stop fighting. Indeed, he fully expected – and perhaps secretly hoped – to be martyred. The faith of these rebels really was central to their cause. It inspired as well as obliged them to resist, by offering the consolation of paradise to all those killed in the line of duty.

I sat back and watched them pray together after supper. There were ten turbaned Talibs in the room by then, shoulder to shoulder towards Mecca, their qari, Mullah Naim, singing the responses from the front. Their turbans, I noted, were all black: another development since 2007, when their allegiance to the cause was necessarily less overt. You could see that it bound these warriors together, this comforting, calming ritual. Abdullah once described his religion as 'peace and perfection: like eating on an empty stomach' – and they did seem almost physically sated by their prayer session. Their worship was, as always, intensely spiritual but at the same time strangely banal. The numinous atmosphere seemed scandalously spoiled to me when, right in the middle of a response, a mobile phone began to chirrup in Mullah Naim's pocket. I was astonished when he actually took the call, held a short conversation and returned to his prayers as though nothing had happened. It showed how intertwined the day-to-day business of being in the Taliban and Islam really were; and that when you pray five times a day, even a qari must learn to live with interruption.

The West, Abdullah was convinced, had already lost the war in Afghanistan. The Taliban would return to national power eventually; the only questions left were how, and when.

'Many, many of Karzai's people, even some high-ups in government, have come to us in secret to tell us they support us . . . everyone knows you foreigners will leave, and they are worried about what will happen when you do.'

I was not surprised to hear that he had no interest whatsoever in peace talks: an accurate reflection of Mullah Omar's publicly stated view. General Petraeus, who took over from General McChrystal in June, had recently begun publicly to encourage President Karzai's efforts at dialogue with the Taliban leadership. He even revealed that Nato intelligence had helped a senior Taliban figure to travel to at least three meetings in Kabul from Pakistan. Abdullah, however, dismissed all reports of rapprochement as 'lies and propaganda'. No one, he said, could speak to Karzai on behalf of the

Taliban without Mullah Omar's authorization, which he was absolutely certain had not been granted.

'Mullah Omar has made his position very clear: the Taliban will not negotiate until all the foreign soldiers have left,' he insisted.

I pointed out that America and Britain were, actually, leaving: had not both Obama and the British Prime Minister given dates for the exit of their combat troops? But Abdullah just shook his head.

'Why wait?' he said. 'Why not just go now?'

'We can't leave all at once. It would be perceived as a defeat for Western arms. Obama needs an "exit with honour".'

'An exit with honour? You should be so lucky. The only reason you are still here now is that we can't shoot down your aircraft. But soon, God willing, we will have the anti-aircraft weapons we need, and when that happens you will be *begging* us to leave.'

Rumours that the Taliban were about to get hold of SAMs – surface-to-air missiles – had been doing the rounds since 2006 at least. They were an iconic weapon in Afghanistan, still revered as the means by which the mujahideen had brought down the Soviets in the 1980s. Did Abdullah know something now that Nato didn't? He wasn't saying. But I suspected he was right about the effect SAMs could have on Western resolve in Afghanistan.

'We don't believe the US and UK are sincere about negotiations,' Mullah Naim offered. 'America doesn't want to leave but to establish a base here – for oil, and to put pressure on Iran.'

'America is here to defend itself against terrorism,' I countered. 'General Petraeus has said many times that we are in Afghanistan for one reason only: to prevent the re-establishment of al-Qaida here.'

'But there are no al-Qaida fighters in Afghanistan any more. I have fought in the south and in the east as well as here, and in seven years of operations I have not seen a single al-Qaida fighter. Not one.'

At twenty-eight, Naim belonged to a generation of Taliban who had nothing to do with Mullah Omar's rise to power. He had taken up arms for the first time in 2003, two years after 9/11, and was fighting less for the restoration of the old regime than in response to the US occupation of his country. Petraeus's al-Qaida argument was so patently ridiculous to him that he had concluded America must be pursuing a hidden agenda.

'There were some foreign fighters operating in Chak for a while last year,' Mullah Naim recalled. 'Arabs, Chechens, Pakistanis. Foreign fighters are found wherever the fighting is fiercest. But they have no link to al-Qaida. They take an oath of loyalty to the Emir, and obey our orders one hundred per cent. They couldn't even get to the front lines without our help.'

The distinction between al-Qaida and 'foreign' fighters, so often lost on the Western public and even on Nato commanders, was a crucial one.

'We don't really like foreigners,' Naim explained. 'We

prefer to do our fighting ourselves; we know the terrain better than they ever will. But when we are short of troop numbers, as we were last year, they are welcome enough as reinforcements.'

He insisted that the welcome extended to al-Qaida in the 1990s would never be shown again.

'Their people are just killers. They have no respect for life, including the lives of civilians. They would create trouble in the end if they came here.'

For all Abdullah's hospitality there remained an underlying tension to our conversation. I overstepped the mark when I asked, jokingly, how much I could get if I betrayed him to the Americans.

'About half a million dollars,' he said.

'Half a million? Is that all?' I teased.

Naim thought this was quite funny but Abdullah eyed me coolly.

'Don't forget there's a price on your head too,' he said.

I thought it best to change the subject.

Not all his subordinates were entirely friendly, either. I recognized one of them, Rahimullah, from my 2007 visit. He had been easy-going then, but his greeting this time was strangely muted. The reason was soon clear. In the intervening period, like one or two others here, he had been captured by the Americans and spent seven months in custody, first at Bagram, then in a jail run by the NDS, whom he had eventually bribed to release him.

Unlike the Zabuli elders I met in Jalalabad, these Taliban did at least distinguish between their American and British enemies – although the distinction they made was an unnervingly slight one.

'We know that the UK is not powerful like the US,' Naim said, 'but you make up for that by being cunning and manipulative: you know how to get what you want. In my opinion, the occupation is a British ploy to gain revenge for the last war.'

It was not the first time I had heard this fantastical suggestion. I presumed he was referring to the Third Anglo-Afghan war of 1919; although he might just as well have been thinking of the previous war that began in 1878. I later overheard Abdullah identifying himself over his field radio as 'Maiwand', after Ayub Khan's famous victory over the British in 1880. Naim's call-sign was 'Shahid', the Koranic word for a martyr, which seemed only marginally less revealing.

Chak was, after all, a very dangerous place – and not just for me. Abdullah said he had lost count of the times he had almost been captured or killed. US Special Forces raids, I learned, were happening 'almost all the time' in the valley. The drone I had heard earlier indicated they might even be preparing another one as we spoke.

'What will you do if the Americans come?' Abdullah asked. 'Will you run? You don't look as though you could run very far.'

The minefield we had negotiated earlier was only a small part of Chak's defences. The mountain tops around about were constantly manned by sentries on the lookout for any unusual helicopter activity in the neighbouring valleys. This was generally the most reliable indicator that a Special Forces raid was due, and a signal for the Taliban to take to the hills themselves. Naim was not exaggerating when he said they knew the terrain better than anyone else. Like all the Taliban here he was born in Chak, and they had hideouts for many miles around.

After supper, Abdullah told me to put my shoes back on: he wanted to show me something, and we were going for a short drive. It was long past midnight, and the air was sharp with frost as we picked our way by moonlight back up to the road where a car was waiting with the engine running. Six of us crammed aboard and we trundled off up the valley. We passed through three villages without seeing a single soul apart from a Taliban sentry who came bounding out of a checkpoint with his gun already in his shoulder: he hadn't recognized the car, and laughed sheepishly when he leant down and saw his commander inside.

We stopped at the far end of the third village and got out. Abdullah began to walk up the middle of the road, beckoning me to follow. A little further on he stopped, rummaged in a plastic bag concealed beneath his cloak and brought out a pair of old Red Army night-vision glasses. It was at this moment I realized we were perhaps 600 yards from the district's main ANA base.

'All this valley belongs to us,' said Abdullah in a low voice, with a sweep of his hand behind him, 'except for about one square kilometre around the district centre. There are about eighty soldiers in there but they never come out. They are too scared; they stay hiding in their trenches. We attack them whenever we want. In fact, we can attack them now if you like. Would you like that?'

I thought he was joking until he passed me the night-vision glasses. High walls topped with barbed wire and sandbagged machine gun posts leapt into ghostly grey-green focus. I politely declined the offer: I dreaded instigating anyone's death. Abdullah merely shrugged, not puzzled but indifferent. Their attitude to war, I thought to myself, was truly alien. They were like school-boys, almost, with their infectious, amateurish enthusiasm for action. Such joie-de-guerre would not have been out of place in a playground. Yet the bullets in their weapons and the risks of their enterprise were not pretend ones. To kill or be killed: it was all the same to them, and if it didn't happen tonight then it would happen tomorrow or the day after or next week. It was hard to imagine living under such pressure for as long and as constantly as these people had. They were like dead men walking. Their serenity was spooky, and was only possible among fighters who believed with the cores of their beings that they were bound for a martyr's paradise.

Abdullah's greatest achievement of the year, in his opinion, was not some spectacular guerrilla attack but the successful sabotaging of parliamentary elections in Chak that September. 'There are eighty-seven polling stations in this district, and eighty-six of them didn't even open,' he said proudly. 'No one voted in this valley – no one!'

According to Abdullah, it had taken very little to persuade the people of Chak to turn away from the Western-backed government in Kabul – although they made sure there were no waverers by attacking the Coalition helicopters forced to bring in the voting forms because the roads were so unsafe. The one polling station that did open had been located in the district centre in front of us. Abdullah explained how a local candidate, Wahedullah Kalimzai, had bribed election officials to stuff the ballot boxes.

'He paid them $400,000. They were up all night filling in the voting slips. And Kabul has the temerity to call these elections a success!'

As the owner of a successful construction firm, Kalimzai was said to have grown immensely rich on contracts to build bases and other infrastructure for ISAF. In Abdullah's view, therefore, the West was ultimately responsible for Kalimzai's monstrous corruption – an irony that was of course not lost on him. There was nothing unusual about what had happened in Chak. The parliamentary elections of 2010 were marred by fraud all over the country, just as the presidential ones of 2009 were. This time, some 1.3 million ballots had to be disqualified: nearly a quarter of all the votes cast.

I was glad we didn't linger longer than necessary in that exposed spot. Our little group must have looked suspicious to any drone operator. Abdullah ordered Naim to take us to a farmhouse in another village, before announcing that he wasn't coming with us but intended to stay up for the rest of the night: if the Americans really were coming, he wanted to be ready for them. He pulled his patou tighter over his head and shoulders and, with a single gunman for company, slipped over the berm at the side of the road and vanished into the night.

Our new quarters smelled deliciously of freshly picked apples. Sacks of them were piled up inside the entrance, waiting for a buyer who came in by truck from as far away as Iran. It was two o'clock in the morning, yet Naim still wasn't ready for sleep. Instead he told us a story of an apple farmer recently killed by the *Amriki*.

'He had gone to sleep in his orchard to protect his ripe apples from thieves,' he said. 'The Americans shot him where he lay through the heart and head . . . They kill innocent people all the time. That is why the people hate them so much, and support us.'

It wasn't hard to see how Abdullah had persuaded the people of Chak to boycott the election. If even half of what Naim said was true, his account of Special Forces operations in the valley spelled disaster for Nato's hearts and minds campaign. He said that the previous month, when a group of students returning to their families were killed out on the highway, the locals rioted in protest, burning cars and blocking the road for hours. Even more recently, just up the road from here, a taxi-driver had been pulped in his car by cannon fire from an Apache helicopter as he innocently made his way home.

'There was a big funeral. The mourners came from miles around, hundreds of them – and when we buried the martyr, they chanted "Death to America".'

A combination of heavy-handed tactics and poor intelligence appeared to have alienated everyone who lived here, while turning the Taliban into heroic defenders of the community.

'One of their night raids went wrong this summer,' Naim recalled. 'They got stuck here and the battle went on for three days. They didn't get any of us, but they took their frustration out on a poor donkey from my village. I don't know what kind of weapons the Americans were using, but when they had finished its flesh was like candy floss. There was nothing left but its hooves.'

His confidence that they were winning their war with the West was great, although not, it turned out, absolute. The Chaki Taliban's weakness, and greatest fear, was the risk of betrayal by 'spies', against whom they took extraordinary precautions. Just before dawn, less than three hours after we had gone to sleep, Naim shook my shoulder and announced that we were on the move again. This was completely normal for them. None of them slept very much, and never in the same place on consecutive nights. They moved about the district with disciplined randomness. In the 24 hours I spent with them we changed location four times.

Naim led me out of the house and set off fast down a rocky hill, as sure-footed as a goat. I stumbled after him, still half asleep and stiff from the cold, to another hujra in another farmhouse where I was promptly ordered to go back to sleep. I was woken again two hours later when

Abdullah bustled in. The Americans, I deduced groggily, had not attacked that night. His men had, however, caught three spies in one of the villages further up the valley. Abdullah began to produce an improbable number of mobile phones from various waistcoat pockets. He explained that half of them belonged to the spies, who had allegedly been spotted taking photographs with them.

'It happens sometimes,' Abdullah said. 'The Americans offer a lot of money for information. It can turn people's heads.'

Naim and another Talib were given a phone each, and the three of them began to scroll through the data they contained with practised thumbs. Naim pressed the Last Number Dialled button and pretended to be a policeman when someone answered. He hung up, laughing, when the voice at the other end failed to respond to this ruse. Abdullah, meanwhile, had found a clip from a Hollywood B-movie on his. Still rubbing my eyes, I watched a group of teenagers on dirt-bikes fleeing a horde of giant man-eating tarantulas.

I asked what was likely to happen to the spies. Abdullah revealed that he had already consulted headquarters in Pakistan by phone. Their office hours were certainly impressive: it wasn't even 7.30 a.m. yet. It had been decided that the three should be tried according to Sharia by the local judge – a dignitary appointed, like Abdullah, by the High Council.

'And if they are found guilty?'

'If there is proof, they will be hanged,' Abdullah replied.

Naim added: 'And the hangings will be popular. Many people will come to watch.'

This was law and order Taliban-style, a system of fast and simple village justice that could also be horribly harsh. The odds of the detainees surviving didn't sound good. It put me in mind of the furore that had broken out in the Western media that autumn about the rights and wrongs of Julian Assange's Wikileaks website, which had publicized some 90,000 supposedly secret US military records relating to Afghanistan – allegedly including the details of many Afghans who had spied or acted as informants for the Americans. Had Wikileaks proved useful in the Taliban's hunt for spies in Chak?

'We don't have internet in the valley, so not yet,' said Abdullah. 'But the documents are still being analysed by headquarters . . . we have learned quite a lot from the documents, in general, about the way Nato operates and thinks.'

It was fascinating to watch Abdullah wearing his other hat, as the district's chief administrator. He had been on the lookout for Special Forces raiders all night and had hardly slept, but there was no let-up for him now. For the first three hours of the day, his phones hardly stopped ringing as he dealt with the routine civilian business of the community. That morning, apart from consulting Quetta on the captured spies, he had dispatched some of his lieutenants to arbitrate in a land dispute between two feuding families, and spoken at length to the Sharia judge about a woman seeking to divorce her husband on the grounds that he beat her. The judge was disinclined to grant her wish. Abdullah, who knew the husband, thought her case was more than justified, and was trying to persuade the judge to change his mind. Abdullah understood that divorce for Afghan women tends to bring a life of singledom, destitution and tragedy. The deciding factor for him was the knowledge that a suitor was waiting in the wings to scoop the woman up if a divorce was granted. Based on acquaintance with the people involved, and closely adapted to local circumstances, this was Taliban justice at its humane and considered best. My fixer was quietly impressed: 'It would never happen like this in Kabul,' he said.

Abdullah was supposed to officiate at a wedding later in the day and, between phone calls, toyed aloud with the idea of taking me along as a guest. But in the end he decided against it, and sent one of his men to deputize for him.

'I think you might attract rather a lot of attention,' he murmured.

He preferred to keep me as far from public view as he reasonably could. The Taliban's control of Chak was not in dispute, but that did not mean they trusted every inhabitant. In the paranoid atmosphere of the valley, the presence of a Westerner could all too easily be misconstrued. Later, when the conversation turned again to the Americans and the weapons they used, he offered to take me to see an apple farmer's house that, he claimed, had been attacked using depleted uranium munitions.

'An apple tree normally grows again after it has been hit by shellfire,' he said. 'The one by this house is sick in a way I have never seen before.'

Depleted uranium ammunition, favoured for its extraordinary density and therefore its armour-piercing qualities, has been used by the US Army since the First Gulf War, although its use is now highly controversial. Some toxicologists think the radiation associated with it is partly responsible for Gulf War Syndrome. Evidence that US Special Forces were using it against the Taliban – a militia not exactly noted for its use of armour – seemed worth investigating.

We travelled this time on two Chinese-manufactured Pamir motorbikes. I rode pillion behind Naim, who insisted on adjusting my patou before we set off so my face was invisible to passers-by. He also carried my camera on the grounds that it would mark me out if it was over my shoulder. I clung on tightly as we veered off the road. Pamirs are sometimes nicknamed 'the Taliban Humvee' and I was beginning to understand why. Naim and Abdullah were skilled off-road riders. We bucketed along a raised and dangerously narrow footpath, forded a deep stream, roared up a hill slippery with gravel and then headlong down a vertiginous shortcut between two high compound walls – and all on a pair of machines that looked designed for a gentle urban commute. I was struck once again by how well these men knew their ground. They seemed to live in primitive symbiosis with every rock and tree and stream. Naim could, and did, point out the house he was born in. His family had lived here for so many generations that, like highland sheep, they had become hefted to the land. In Naim's view it was not just presumptuous for infidel foreigners to try to dislodge them from it, but absurd. And it went without saying that the attempt would fail.

I could see there was a problem with the depleted uranium story the moment we arrived. Abdullah and Naim, who had obviously not visited the apple farmer's house for a while, were embarrassed to find that the tree had recovered. Its bark was still smoke-blackened, certainly; but the tiny buds sprouting along the branches suggested the core of the tree was in rude health. There was no further talk of sinister American weaponry.

Even so, the trip was worth it. The mud-brick walls of the farmhouse, which was really a two-roomed shack, were pockmarked with bullet holes; the roof and one end of the building had been demolished by a missile or a bomb. We peered through a hole where the window had once been, and saw mangled floor timbers liberally splattered with dried blood. According to Abdullah, a poor family of seven had lived in this hovel – and all of them, women and young children included, had been killed in their beds by US Special Forces that summer.

'We still have no idea why they attacked this house,' said Abdullah. 'They always say afterwards that they had information that there were insurgents here. But this family had nothing to do with us.'

The tree by the front door, the dead family's former pride and joy, had sprouted more than blossom buds. Its branches were festooned with strips of green and white silk cloth: the mark, Abdullah explained, of a spontaneous public shrine.

'The people do this of their own accord: it is nothing to do with the Taliban. This family was martyred. The people dip their fingers in the blood they spilled to bring good luck . . . they think the blood of a martyr has magic powers. Maybe that is why the tree is doing so well,' he added with a smile.

The Taliban disapprove of this type of rural superstition, which they regard as un-Islamic. But Abdullah needed the support of the people; he was too canny a shadow governor to try to suppress their mystical traditions, which predate Islam in Afghanistan by millennia. The cruelty and clumsiness of attacks like this one made him look not just accommodating but sensitive towards local beliefs. As he well understood, the US's military-driven policy had pushed the people of Chak straight into the Taliban's hands. But he was not cynical: his war against the foreigners was heartfelt, his anger genuine.

'You foreigners can never win here,' he said. 'If you sent a million troops here, you would still lose.'

Later, as we prepared to return to Kabul, I asked if he had any particular message for the West. It was late afternoon by then, with the sun slanting through another apple orchard casting spiky shadows on the leafy ground. He paused, and thought, and said portentously:

'In the friendliest way possible, please tell the British people – tell your Prime Minister – that you should leave our country now.'

'Right,' I said, lightly. 'Anything else?'

But he was no longer in joking mood.

'Please,' he repeated, pulling his patou tighter about his shoulders and looking me in the eye. 'The foreigners must leave. As soon as possible, before it is too late.'

Then without further ceremony he turned on his heel and slipped silently away through the trees.

Postscript

By the time this edition of *Taliban* went to press in the winter of 2010, Operation Moshtaraq in the Helmandi district of Marjah was over, and the next phase of the campaign against the Taliban was well under way: Operation Omid, the domination of greater Kandahar.

The Americans said they were pleased with the way Moshtaraq had gone. General McChrystal called it 'a model for the future: an Afghan-led operation supported by the Coalition, deeply engaged with the people'. But even as his troops moved on to the main objective, it was clear they had achieved only partial success in Marjah. The Taliban were still there, killing the occasional ISAF soldier with sniper fire and threatening local contractors who cooperated with the Americans; while the locals, however much they appreciated work clearing canals at $5 a day for ISAF's Civil Affairs unit, had yet to throw in their lot with the central government.

'The local residents don't trust we will provide security,' said Naimatullah, the acting district governor of Marjah. 'They are taking a wait-and-see attitude ... they are worried that the Taliban will return and punish them for supporting the government.'[1]

Some 23,000 Coalition troops are now engaged around Kandahar: by far the largest operation of the war. Will they really succeed in establishing true security there when so many questions remain about Marjah, a district of just 80,000 compared to Kandahar's population of one million? The indications are not good. Notional front lines have disintegrated and been replaced by random IED kill-zones. US Special Forces have also secretly trained and armed an assortment of tribal militias in the hope that they might police their own communities,[2] but it remains to be seen if they are really in control of them. Locals and the Taliban alike complain that the new militias are already operating above the law. If they are right, then the American policy is in danger of reinforcing the insurgency. It was precisely to get rid of out-of-control militias that the Taliban came into being in 1994.

Western military leaders have gone on reaffirming their commitment to Afghanistan. 'The worst of all things would be to get out before we finish the job properly,' said the head of the British Armed Forces, General David Richards, who insisted that the 10,000 UK personnel currently stationed there would need to stay for 'as long as it takes'.[3] In the US, similarly, General Petraeus remarked in September that President Obama's

July 2011 deadline for the start of troop withdrawal was 'not a date when we rush for the exit and reach for the light switch'.[4] Yet in his end-of-year strategy review, President Obama – who did not do as badly in November's mid-term Congressional elections as some had predicted – did not retract his 2011 pledge; while Prime Minister David Cameron has so far shown every sign of sticking to his promise that UK combat operations in Afghanistan will end by 2015.

At a summit of Nato leaders in Lisbon in November, the agenda was dominated by plans for Western withdrawal. General Petraeus presented a colour-coded map that, district by district, time-tabled when he thought responsibility for security could be handed over to local forces. The map's details were kept secret, but two-thirds of the country's 300-plus districts were reportedly coloured green, meaning that in his opinion they could be handed back without risk almost immediately. But are Afghanistan's newly trained security forces really ready? Responsibility for security in districts such as Chak has, in effect, already been handed over. Was Chak one of the green-coloured districts on the Lisbon map? Afghans could be forgiven for being sceptical if so.

In the course of 2010, Washington at last began to soften its position on the exit strategy's other pillar: a political settlement with the insurgents. For the first time, the US offered public support for President Karzai's attempts at dialogue. A 'High Peace Council', convened in October to explore ways of reconciling with the Taliban leadership, attracted the participation, among others, of three senior ex-Taliban figures. Among them was Abdul Salaam Zaeef, who said he felt 'optimistic' about these 'first steps towards peace'.

President Obama, however, still seems unwilling to instigate the direct talks with the Taliban that many Afghans think are needed if a political settlement is to mean anything. The main reason, no doubt, is his electorate. Most Americans still make no distinction between the Taliban and al-Qaida. An astonishing number of them, indeed, appear to confuse Islam as a whole with al-Qaida – as was perhaps demonstrated by the ferocious resistance to Feisal Abdul Rauf's plan to build a Muslim community centre two blocks from the World Trade Centre in New York in the summer of 2010. (Rauf, described by *The Economist* as 'a well-meaning American cleric who has spent years trying to promote interfaith understanding', is a peace-promoting Sufi – almost the polar opposite, within Islam, of the militant Wahhabism espoused by al-Qaida.) To many ordinary Americans, 'talking to the Taliban' remains tantamount to appeasing terrorists. With the memory of 9/11 still painful, it could be electorally disastrous for any American president to proceed too quickly with what one journalist called 'as massive a U-turn in US policy as it was for the British government to talk to the IRA'.[5] Obama, a leader mistakenly believed by a quarter of Americans to be a Muslim himself, has especial reason to be wary.

As Washington hesitates, so the Taliban position on

negotiations seems to harden. In his annual Eid al-Adha address in November, Mullah Omar warned his followers that the 'cunning enemy ... wants to throw dust into the eyes of the people by spreading rumours of negotiation'. He dismissed claims that the leadership might show any flexibility in its position as 'baseless propaganda', just as Commander Abdullah in Wardak had done. He also fired an unprecedented blast at Mullah Zaeef and the other ex-Taliban in Kabul who had shown support for Karzai's High Peace Council. 'We can't figure out why you are unilaterally co-operating with the invaders,' he said. 'Can the present regime reflect your objectives of jihad? Was the aim of your fourteen-year-long jihad only to let the Russians be replaced by the Americans?'

For several weeks in 2010, Nato intelligence officials believed that Omar's fiery rhetoric was for public consumption only, and that he was privately keen to explore the terms of a deal via his deputy, the former Transport Minister Mullah Akhtar Mohammed Mansour. But in a twist that might have been lifted from a spy novel, it emerged just one week after Omar's Eid al-Adha address that 'Mansour' was an impostor. According to some reports he was actually a shopkeeper from Quetta – a courageous con-artist who guessed, correctly, that no one in Kabul would know what the real Mansour looked like, and would be unable to verify his identity because photographs of the image-averse Taliban are so rare.

The fake Talib attended at least three meetings in

Kabul, allegedly including one with President Karzai himself; MI6 was said to have flown him in from Kandahar on an RAF Hercules, and to have paid out as much as half a million dollars to persuade him to attend further meetings. This embarrassing episode hurt more than the pride of a few secret agents. The unmasking of 'Mansour' showed that Omar had not been posturing in his Eid al-Adha address: he really meant it when he described the possibility of negotiations before Nato leaves as 'baseless propaganda'. The affair dealt another heavy blow to the hunt for political compromise.

And yet attempts to establish dialogue with the leadership are not quite back to square one. At least the possibility of talks is firmly on the table now – and neither side can afford to ignore indefinitely the wishes of the war-weary Afghan people, who have suffered more than any other group in this conflict. At least 11,400 civilians have been directly killed since 2001, and the casualty rate is still accelerating. More than 1,200 were killed and 2,000 injured in the first seven months of 2010 alone.[6] No wonder 83 per cent of Afghans are now in favour of talks.[7] Who would not choose compromise and the chance of peace over continued war, poverty and corruption? The alternative is to persevere with a war that looks increasingly unwinnable: a strategy that could lead both Afghans and the West into a crisis potentially far more dreadful than the one we are in now. If ordinary Afghans are ready to give the Taliban the benefit of the doubt, is it not time that the West did too?

Notes

Introduction
1 *Channel 4 News*, 28 January 2010.
2 Bernd Debusman, Reuters, 14 May 2010.
3 Jonathan Steele, *Guardian*, 5 May 2010.

Chapter 1 The Tank of Islam: Kandahar, 1994
1 David Loyn, *Butcher and Bolt*, p231.
2 Christina Lamb, *The Sewing Circles of Herat*.
3 For some of the detail in this section, as elsewhere throughout this book, I am indebted to Mullah Abdul Salam Zaeef and his excellent *My Life with the Taliban*.
4 Quoted in David B. Edwards, *Before Taliban*.

Chapter 2 The Army of Orphans: Peshawar, 1996
1 Nancy Hatch Dupree, *An Historical Guide to Afghanistan*.
2 Christina Lamb, *The Sewing Circles of Herat*, p14.
3 Declan Walsh, *Guardian*, 30 January 2010.
4 Amnesty International.

5 AFP, 19 June 1999, quoted in Michael Griffin, *Reaping the Whirlwind*, p221.
6 CIA World Fact Book.
7 CIA World Fact Book.
8 Ahmed Rashid, *Descent into Chaos*, p236.

Chapter 3 'Try Not to Hurt the People!': Kabul, 1996–1998

1 Michael Griffin, *Reaping the Whirlwind*.
2 Michael Griffin, *Reaping the Whirlwind*, p66.
3 *New York Times*, 30 September 1997.
4 Ahmed Rashid, *Taliban*, p207.
5 Ahmed Rashid, *Taliban*, p111.
6 Michael Griffin, *Reaping the Whirlwind*, p67.

Chapter 4 The Government that Might Have Been, 1998–2000

1 Gretchen Peters, *Seeds of Terror*, p81.
2 A. Ghani Khan, *The Pathans*.
3 Ahmed Rashid, *Taliban*, pp74–5.
4 Reuters, 21 August 1998.

Chapter 5 The Al-Qaida Hijack, 1999–2001

1 Ahmed Rashid, *Descent into Chaos*, p60.
2 G8 Summit Press Conference, 9 July 2009.
3 Fatwa quoted by Ahmed Rashid, *Taliban*, p134.
4 2001 Census.
5 Zahid Hussain, *The Times*, 4 May 2010.
6 James Hider, *The Times*, 10 January 2010.
7 *New York Times*, 5 January 2007.
8 Ahmed Rashid, *Taliban*, p133.

9 E.g.http://news.bbc.co.uk/1/hi/world/south_asia/ 1550419.stm

10 AFP, 11 October 1999, quoted in Michael Griffin, *Reaping the Whirlwind*, p234.

11 Gretchen Peters, *Seeds of Terror*, p88.

12 Patrick Robinson, *Lone Survivor: The Eyewitness Account of Operation Redwing and the Lost Heroes of SEAL Team 10*.

13 Hugh Beattie, *Imperial Frontier: Tribe and State in Waziristan*.

14 *New York Times*, 13 April 1999.

15 Ahmed Rashid, *Taliban*, p79.

16 Nancy Hatch Dupree, *An Historical Guide to Afghanistan*.

17 Ahmed Rashid, *Descent into Chaos*.

18 Christina Lamb, *The Sewing Circles of Herat*.

Chapter 6 Surviving the Daisycutters: 2001–2003

1 For some of the detail in this chapter, I am particularly grateful to Ahmed Rashid and his masterly study, *Descent into Chaos*.

2 Professor Marc Herold, University of New Hampshire.

3 Jonathan Steele, 'Forgotten Victims', *Guardian*, 20 May 2002.

4 Quoted by Gretchen Peters, *Seeds of Terror*, p107.

5 Human Rights Watch.

Chapter 7 Like a Jam-jar to a Swarm of Wasps: The Insurgency Explodes, 2003–2009

1 James Dao, *New York Times*, 3 November 2002.

2 Jane Perlez, 'Rebuffing US, Pakistan Balks at Crackdown', *New York Times*, 14 December 2009.

3 *Asia Times* online, 5 May 2004.

4 Bill Roggio, 'Taliban Losses in Afghanistan, Gains in Pakistan', *Long War Journal*, 25 June 2006.

5 United Nations Assistance Mission in Afghanistan.

6 Soraya Sarhaddi Nelson, 'Disabled Often Carry Out Afghan Suicide Missions', National Public Radio, 15 October 2007.

7 *The Times*, 1 March 2010.

8 ISAF.

9 US Government Accountability Office, May 2010.

10 Richard Pohle, *The Times* online/Afghanistan, 17 May 2010.

11 For a full account of this meeting, see *A Million Bullets*, Chapter 9.

12 Bernd Debusman, Reuters, 14 May 2010.

13 *Financial Times* interview, 25 January 2010.

Chapter 8 The McChrystal Plan: Sawing Wood with a Hammer

1 thehill.com, 26 December 2009.

2 *USA Today*, 6 March 2010.

3 UNAMA.

4 Special Inspector General for Afghanistan Reconstruction, 30 October 2009.

5 UN/Antonio Giustozzi.

6 Gareth Porter, Inter Press Service, 29 November 2009.

7 UNAMA.

8 *The Times*, 15 April 2009.

9 *The Times*, 15 April 2009.

10 Michael Evans, *The Times*, 1 May 2010.

11 William Polk, MEC Analytical Group, 5 April 2010.

12 Ben Mcintyre, *The Times*, 30 March 2010.

Chapter 9 'This One, This is the Big One': Mullah Zaeef and the Prospects for Peace

1 Craig Whitlock, *Washington Post*, 23 January 2010.
2 US Government Accountability Office, May 2010.
3 David Loyn, *Butcher and Bolt*, p236.
4 *My Life with the Taliban*.
5 *Dawn*, 7 October 2008.
6 http://www.guardian.co.uk/news/datablog/2009/nov/19/afghanistan-civilian-casualties-statistics
7 Jerome Starkey, *The Times*, 25 February 2010.
8 Jerome Starkey, *The Times*, 5 April 2010.
9 Tim Reid and Michael Evans, *The Times*, 5 June 2010.
10 Michael Evans, *The Times*, 2 April 2010.
11 Jerome Starkey, *The Times*, 9 April 2010.
12 'The Year of the Drone', New America Foundation, February 2010.
13 Ali Ezzatyar and Shahpur Kabraji, *Beirut Daily Star*, quoted by MEC Analytical Group, 12 April 2010.
14 Jerome Starkey, *The Times*, 25 February 2010.
15 Kathy Gannon, AP, 4 March 2010.
16 Kathy Gannon, AP, 4 March 2010.
17 Carlotta Gall, *New York Times*, 26 March 2009.

Chapter 10 The Trouble with President Karzai

1 *The Times*, 20 October 2009.
2 Jeremy Page, *The Times*, 29 September 2009.
3 Lyse Doucet, BBC, 3 April 2010.
4 Jerome Starkey, *The Times*, 7 April 2010.
5 PBS Profile, December 2001.
6 Ann Marlowe, *Washington Post*, 11 February 2008.

7   David Blair, *Daily Telegraph*, 12 April 2008.
8   *Daily Mail*, 31 March 2009.

Chapter 11 Getting Rich Quick in Tajik Kabul

1   Azadi Radio, 5 April 2006.
2   Julian Borger and Ewen MacAskill, *Guardian*, 22 March 2009.
3   Tom Coghlan, *The Times*, 21 April 2010.
4   John Aston, *Scotsman*, 20 April 2010.
5   Tom Coghlan, *The Times*, 21 April 2010.
6   Dexter Filkins, *The Forever War*.
7   Jon Boone, *Guardian*, 24 August 2009.

Chapter 12 Not Black and White, but Grey: Hizb-i-Islami and the Afghan Parliament

1   Centre for Women and Democracy.
2   Syed Saleem Shahzad, *Asia Times*, 3 June 2008.
3   Giles Whittell, *The Times*, 30 March 2010.
4   Ben Farmer and Rob Crilly, *Daily Telegraph*, 13 April 2010.

Chapter 13 How to Talk to the Taliban

1   Michael Semple, *Reconciliation in Afghanistan*.
2   Michael Semple, *Reconciliation in Afghanistan*.
3   Tim Weiner, *New York Times*, 24 July 1993.

Chapter 14 In the Jalalabad Fief of Shirzai

1   See *Kandahar Cockney*, p285.
2   Doug Saunders, *Toronto Globe & Mail*, 3 May 2008.
3   Tom Coghlan, *The Times*, 15 May 2010.

Chapter 15 The Taliban of Chak

1 See, for example, Tom Coghlan and Jerome Starkey, 'Taleban hierarchy crumbles after SAS raids', *The Times*, 8 November 2010.

2 See Julius Cavendish's account in *The Times*, 29 May 2009.

Postscript

1 Marie Colvin, *Sunday Times*, 9 May 2010.

2 Stephen Grey, *Channel 4 News*, 16 May 2010.

3 *The Times*, 8 November 2010.

4 Deborah Haynes, *The Times*, 23 September 2010.

5 Jonathan Steele, *Guardian*, 5 May 2010.

6 UNAMA.

7 Asia Foundation opinion poll. See Francis Elliot, *The Times*, 10 November 2010.

Bibliography

Adamec, Ludwig W. – *Historical Dictionary of Afghanistan*, Scarecrow Press 2002

Ali, Mohammed – *The Afghans*, Punjab Educational Press 1958

Beattie, Hugh – *Imperial Frontier: Tribe and State in Waziristan*, Curzon 2002

Borovik, Artyom – *The Hidden War, A Russian Journalist's Account of the Soviet War in Afghanistan*, Faber and Faber 1991

Chayes, Sarah – *The Punishment of Virtue: Inside Afghanistan After the Taliban*, Portobello Books 2007

Dupree, Nancy Hatch – *The Road to Balkh*, Afghan Tourist Organization 1967

Dupree, Nancy Hatch – *An Historical Guide to Afghanistan*, Afghan Tourist Organization 1977

Edwards, David B. – *Before Taliban*, University of California Press 2002

Fergusson, James – *Kandahar Cockney: A Tale of Two Worlds*, Harper Collins 2004

Fergusson, James – *A Million Bullets: The Real Story of the British Army in Afghanistan*, Corgi 2009

Filkins, Dexter – *The Forever War*, Vintage Books 2009

Fodio, Sheikh Uthman – *Handbook on Islam*, Madinah Press 1991

Ghani, Ashraf and Clare Lockhart, *Fixing Failed States*, Oxford University Press 2008

Giustozzi, Antonio – *Koran, Kalashnikov and Laptop: The Neo-Taliban Insurgency*, Columbia University Press 2008

Giustozzi, Antonio – *Decoding the New Taliban: Insights from the Afghan Field*, Columbia University Press 2009

Grey, Stephen – *Operation Snakebite, The Explosive True Story of an Afghan Desert Siege*, Viking (Penguin) 2009

Griffin, Michael – *Reaping the Whirlwind: The Taliban Movement in Afghanistan*, Pluto Press 2001

Khan, A. Ghani – *The Pathans, A Sketch*, UNO Printing Press 2008 (first published 1947)

Lamb, Christina – *The Sewing Circles of Herat*, HarperCollins 2002

Loyn, David – *Butcher and Bolt: Two Hundred Years of Foreign Engagement in Afghanistan*, Hutchinson 2008

Marsden, Peter – *The Taliban: War, Religion and the New Order in Afghanistan*, Zed Books 1998

Peters, Gretchen – *Seeds of Terror: How Heroin is Bankrolling the Taliban and Al Qaida*, Oneworld 2009

Rashid, Ahmed – *Taliban: The Story of the Afghan Warlords*, Pan Books 2001

Rashid, Ahmed – *Descent into Chaos*, Allen Lane (Penguin) 2008

Robinson, Patrick – *Lone Survivor: The Eyewitness Account of*

Operation Redwing and the Lost Heroes of SEAL Team 10, Back Bay Books 2007

Roy, Olivier (with Mariam Abou Zahab) – *Islamist Networks: The Afghan-Pakistan Connection*, C. Hurst & Co 2004

Semple, Michael – *Reconciliation in Afghanistan*, United States Institute of Peace Press 2010

Zaeef, Abdul Salam – *My Life with the Taliban*, C. Hurst & Co 2010

Picture Credits

Every effort has been made to trace copyright holders; those overlooked are invited to get in touch with the publishers. Credits run clockwise from top left image.

Section One

Small photo, Mohammad Omar, Khandahar, 1996: BBC News/ Newsnight/AFP/Getty Images

Taliban fighters in a jeep: AP/Zaheeruddin Abdullah; Taliban fighters near Kabul, 21 October 1996: Roger Lemoyne/ Liaison/Getty Images; group of Taliban praying, early nineties: Stephan Gladieu/L'Express/ Gamma, Camera Press, London; Abdul Salam Zaeef, 19 October 2001: Getty Images; Mullah Dadullah, TV screen shot 19 May 2006: Farzana Wahidy/AFP/Getty Images; Jaluddin Haqqani, 14 March 1994: Robert Nickelsberg/Liaison/Getty Images; Mohammad Rabbani, 2 February 2000: Tanveer Mughal/AFP/Getty Images

Maps by Tom Coulson, Encompass Graphics

Afghan women walking home, Kabul, December 2000: Arthur Fox/ Gamma, Camera Press, London; Ahmed Shah Massoud with his commanders, 15 August 1997; Hekmatyar, Mazar, 1998: author's photo; girls' school, Kabul, June 2001: Stephan Gladieu/L'Express/ Gamma, Camera Press, London; Kandahar street scene, 13 March 1996: Topfoto/Ullstein; Taliban beating a woman, Kabul, 2001: RAWA/WPN

Main image, Bamiyan, 1992: Steve McCurry/Magnum Photos; destruction of the Buddhas of Bamiyan, 12 March 2001: CNN/Getty Images

Section Two

Taliban prisoners, Shibarghan, 8 December 2001: Oleg Nikishini/Getty Images

Main image, bombing of village near Bagram, 12 November 2001: Marco di Lauro/Associated Press; Ulema meeting, 20 September 2001: Barry Iverson/Time & Life Images/Getty Images; Northern Alliance troops enter Kabul, 13 November 2001: Scott Peterson/Getty Images; Northern Alliance troops check Taliban bodies, Mazar-i-Sharif, 28 November 2001: Oleg Nikishini/Getty Images; Rashid Dostum near Mazar-i-Sharif, 28 November 2001

Donald Rumsfeld visits Bagram Airbase, 27 April 2002: Natalie Behring-Chisholm/Getty Images; US trooper and remains of Humvee, May 2010: Richard Pohle; Royal Marines attack Taliban, Barikju, Northern Helmand, 2007; journalists photograph the body of Mullah Dadullah, Kandahar, 13 May

Index